MY PAST AND THOUGHTS

MY PAST AND THOUGHTS

The Memoirs of Alexander Herzen

VOLUME V

*Translated from the Russian
by Constance Garnett*

faber and faber

This edition first published in 2008
by Faber and Faber Ltd
3 Queen Square, London WC1N 3AU

Printed by Books on Demand GmbH, Norderstedt

All rights reserved
Translation © Constance Garnett, 1926

The right of Constance Garnett to be identified as translator of this work
has been asserted in accordance with Section 77 of the
Copyright, Designs and Patents Act 1988

This book is sold subject to the condition that it shall not, by way of
trade or otherwise, be lent, resold, hired out or otherwise circulated
without the publisher's prior consent in any form of binding or cover other than
that in which it is published and without a similar condition including this
condition being imposed on the subsequent purchaser

A CIP record for this book is available from the British Library

ISBN 978–0–571–24545–1

Our authorised representative in the EU for product safety is
Easy Access System Europe, Mustamäe tee 50, 10621 Tallinn, Estonia
gpsr.requests@easproject.com

CONTENTS

SECTION FOUR (continued)

LONDON EXILES OF THE 'FIFTIES

CHAPTER VI:—Ordinary Misfortunes and Political Misfortunes—Teachers and Commissionaires—Agents and Salesmen—Orators and Letter-writers—Do-nothing Factotums and ever-busy Drones—Russians—Thieves—Spies

page 2

CAMICIA ROSSA	*page* 33
1. AT BROOKE HOUSE	*page* 35
2. AT STAFFORD HOUSE	*page* 51
3. AT HOME	*page* 59
4. 26 PRINCE'S GATE	*page* 68
APOGEE AND PERIGEE	*page* 81
BEHIND THE SCENES (1863 TO 1864)—	
V. I. KELSIEV	*page* 101
THE COMMON FUND	*page* 117
BAKUNIN AND THE CAUSE OF POLAND	*page* 131
APPENDIX—	
1. THE STEAMER 'WARD JACKSON'	*page* 161
2. COLONEL LAPINSKI AND AIDE-DE-CAMP POLLES	*page* 168
FRAGMENTS (1867 TO 1868)—	
1. SWISS VIEWS	*page* 176
2. CHATTER ON THE ROAD AND FELLOW-	
COUNTRYMEN IN THE BUFFET	*page* 186
3. BEYOND THE ALPS	*page* 189
4. ZU DEUTSCH	*page* 192
5. THIS WORLD AND THE OTHER:—I. The Other World —II. This World—III. The Flowers of Minerva	*page* 196

VENEZIA LA BELLA (February 1867) *page* 220

LA BELLE FRANCE—

1. ANTE PORTAS *page* 240
2. INTRA MUROS *page* 246
3. ALPENDRÜCKEN *page* 255
4. THE DANIELS *page* 263
5. SPOTS OF LIGHT *page* 270
6. AFTER THE INVASION *page* 272

THE EMPEROR ALEXANDER I. AND

V. N. KARAZIN—

1. DON CARLOS *page* 276
2. THE LETTER *page* 285
3. MARQUIS VON POSA *page* 299
4. THE SINS OF THE FATHERS *page* 304
5. FAREMO DA SE *page* 318
6. ON THE FURTHER SIDE *page* 325

SECTION FOUR (continued)

LONDON EXILES OF THE 'FIFTIES

THIS fragment follows upon the description of the 'Mountain Heights of the Exile World'—from their eternally red crags down to their lowest bogs and 'sulphur mines.'[1] I beg the reader not to forget that in this chapter we are plunging with him below the level of the sea and are concerned exclusively with its slimy bottom, as it was after the tempest of February.

Almost everything here described has changed and vanished; the political dregs of the' fifties are overlaid by fresh sand and fresh mud. This underworld of agitations and oppressions has ebbed, subsided, died away; all that is left of it is covered by fresh formations. Its surviving figures are becoming a rarity, and now I like to meet them.

Some of the specimens I want to preserve are mournfully grotesque, mournfully ludicrous, but they are all drawn from nature—and they ought not to vanish without a trace.

[1] *Die Schwefelbande.*—(*Author's Note.*)

Chapter 6

ORDINARY MISFORTUNES AND POLITICAL MISFORTUNES—
TEACHERS AND COMMISSIONAIRES—AGENTS AND SALESMEN
—ORATORS AND LETTER-WRITERS—DO-NOTHING
FACTOTUMS AND EVER-BUSY DRONES—
RUSSIANS—THIEVES—SPIES

(Written in 1856 and 1857)

... FROM the *sulphurous gang*, as the Germans themselves called the Marxists, it is an easy and natural transition to the muddy slime, to the lowest dregs which drift from continental shocks and commotions to the shores of Britain, and most of all to London.

It may well be imagined what incongruous elements are caught up from the Continent and deposited in England by those ebbs and flows of revolution and reaction which exhaust the constitution of Europe like an intermittent fever; and what amazing types of people are cast down by these waves and stray about in the damp swamps of London. What must be the chaos of ideas and theories in these specimens of every kind of moral formation and reformation, of every protest, every Utopia, every disillusionment, and every hope, who meet in the alleys, eating-houses and beer-shops of Leicester Square and the adjoining back streets? 'There,' as *The Times* puts it, 'lives a wretched population of foreigners wearing hats such as no one wears, and hair where none should be, a miserable, poverty-stricken, harassed population who set all the powerful monarchs of Europe trembling except the Queen of England.'

Yes indeed, there in the public-houses and beer-shops sit these foreign visitors over their gin with hot or cold water or without water at all, or with a mug of bitter porter, and still bitterer words on their lips, waiting for a revolution, for which they are no longer adapted, and money from relations, which they will never get.

What original, what odd figures I have studied among them! Here, side by side with the Communist of the old faith, hating every man of property in the name of universal brotherhood, is the old Carlist who had shot at his own brothers in the name of patriotism from devotion to a Montemolin[1] or a Don Juan, of whom he knew nothing and knows nothing. There, side by side with the Hungarian who describes how with five *honveds*[2] he sent a squadron of Austrian cavalry flying, and to make himself look more martial buttons his Hungarian coat up to the throat, though its proportions betray that its youth belonged to another wearer, sit the German who gives lessons in music, Latin, every literature and every art, for his daily beer; the cosmopolitan and atheist who despises every nationality except Kur-Hesse or Hesse-Cassel, according to which of the Hessen he happens to have been born in; the Pole of the old-fashioned pattern who loves independence as a Catholic may; and the Italian for whom independence means hatred of Catholicism.

Beside the revolutionary *émigrés* are the *conservative émigrés*: the business man or the notary who has absconded *sans adieux* from his fatherland, creditors and guarantors, and who also reckons himself unjustly persecuted; the *honest* bankrupt convinced that he will soon clear his character and obtain fresh credit and capital; just as his neighbour on the right knows for certain that in a day

[1] Don Carlos, born 1818, usually called Count of Montemolin to distinguish him from the better known Don Carlos, his father. Both were unsuccessful pretenders to the throne of Queen Isabella of Spain. Don Juan was the brother of the Count of Montemolin, and at the latter's death succeeded to his claims.

[2] *Honveds* ('Land-defenders'), the name given to the old national heroes of Hungary, was in 1848 adopted by the revolutionary armies.—(*Translator's Notes*.)

or two 'La Rouge' will be proclaimed by 'Marianne' in person; while his neighbour on the left is equally certain that the Orleans family is packing up in Claremont and the princesses are ordering splendid dresses for a triumphal entry into Paris.

To the *conservative* group of the 'guilty but not convicted through absence of the accused' belong also more thorough-going persons than bankrupts or notaries of too ardent imagination; these were persons who had had *great misfortunes* in their native land and were trying with all their might to pass off their *ordinary misfortunes* for *political misfortunes*. This peculiar nomenclature calls for explanation.

One of our friends went as a joke to a matrimonial agency. He was asked for ten francs and questioned as to what kind of bride he desired, whether fair or dark, how much dowry she must have, and so on. The sleek little old man, after noting down his answers, began with apologies and circumlocutions to question him about his origin and was greatly rejoiced on learning that he was of noble rank; then, redoubling his apologies and observing that the silence of the grave was their rule, asked him: '*Have you not had misfortunes?*'

'I am a Pole and in exile, that is without country, without rights, without property.'

'The last item is unfortunate, but excuse me, for what reason did you leave your *belle patrie?*'

'By reason of the last rebellion.' (This happened in 1848.)

'That is of no consequence. *Political misfortunes we do not count*, they are rather to the good, *c'est une attraction*. But allow me, can you assure me that you have had no *other misfortunes*?'

'I should think I have had; why, my father and mother are dead.'

'Oh, no, no . . .'

SCHOELCHER AND A FRENCH EXILE

'What then do you mean by the words, *other misfortunes*?'

'You see, you might have left your lovely fatherland for *private* reasons and not for political ones. Sometimes in youth imprudence, bad example, the temptations of great cities—you know how it is. . . . An I.O.U. thoughtlessly given, a sum of money not your own spent somewhat irregularly—a signature or something . . .'

'I understand, I understand,' said my friend. 'No, I assure you I have not been tried either for theft or forgery.'

. . . In the year 1855 a Frenchman, *exilé de sa patrie*, went from one to another of his comrades in misfortune, proposing they should assist him to publish a poem after the style of Balzac's 'Comédie du Diable,' which he had written in prose and verse with new orthography and newly invented syntax. Among the characters in the poem were Louis-Philippe, Jesus Christ, Robespierre, Maréchal Bugeaud, and God Himself.

Among others he approached with this request Schoelcher, the most honest and rigid of mortals.

'Have you been in exile long?' the champion of the negroes asked him.

'Since 1847.'

'Since 1847? And you came here?'

'From Brest, from penal servitude.'

'What affair was that? I don't remember it at all.'

'Oh, well, the case was very famous at the time Of course, it was more of an individual case.'

'What was it, though?' . . . Schoelcher asked, somewhat perturbed.

'*Ah, bah, si vous y tenez*, I protested in my own way against the rights of property, *j'ai protesté à ma manière*.'

'And you . . . you have been in Brest?'

'*Parbleu oui*, seven years of penal servitude for *burglary (vol avec effraction)*,' and Schoelcher, with the voice of the chaste Susannah dismissing the indiscreet old men, bade the independent protester leave him.

The persons, whose misfortunes were fortunately *general* and whose protests were collective, whom we have left in grimy public-houses and black cook-shops at unpainted tables with gin or porter before them, had their fill of suffering, and, what was most distressing, without the faintest idea what they suffered for.

Time passed with terrible leisureliness, but it passed; revolution was nowhere in sight, except in their imaginations, while poverty, actual and merciless, mowed closer and closer the pastures on which they grazed, and all this mass of people, for the most part good people, went hungrier and hungrier. They had no habit of work; their thoughts, bent on the political arena, could not concentrate on the practical; they caught at anything, but with exasperation, with annoyance, with impatience, without perseverance, and everything slipped through their fingers; those who had the strength and manliness for work were gradually detached and swam up out of the bog, but the others!

And what an endless number there were of those others! Since those days the French amnesty and the amnesty of death has carried off many, but in the early 'fifties I came upon the great tide.

The German refugees, especially those not of the working class, were very poor, not less so than the French. They were rarely successful. Doctors who had studied medicine thoroughly, and in any case knew their work a hundred times better than the English sawbones who were called surgeons, could hardly get together a meagre practice. Painters and sculptors, with pure and platonic dreams of art and its sacred service, but without productive talent, without intensity and persistence, without unerring instinct, perished in the crowd of competing rivals. In the simple conditions of their little native town, on the cheap German food, they might have led long and tranquil lives, preserving their virginal worship of their ideals and their faith in their sacred vocation. There they would have lived and died, suspected of talent. Torn up from their little native gardens by the French upheaval, they were lost in the forest jungles of London life.

If one is not to be crushed and stifled in London, one must do a great deal of work, and do it smartly, at once, and do what comes first, what is in demand. One must fix the distracted attention of the blasé crowd by intensity, impudence, mass or variety. Ornaments, patterns for embroidery, arabesques, models, sketches, portraits, frames, water-colours, cameos, flowers—anything, so long as it is done quickly, so long as it is done in the nick of time and in immense quantity. Twenty-four hours after the news of Havelock's victory in India, Julien, *le grand Julien*,[1] had composed a musical performance with the cries of African birds and the tramp of elephants, with Indian chants and firing of cannon, so that London read the news in the newspapers and listened to its presentation at the concert simultaneously. He made immense sums out of this composition, which ran for a month. Meanwhile the dreamers from beyond the Rhine fell by the roadside in this inhuman race for money

[1] Sir George Grove in his *Dictionary of Music and Musicians* says of Jullien (originally Julien): 'No one at all in the same category has occupied anything like the same position in public favour. His name was a household word and his face and figure household shapes during a period of nearly twenty years.' 'To Jullien is attributed the immense improvements made in our orchestras during these twenty years.' Among other works he composed The Allied Armies Quadrille (Crimean War, 1854), The Indian Quadrille and Havelock's March (Indian Mutiny, 1857), The English Quadrille, and The French Quadrille.—(*Translator's Note.*)

and success; exhausted, they folded their hands in despair, or worse still, raised them against themselves to put an end to the unequal and humiliating struggle.

Apropos of concerts, those of the Germans who were musical were better off altogether; the number of such employed every day by London and its suburbs is colossal. Theatres and private lessons, modest working-class balls and immodest ones at the Argyle Rooms, at Cremorne and the Casino, *cafés chantants* with dancing, *cafés chantants* with living pictures in tights, Her Majesty's, Covent Garden, Exeter Hall, the Crystal Palace, St. James's at the top and the corners of all the main streets at the bottom occupy and maintain the whole population of two or three German duchies. A poor fellow will dream of the Music of the Future and of Rossini doing homage to Wagner, will read Tannhäuser at home from the score with no instrument, and then, sitting behind a retired tambour-major and a mummer with an ivory stick, play some Mary Anne polka or Flower and Butterfly *redowa* for four hours in succession and be given two shillings to four-and-sixpence for his evening. Then he will go out into the dark night, through the rain to an underground beer-shop, chiefly frequented by Germans, and there find my old friends Kraut and Müller: Kraut, who has been working for six years at a bust, which keeps growing worse and worse; and Müller, who has been for twenty-six years writing a tragedy called 'Eric,' which he read to me ten years ago and again five years ago, and would be reading to me again now if we had not quarrelled. And we quarrelled about General Urban, [1] but of that another time. . . .

. . . And what did not the Germans do to win the

[1] The Austrian Field-Marshal Urban defeated Garibaldi's volunteers and took Varese, but was obliged to abandon it (June 1859).—(*Translator's Note*.)

favourable notice of the English, and all without success?

Germans, who all their lives have smoked in every corner of their dwellings, at dinner and at tea, in bed and at their work, do not in London smoke in their smutty, smoke-begrimed drawing-room, and will not allow their guests to do so. Men who have always in their own country been in the habit of going to a tavern to drink and sit over a pipe in good company will pass the London public-houses without looking at them, and send a maid there for beer with a mug or a milk-jug.

I once happened in the presence of a German *émigré* to fold up a letter addressed to an Englishwoman. 'What are you about?' he cried in excitement. I started, and involuntarily dropped the letter, supposing that there was a scorpion in it at least. 'In England,' he said, 'a letter is always folded in three and not in four, and you writing to a lady too! and such a lady!'

On my first arrival in London I went to look up a German doctor of my acquaintance. I did not find him at home, and wrote on a sheet of paper that was lying on the table something of this kind: '*Cher docteur*, I am in London and should very much like to see you. Won't you come this evening to such-and-such a tavern to have a bottle of wine as in old days, and to have a good talk?' The doctor did not come, and next day I received a note from him to this effect: 'M. Herzen, I am very sorry that I could not take advantage of your kind invitation. My duties do not leave me much leisure. I will try, however, to visit you in a day or two, etc. . . .'

'. . . Why, it seems the doctor has got a practice then?' I inquired of the German patriot to whom I was indebted for the information that the English fold their letters in three.' Not at all; *der Kerl hat Pech gehabt* in London, *es geht ihm zu ominös*.' 'Then what is he doing?' and I handed my friend the note. He smiled, but observed that I should not have left on any doctor's table an open letter in which I invited him to have a bottle of wine: 'And besides, why ask him to such a tavern, where there is always a crowd? Here people drink at home.' 'It is a pity,' I observed, 'that knowledge always comes too late; now I know how to invite the doctor and where to bid him come, but I certainly shall not ask him.'

Now we will go back to our exiles dreaming of revolution, of remittances from relations, and of earning without working.

For a man who has not been a workman to begin working is not so easy as it seems; many people imagine that if need has arisen, if there is work, if there are tools, the workman too is ready. Work requires not only its special education and training but also self-sacrifice. The exiles, for the most part, came from second-rate drawing-rooms and literary circles, and were journalistic hacks or budding lawyers. They could not live in England by the work they were accustomed to, and any other was unnatural to them; moreover, they felt it not worth while to begin anything new, they were always listening for the bugle-call: ten years passed, fifteen years passed, no call to battle came.

In despair, in vexation, without clothes, without a secure prospect for the morrow, surrounded by growing families, they shut their eyes and fling themselves headlong into schemes and speculations. Their schemes do not succeed, their speculations come to grief, both because the schemes they hatch are nonsensical and because instead of capital all they bring to them is a sort of helpless clumsiness, an excessive irritability, an incapacity to find their bearings in the simplest position, and again an incapacity for sustained labour and for enduring the first thorny steps. When they fail they find their solace in blaming their poverty: 'With two or three hundred pounds everything would have gone splendidly!' The lack of capital really is of course a drawback, but that is the common lot of working people. There is no scheme too wild for them, from a joint-stock society for procuring eggs from Havre to the invention of special inks for trade-marks and of some sort of essences by which the vilest spirits can be transformed into excellent liqueurs. But while the societies are being formed and capital is being collected for all these marvels, they must have food to eat and some sort of clothing to shield them from the north-east wind and the modest eyes of the daughters of Albion.

Two palliative measures were undertaken with this view: one very tiresome and very unprofitable, the other also unprofitable, but attended with more entertainment. Quiet people with *Sitzfleisch* took to giving lessons in spite of the fact that they had not only given no lessons before, but had very probably never received any. The fees were terribly lowered by competition.

Here is a specimen of the advertisement published by an old man of seventy, who, I fancy, belonged rather to the class of *independent* than of *collective* protestors:—

Monsieur N. N.
Teaches the French Language
on a new and easy System of rapid proficiency;
has attended members of the British Parliament
and many other persons of respectability,
as vouchers certify; translates and interprets
that universal continental language,
and English,
In a Masterly Manner.
Terms Moderate:
Namely, Three Lessons per week for Six Shillings.

Giving lessons to English people is not a particularly pleasant task; an Englishman does not stand upon ceremony with any one whom he employs for payment.

One of my old friends received a letter from an Englishman asking him to give French lessons to his daughter. My friend went at the hour fixed to arrange terms. The father was having an after-dinner nap, but the daughter greeted him rather civilly; then the old man came out, looked B. up and down and asked: '*Vous être le* French teacher?' B. admitted it. '*Vous pas convenir a moa.*' With this the British ass pointed to his visitor's moustache and beard. 'Why didn't you give him a punch?' I asked B. 'Well, I thought of it, but when the bull had turned away, the daughter with tears in her eyes mutely begged my forgiveness.'

Another resource is simpler and not so tedious; it consists in a spasmodic and artistic selling of things on commission, pressing all sorts of goods on people regardless of whether they want them. The French for the most part dealt in wines and spirits. One Legitimist used to offer his acquaintances and co-religionists brandy which he obtained in an exceptional way through connections, of which in the present state of France he could not and ought not to speak, and, moreover, through a ship's captain whom it would be a *calamité publique* to compromise. The brandy was nothing special and cost sixpence more than at the shops. The Legitimist, accustomed to plead 'with declamation,' would add insult to his insistence: he would take a wine-glass in two fingers by the foot, would slowly describe circles with it, splash a few drops, sniff them in the air and invariably be astonished at the extraordinarily fine aroma of the brandy.

Another comrade in affliction who had once been a provincial professor of literature had recourse to the seductions of wine. He obtained his wine straight from the Côte d'Or, from Burgundy, from his old pupils, and was extraordinarily successful in his choice of it.

'*Citoyen,*' he wrote to me, 'ask your brotherly heart (*votre cœur fraternel*) and it will tell you that you ought to grant me the agreeable privilege of furnishing you with French wine. And in so doing your heart will be at one with taste and with economy. While you drink excellent wine at the very lowest price you will have the happiness of thinking that in purchasing it you are alleviating the lot of a man who has sacrificed all to the cause of his country and of freedom.

'*Salut et fraternité!* P.S.—I have taken the liberty of despatching you with this a few samples.'

These samples were in half-bottles on which he had with his own hand inscribed not only the name of the wine but various incidents from its biography: Chambertin (*Gr. vin et très rare!*), Côte Rôtie (*Comète*), Pommard (1823!), Nuits (*provision Aguado!*).'

Two or three weeks later the professor of literature would send a fresh set of samples. A day or two after sending them he would usually appear himself and sit on for two or three hours until I had consented to keep almost all the samples and paid for them. As he was relentless and this was repeated several times, I used in the end to praise some of the samples, pay him for them, and give him back the rest as soon as he opened the door. 'I do not want to encroach on your valuable time, *citoyen*,' he would say to me, and spare me for a fortnight from the sour Burgundy born under the comet and the sugary Côte Rôtie from the cellars of Aguado.

The Germans and Hungarians applied themselves to other branches of industry.

One day at Richmond I was lying down with a terrible attack of headache. François came up with a visiting-card saying that a gentleman urgently desired to see me, that he was an Hungarian, *ajutante del generate* (all the Hungarian exiles who had no honest calling dubbed themselves Kossuth's adjutants). I glanced at the card—it was an absolutely unknown name adorned with the title of captain.

'Why have you admitted him? How many thousand times have I told you of it?'

'This is the third time he has called to-day.'

'Well, ask him into the drawing-room.' I went down like a raging lion, fortifying myself with a dose of a sedative.

'Allow me to introduce myself, Captain So-and-so. I was for a long time a prisoner of the Russians with Rüdiger after Vilagosz. The Russians treated us extremely well. I was particularly favoured by General Glazenap and Colonel . . . What was it . . .? Russian surnames are very difficult . . . itch . . . itch . . .'

'Please don't trouble. I do not know any colonel. Very glad that you were comfortable. Won't you sit down?'

'Very, very comfortable . . . we used to play every day with the officers *shtoss* and *bank* . . . very fine fellows and they can't endure the Austrians. I even remember a few words of Russian—*gleba, sheverdak, une piéce de vingt-cinq sous.*'

'Allow me to inquire to what I am indebted . . .?'

'You must excuse me, baron . . . I was taking a walk in Richmond . . . lovely weather, only it's a pity it has come on to rain. I have heard so much about you from the *old man himself* and from Count Sandor—Sandor Téléki—and also from the Countess Teresa Pulszky[1] . . . What a woman the Countess Teresa!'

[1] This lady was the wife of the Count F. A. Pulszky, who was a friend of Kossuth and associated with him in the efforts to throw off the yoke of the Austrian Government. He wrote several books

'Quite so, *hors ligne!*'

Silence.

'Ye—es, and Sandor . . . we were in the *honveds* together. . . . I particularly wanted to show you . . .' and he drew out from under his chair a portfolio, untied it, and took out portraits of the armless Raglan,[1] the revolting countenance of St.-Arnaud,[2] and Omer Pasha[3] in a fez. 'A remarkable likeness, baron. I have been in Turkey myself. I was at Kutais in 1849,' he added, as though to guarantee the likeness in spite of the fact that neither Raglan nor St.-Arnaud were there in 1849. 'Have you seen this collection before?'

'Of course I have,' I answered, moistening my head with lotion. 'These portraits are hung up everywhere in Cheapside, along the Strand, and in the West End.'

'Yes, you are right, but I have the whole collection, and those are not on Chinese paper. In the shops you would pay a guinea for them, and I can let you have them for fifteen shillings.'

'I am really very much obliged to you, but tell me, captain, what do I want with the portraits of St.-Arnaud and all this crew?'

'Baron, I will be open with you. I am a soldier

describing his adventures, and his wife wrote her memoirs, known in English as *Memoirs of an Hungarian Lady* (published in London, 1850), and other books, such as *Tales and Traditions of Hungary* (1851).

[1] The famous Lord Raglan, who distinguished himself in the campaigns against Napoleon and still more so in the Crimean War, lost his right arm at Waterloo and is said to have practised writing with his left hand the very next day. The 'Raglan sleeve' is doubtless so named in his honour.

[2] St.-Arnaud, Jacques Leroy de (1801-1854), one of the leading organisers of the Coup d'État of December 2, defeated the Russians at Alma.

[3] Omer Pasha, Turkish General in the Crimean War.—(*Translator's Notes.*)

and not one of Metternich's diplomats. Having lost my estates near Temesvar, I am temporarily in straitened circumstances and am therefore selling *objets d'art* on commission (and also cigars—Havanna cigars and Turkish tobacco—Russians and we Hungarians know what is good in that line!), and so I make the poor halfpence with which to buy the bitter bread of exile, *wie der Schiller sagt*.'

'Captain, be completely open and tell me what will you make off each collection?' I asked (though I doubt whether Schiller did utter that line of Dante).

'Half a crown.'

'Then let us settle the matter like this: I will offer you a whole crown if you will let me off buying the portraits.'

'Really, baron, I am ashamed, but my position . . . but you know it all, you feel it all. . . . I have so long cherished a respect for you . . . the Countess Pulszky . . . and the Count Sandor, Sandor Téléki. . . .'

'Excuse me, Captain, I have such a headache that I can hardly sit up.'

'Our governor (namely Kossuth), our old man, often has a headache too,' the *honved* observed by way of encouragement and consolation; then he hurriedly tied up his portfolio, and together with the striking likenesses of Raglan and company carried off a fairly good portrait of Queen Victoria on a coin.

Among these pedlars of exile who offer profitable purchases and the *émigrés* who have been for the last ten years stopping every man wearing a beard in the streets and squares, begging for two shillings to make up their fare to America or sixpence to pay for the coffin of a baby who has died of scarlet fever, there are the exiles who write letters, sometimes on the grounds of acquaintance, sometimes of non-acquaintance, expatiating on extreme straits of all kinds and temporary money difficulties, often with prospects of growing wealthy in the far future and always with an original taste in epistolary composition.

I have a portfolio of such letters. I will quote two or three particularly characteristic.

'*Herr Graf!* I was a lieutenant in the Austrian army, but fought for the freedom of the Magyars, was forced to flee, and have worn out all my clothes; if you have any old trousers to spare, you will confer an unspeakable obligation on me.

'*P.S.* —To-morrow at nine o'clock I will wait upon your *courier*.'

That is an example of the naive style, but there are letters that are classical both in language and in their clear-cut incisiveness: '*Domine, ego sum Gallus, ex patriâ meâ profugus pro causâ libertatis populi. Nihil habeo ad manducandum, si aliquod pro me facere potes, gaudeo, gaudebit cor meum.*

'*Mercuris dies* 1859.'

Other letters neither laconic nor classical in form are distinguished by a peculiar method of reckoning.

'*Citoyen*, you were so kind as to send me three pounds last February (you may not remember it, but I remember it). For a long time past I have been meaning to repay you, but have received no money at all from my relations; I am expecting a rather considerable sum in a few days. If I were not ashamed, I would ask you to send me another two pounds, and then I could repay you the five pounds in a *round sum*.'

I preferred the sum to remain triangular. The gentleman who was so set upon round sums began to spread it abroad that I was in touch with the Russian Embassy.

Then come business letters and oratorical letters, and both kinds lose a great deal in translation.

'*Mon cher Monsieur!* No doubt you know of my

discovery. It should bring glory to our century and a crust of bread to me. And this discovery remains buried in obscurity because I have not the credit for a paltry two hundred pounds, and instead of working at it am obliged to *courir le cachet* for wretched pay. Every time that permanent and profitable work presents itself an ironical destiny breathes upon it (I am translating word for word), it flies away—I pursue it, its obstinate insolence baffles my projects (*son opiniâtre insolence bafoue mes projets*), again my hopes are raised and I fly after it—after it. I am flying after it now. Shall I catch it? I almost believe so—if you have confidence in my talent, are willing to *embarquer votre confiance en compagnie de mon esprit et la livrer au souffle peu aventureux de mon destin.*'

Further on he explains that he has eighty pounds, even eighty-five pounds in prospect; the remaining hundred and fifteen pounds the inventor seeks to borrow, promising thirteen or at least eleven per cent. in case of success. 'Could capital be better, more safely invested in our day when the finances of the whole world are unstable and states are tottering, propped on the bayonets of our foes?'

I did not give the hundred and fifteen. The inventor began to admit that there was something a little dubious in my behaviour, '*il y a du louche,*' and that it would be as well to be on one's guard with me.

In conclusion here is a purely oratorical letter:—

'Generous fellow-citizen of the future republic of the world! How many times have you and your distinguished friend Louis Blanc assisted me, and again I am writing to you and to *citoyen* Blanc to beg for a few shillings. My heart-rending position has not changed for the better, far from my Lares and Penates, on the inhospitable island of egoism and greed. With what profound truth have you said in your works (I am con-

STREET BEGGARS 19

tinually re-reading them), "The talent dies out without money like a lamp without oil" —' and so on.

I need hardly say that I never did write such bosh, and my fellow-citizen of the *république future et universelle* had never once opened my works.

After the orators by letter come the orators by word of mouth who 'work the pavement and the street corner.' For the most part they only pretend to be exiles, but are in reality foreign workmen who have sunk from drink or men who have had *misfortunes* at home. Taking advantage of the immense size of London, they work thoroughly through one quarter after another and then return to the Via Sacra—that is to Regent Street, with the Haymarket and Leicester Square.

Five years ago a young man rather neatly dressed and of a sentimental appearance approached me on several occasions in the dusk with a question in French spoken with a German accent: 'Could you tell me where such-and-such a part is?' and he handed mean address half a dozen miles from the West End, somewhere in Holloway or Hackney. Everybody tried, as I did, to explain where it was. He was overwhelmed with horror. 'It is nine o'clock in the evening already. I have had nothing to eat yet . . . when shall I get there? . . . Not a penny for an omnibus. . . . I did not expect this. I do not like to ask you, but if you could lend me . . . one shilling would be enough. . . .'

I met him twice more. At last he disappeared, and not without satisfaction I came upon him some months later in his old pitch with a different beard and wearing a different cap. Raising the latter with feeling, he asked me: 'No doubt you know French?' 'I do, 'I answered, 'but I know also that you have an address, that you have to go a long distance, that the hour is late, that you have had nothing to eat, that you have no money for an omnibus and that you need a shilling . . . but this time I will give you sixpence because I have told you all that instead of your telling me.'

'I can't help it, 'he answered, smiling, without the slightest resentment,' of course you won't believe me again, but I am going to America. You might add something for my fare.'

I could not resist that, and gave him another sixpence.

There were Russians, too, among these gentry—for instance, Stremouhov, a former officer from the Caucasus who had been begging in Paris as long ago as 1847, telling a very plausible tale of some duel, an escape, and so on, and carrying off to the intense exasperation of the servants everything he could get: old clothes and slippers, winter vests in summer and cotton trousers in the winter, children's clothes, ladies 'frippery. The Russians got up a subscription for him and sent him off to the Foreign Legion in Algiers. He served there for five years, brought away a testimonial and again went begging from house to house, telling about the duel and the escape and adding various Arab adventures. Stremouhov was growing old and people were both sorry for him and terribly sick of him. The Russian priest attached to the London Embassy got up a subscription to send him to Australia. He was given introductions in Melbourne, and he himself and, what was more important, his fare were put in the captain's special care. Stremouhov came to say good-bye to us. We gave him a complete outfit. I provided him with a warm overcoat, Haug with shirts and so on. Stremouhov shed tears at parting and said:' Say what you like, gentlemen, but it is no easy thing to go so far away. To break with all one's habits, but it must be . . .' and he kissed us and thanked us most warmly.

I thought that Stremouhov had been for long ages on the banks of the Victoria River when suddenly I read in *The Times* that a Russian officer called Stremo-uhov had been sentenced to three months 'imprisonment for disorderly behaviour and fighting some one in a tavern after mutual accusations of theft and so on. Four months after that I was walking along Oxford Street when it began to rain heavily, and as I had no umbrella I stood under a gateway. At the very moment when I stopped, a lanky figure under a wreck of an umbrella whisked hurriedly under another gateway. I recognised Stremouhov.' What, have you come back from Australia?' I asked him, looking him straight in the face.

'Ah, it's you, and I didn't recognise you,' he answered in a faint and sinking voice, 'no, not from Australia, but from the hospital where I have been lying for three months between life and death . . . and I don't know why I recovered.'

'In which hospital have you been—St. George's?'

'No, not here, in Southampton.'

'How was it you fell ill and did not let any one know, and how was it you did not go?'

'I missed the first train. I went by the next, but the steamer had left. I stood on the quay. I stood there and almost threw myself into the briny depths; I went to the Reverend to whom our priest had recommended me. "The captain," he said, "has gone; he would not wait an hour."'

'And the money?'

'He left the money with the Reverend.'

'You took it, of course?'

'I did, but I got no good out of it. While I was ill they stole everything from under my pillow, wretches that they are. If only you can help me!'

'And here in your absence another Stremouhov has been clapped into prison, and for three months too, for fighting with a courier. Didn't you hear of it?'

'How could I hear of it, lying between life and death? I believe the rain is giving over. Good-bye.'

'You must be careful how you go out in the damp or you will be getting into hospital again.'

After the Crimean War several prisoners of war, both sailors and soldiers, were left in London, though they could not themselves say why. For the most part given to drink, it was some time before they realised their position. Some of them asked the Embassy to intercede for them, to take up their cause, *aber was macht es denn dem Herrn Baron von Brunow!*

They were an extremely melancholy spectacle, tattered and emaciated; they would sometimes cringingly, sometimes with insolence (rather unpleasant in a narrow street after ten o'clock at night), ask for money.

In 1853 several sailors ran away from a man-of-war at Portsmouth. Some of them were brought back in accordance with the absurd law which applies exclusively to sailors. Several of them escaped and walked on foot from Portsmouth to London. One of them, a young man of two-and-twenty with a good-natured and open face, was a shoe-maker and could make *schlippers* as he called them. I bought him tools and gave him money, but he could not get work.

It was just then that Garibaldi was sailing with his ship, *The Commonwealth*, to Genoa, and I asked him to take the young man with him. Garibaldi engaged him at a wage of £1 a month, promising to raise it to £2 a month in a year's time if he should behave well. The sailor of course agreed, took £2 in advance from Garibaldi and brought his belongings on to the ship.

The day after Garibaldi had left, the sailor came to me, red in the face, drowsy and bloated-looking.

'What has happened?' I asked him.

'A misfortune, your honour. I was too late for the ship.'

AN UNGRATEFUL SAILOR

'How did you come to be late?'

The sailor fell on his knees and whimpered unnaturally. The position was not hopeless. The boat had gone to Newcastle-on-Tyne for coal. 'I will send you there by rail,' I said to him, 'but if you are too late again this time, remember that I will do nothing for you even if you are starving. And as the fare to Newcastle is over £1, and I would not trust you with a shilling, I shall send for a friend and ask him to take charge of you all night and put you into the train.'

'I will pray for your honour all my life long!'

The friend who undertook to despatch him came to me and reported that he had seen the sailor off.

Imagine my amazement when three days later the sailor appeared with a Pole.

'What is the meaning of this?' I shouted at him, shaking with genuine fury. But before the sailor could open his lips, his companion proceeded to defend him in broken Russian, bathing his words in an atmosphere of tobacco, wine and spirits.

'Who are you?'

'A Polish nobleman.'

'Every one is a nobleman in Poland. Why have you come to me with this scoundrel?'

The nobleman was cheeky. I observed dryly that I was not acquainted with him, and that his presence in my room was so strange that I might call a policeman and have him removed.

I looked at the sailor. Three days of the aristocratic company of a nobleman had greatly advanced his education. He was not crying, but was looking at me with drunken insolence.

'I was taken very ill, your honour, I thought I should give up my soul to God, but I got a little better when the train had gone.'

'Where were you taken ill, then?'

'On the way, that is, at the railway station.'

'Why didn't you go by the next train?'

'I never thought of it, and besides, not knowing the language . . .'

'Where is your ticket?'

'Why, I have no ticket.'

'How is that?'

'I gave it up to a man.'

'Well, now you can look out for other people; only be sure of one thing, I will never help you in any case.'

'But excuse me,' the nobleman interposed.

'Sir, I have nothing to say to you and desire to hear nothing from you.'

Swearing at me through his teeth, he went off with his Telemachus, probably to the nearest public-house.

Another step downward. . . .

Perhaps many people will ask me wonderingly what further step downward there can be. But there *is* a rather *great* one—only here things are obscure and one must step warily. I had not the *pruderie* of Schoelcher, and the author of the poem in which Christ converses with Marshal Bugeaud seemed to me even more amusing after his heroic sufferings *pour un vol avec effraction*. Even if he did steal something and break a lock, goodness knows what he had suffered for it, and then he had toiled for some years, perhaps with a cannon-ball chained to his legs. He had ranged against him not only the man he had robbed but the whole State and society, the church, the army, the police, the law, all honest men who do not need to rob, as well as all dishonest ones who have not been caught and tried. There are thieves of another kind, rewarded by the Government, cherished by the authorities, blessed by the Church, protected by the army, and not persecuted by the police, because they themselves belong to it; these men do not filch handkerchiefs, but conversations, letters, glances. Exile-spies are doubly spies. . . . With them the utmost limit of vice and depravity is reached; below them, as below Dante's 'Lucifer,' there is nothing, every step from that lowest depth is upward.

The French are great artists in this line. They are capable of adroitly combining the externals of culture, enthusiastic phrases, the *aplomb* of a man whose conscience is clear and whose *point d'honneur* is sensitive, with the duties of a spy. Begin to suspect him, and he will challenge you to a duel; he will fight, and fight bravely too.

The memoirs of Delahodde,[1] of Chenu,[2] and of Schnepf are a treasure-house for the study of the filth to which civilisation leads its vicious children. Delahodde naively prints that in betraying his friends he was obliged to be as artful with them 'as a sportsman is with game.'

Delahodde is the Alcibiades of espionage.

A young man of literary education and radical views, he came from the provinces to Paris, poor as Job, and asked for work at the offices of La Réforme. He was given work of some sort and did it well; little by little he got on to friendly terms with the staff. He obtained an entry into political circles, learnt a great deal of what was being done in the Republican party, and continued working for several years, still on the most friendly terms with his colleagues.

When, after the revolution of February, Caussidière went through the papers at the Prefecture, he found that Delahodde had all this time with the greatest accuracy furnished reports to the police of what was being done at the office of La Réforme. Caussidière

[1] Delahodde (or De Lahode), Lucien, wrote *Histoire des Sociétés Secrètes de 1830 à 1848*, and *La Naissance de la République*.
[2] Chenu, J. A., wrote *Les Conspirateurs*, which called forth a reply, *Réponse aux deux libelles de Chenu et Delahodde*, by J. Miot.—(*Translator's Notes*.)

sent for Delahodde to come to Albert's; there witnesses awaited him. Delahodde came, suspecting nothing, tried to defend himself, but then, seeing the impossibility, admitted that he had written letters to the Prefect. The question arose what was to be done with him. Some thought, and they were perfectly right, that he should be shot on the spot like a dog. Albert opposed this more than any one, and did not want to have a man killed *in his flat*. Caussidière offered him a loaded pistol to shoot himself. Delahodde refused. Some one asked him whether he would like poison. Poison, too, he refused, but on his way to prison, like a sensible person, asked for a mug of beer. This is a fact told me by the deputy-mayor of the twelfth arrondissement, who accompanied him.

When the reaction began to get the upper hand and Delahodde was let out of prison, he went away to England, but when the reaction was completely triumphant he returned to Paris, and was a prominent figure at the theatre and at public gatherings as a lion of a peculiar species; after that, he published his memoirs.

Spies are invariably to be found in all groups of exiles; they are recognised, discovered, beaten, but they do their job with complete success. In Paris the police know all the secrets of London; the day of Delescluze's,[1] and afterwards of Boichot's,[2] secret arrival in France was so well known that they were seized at Calais as soon as they stepped off the boat. At the

[1] Delescluze, Charles (1809-1871), a French journalist and politician, was a member of the Commune in 1871 and killed at the barricades.

[2] Boichot, Jean Baptiste (born 1820), elected a Representative of the People, appeared in uniform at the demonstration of June 13, 1849, escaped to Switzerland and afterwards to London, where he wrote books in conjunction with Felix Pyat and was head of the society called 'La Commune Révolutionnaire.' He returned to Paris in 1854, was captured and imprisoned,—(*Translator's Notes*.)

trial of the Communists at Cologne, documents and letters were read that had been 'bought in London,' as the Prussian commissioner of police naively admitted at the trial.

In 1849 I made the acquaintance of an exiled Austrian journalist called Engländer. He was very clever and very sarcastic, and later on published a series of lively articles on the historical development of Socialism in Kolatchek's *Jahrbücher*. This Engländer had been imprisoned in Paris in connection with the case called the 'Case of the Correspondents.'

All sorts of rumours were current about him; at last he turned up himself in London. Here another Austrian exile, Dr. Hefner, who was greatly respected by his fellow-countrymen, said that Engländer had been in the pay of the Prefect in Paris, and that he had been put in prison for infidelity to the French police, who were jealous of the Austrian embassy in whose service he was also employed. Engländer led a dissipated life, which needs plenty of money, and the Prefect alone apparently did not provide enough.

The German exiles discussed it and discussed it, and sent for Engländer to answer these charges. Engländer tried to turn it off with a joke, but Hefner was relentless. Then the unfaithful consort of the two polices leapt up with a flushed face and tears in his eyes, and said: 'Well, then, I *am* guilty to a great extent, but it is not for him to accuse me'; and he flung on the table a letter from the Prefect which made it clear that Hefner, too, was receiving payment from him.

There was living in Paris a certain N., also an Austrian refugee. I made his acquaintance at the end of 1848. His comrades used to describe an extraordinarily valiant action performed by him during the revolution in Vienna. The insurgents were short of gunpowder. N. undertook to bring it by rail, and brought it. A married man with children, he was in great poverty in Paris. In 1853 I found him in London in great straits; he was living with his family in two small rooms in one of the poorest back-streets of Soho. Nothing succeeded that he undertook. He set up a laundry in which his wife and another exile washed the linen, while N. delivered it; but the comrade went away to America and the laundry failed.

He wanted to get a job in a commercial office, and being a very intelligent fellow and well educated, he might have earned a good salary but for references; without references you cannot take a step in England.

I gave him my name as one: and in connection with this introduction a German refugee, O., observed to me that it was a mistake on my part to do so, that the man did not enjoy a good reputation and was supposed to be in relations with the French police.

About that time Reihel brought my children to London. He took great interest in N. I told him what was said about the latter.

Reihel laughed heartily; he was ready to answer for N. as for himself, and pointed to his poverty as the best refutation of the charge. This last consideration to some extent convinced me, too. In the evening Reihel went out for a walk and came back late, looking pale and upset. He came in to me for a minute, and complaining of a violent sick headache was about to go to bed. I looked at him and said:—

'You have something on your mind. *Heraus damit!*'

'Yes, you have guessed right . . . but first give me your word of honour that you will tell no one.'

'I daresay, but what nonsense! Leave it to my conscience.'

'I could not rest after hearing from you about N., and in spite of the promise I had given to you I made up my mind to question him, and have been to see him.

His wife is going to be confined in a day or two, their poverty is awful. . . . What it cost me to begin to speak! I called him out into the street, and at last, plucking up all my courage, said to him: "Do you know that Herzen was warned of this and that? I am convinced that it is a calumny. Do let me clear up the business." "I thank you," he answered me gloomily, "but that is not necessary; I know where the story comes from. In a moment of despair, starving, I offered the Prefect in Paris my services to keep him *au courant* with news of the exiles. He sent me three hundred francs and I have never written to him since."'

Reihel was almost weeping.

'Listen,' I said: 'until his wife has been confined and is recovered, I give you my word not to speak. Let him get a job in an office and leave political circles, but if I hear fresh evidence and he is still in relations with the exiles I will show him up. Damn the fellow!'

Reihel went away. Ten days later at dinner-time N. came in to see me, pale and in distress. 'You can imagine,' he said, 'how hard it is for me to take this step; but look where I will, I can see no hope of help except from you. My wife will be brought to bed within a few hours, we have neither coal nor tea nor a cup of milk in the house, not a farthing, nor one woman who will help, nor means to send for a doctor.' Utterly exhausted, he sank on to a chair, and hiding his face in his hands said: 'The only thing left for me is to blow out my brains, anyway I shall not see this misery.'

I sent at once to kind-hearted Paul Darasz, gave N. some money, and soothed him as far as I could. Next day Darasz came to tell me that the birth had gone off well.

Meanwhile the rumour, which had probably originated in personal enmity, of N.'s connections with the French police was more and more widely circulated, and at last T., a well-known Vienna *clubiste* and agitator, whose speech led the populace to hang Latour,[1] asserted right and left that he had himself read a letter from the Prefect accompanying a despatch of money. Evidently N. 's exposure was of great moment to T. He came himself to me to confirm N.'s guilt.

My position was becoming difficult. Haug was living with me; hitherto I had said no word to him, but now this reticence was becoming indelicate and dangerous. I told him about it, making no mention of Reihel, as I did not want to mix him up in the drama, which seemed to offer every possibility of a fifth act in a police court or at the Old Bailey. What I had dreaded beforehand was just what happened, 'the Bouillon boiled over.'[2] I could scarcely pacify Haug and restrain him from marching off to N.'s garret. I knew that N. must come to us with some manuscripts he had been copying, and advised him to await his arrival. Haug agreed, and one morning ran in to me, pale with fury, and announced that N. was below. I made haste to throw my papers into the table drawer and go down. Haug was shouting and N. was shouting. The interchange was already rather violent. The strength of the bad language was increasing and increasing. The expression of N, 's face, contorted by resentment and shame, was sinister. Haug was intensely excited and confused. As things were going, it was far easier to come to splitting skulls than reaching the truth.

'Gentlemen,' I said suddenly in the midst of their talk, 'allow me to stop you for a moment.'

They stopped.

'It seems to me that you are spoiling your case by overheat; before abusing each other you ought to put the question quite clearly—'

[1] Latour was Austrian War Minister, murdered by an infuriated crowd on October 6, 1848.
[2] An unconscious pun which occurs in an old Russian poem on the Crusades,—(*Translator's Notes*.)

N.'S EXPOSURE

'Whether I am a spy or not?' shouted N. 'I will allow no man on earth to put such a question to me.'

'No, that is not the question I meant; you are accused by a certain person, and not by him alone, of having received money from the Prefect of Police at Paris.'

'Who is that person?'

'T.'

'He is a blackguard.'

'That is not the point. Have you received money or not?'

'I have,' said N. with strained composure, looking Haug and me in the face. Haug made a convulsive grimace and uttered a sort of moan of impatience to begin reviling N. again. I took Haug by the hand and said: 'Well, that is all we want.'

'No, it is not all,' answered N. 'You ought to know that I have never compromised any one by a single line.'

'That fact can only be confirmed by your correspondent Pietri, and he is not an acquaintance of ours.'

'Well, am I a criminal and you my judges or what? What makes you imagine that I am bound to justify myself to you? I think too highly of my own dignity to let it depend on the opinion of any one like Haug or you. I will never set my foot again within this house,' added N., proudly putting on his hat and opening the door. 'You may be perfectly sure of that,' I said after him. He slammed the door and went out. Haug was for plunging after him, but, laughing, I held him back and paraphrased the words of Siéyès: '*Nous sommes aujourd'hui ce que nous avons été hier—déjeunons!*'

N. went straight off to T. The bulky, shiny Silenus of whom Mazzini once said, 'I always think that he has been fried in olive oil and not wiped afterwards,' had not yet left his bed. The door opened, and before him stood N. with drowsy and puffy eyes.

'You told Herzen that I received money from the Prefect?'

'I did.'

'What for?'

'Because you have.'

'Though you knew that I have sent no report. Take that for it.' With these words N. spat into T.'s face and walked out. . . . The infuriated Silenus, determined to be quits with him, leapt from his bed, snatched up the chamber-pot, and seizing his chance as N. descended the stairs, emptied the contents on his head, saying as he did so: 'And you take that.' This epilogue diverted me unspeakably.

'You see how well I did,' I said to Haug, 'to stop you. Why, what could you have done to the head of the luckless correspondent of Pietri equal to that? He won't be dry till the Second Coming.'

One would have thought the thing must have ended with this German vendetta, but there is still a little sequel to this epilogue. An old gentleman called V., I am told a kind and honest man, undertook to defend N. He called together a committee of Germans, and invited me as *one of the accusers*. I wrote to him that I should not come to the committee, that all I knew about it was limited to the fact that N. in my presence had confessed to Haug that he had received money from the Prefect. V. was not satisfied with this; he wrote to me that N. was guilty in fact, but morally blameless, and enclosed a letter of N. 's to him. N., among other things, drew his attention to the *strangeness* of my behaviour.' Herzen,' he said, 'knew about that money long before from Mr. Reihel, and not only said nothing till T. made his accusation, but even gave me two pounds after that, and when my wife was ill, sent the doctor at his own expense!'

Sehr gut!

CAMICIA ROSSA

SHAKESPEARE'S DAY has been transformed into Garibaldi's day. This is one of the far-fetched coincidences of history, which alone is successful in achieving such improbabilities.

The people who gathered together on Primrose Hill to plant a tree in memory of the Shakespeare Tricentenary remained there to talk of Garibaldi's sudden departure. The police dispersed the crowd. Fifty thousand men (according to the police report) obeyed the orders of thirty policemen and, from profound respect for the law, half-destroyed the grand right of open-air meeting, or, at any rate, helped to support the illegal intervention of the authorities.

Truly, something like a Shakespearian fantasy had passed before our eyes against the grey background of England with a truly Shakespearian juxtaposition of the grand and the revolting, of the heart-rending and the jarring: the holy simplicity of the man, the naive simplicity of the masses, and the secret conclaves behind the scenes, the intrigues and the lies. Familiar shades seemed to flit before our eyes in other forms—from Hamlet to King Lear, from Goneril and Cordelia to *honest* Iago. The Iagos are all in miniature, but what a number there are of them, and how honest they are!

Prologue: Alarums and excursions. The idol of the masses, the one grand popular figure that has appeared since 1848, enters in all the brilliance of its glory. Everything bows down before it, everything celebrates its triumph; this is Carlyle's hero-worship in real life. Cannon-shots, bells ringing, streamers on the boats, and no music only because England's hero has arrived on a Sunday, and Sunday here is kept as a day of mortification. . . . London stands for seven hours on its feet awaiting its guest; the triumphant ovations increase with every day; the appearance in the street of the man in the *red shirt* calls forth an outburst of enthusiasm, crowds escort him at one o'clock in the night from the opera. Workmen and clerks, lords and sempstresses, bankers and High-church clergymen; the feudal wreck, Lord Derby, and the relic of the February revolution, the republican of 1848; Queen Victoria's eldest son and the barefoot swiper born without father or mother, vie with one another in trying to capture a hand-shake, a glance, a word. Scotland, Newcastle-on-Tyne, Glasgow, Manchester are tremulous with expectation—while he vanishes into the impenetrable fog, into the blue of the ocean.

Like the ghost of Hamlet's father, the guest stepped upon some ministerial trap-door and vanished. Where was he? He was in such a place a moment since, but now he is not. . . . All that is left is a point, a sail just floating out of sight.

The English people were bewildered—'the great foolish people,' as the poet said of them. John Bull is good-natured, powerful, stubborn, but heavy, slow and unresourceful, and one is sorry for him while one laughs! A bull with the gestures of a lion, he was just shaking his mane and preening himself to greet a guest as he had never greeted any monarch—still on duty or dismissed from service—and his guest was snatched from him. The lion-bull stamps with his cleft hoof, tears at the ground in his rage . . . but his guards know all the subtle mechanism of the locks and screws of freedom in which he is confined, babble some nonsense to him and keep the key in their pocket, while the point vanishes on the ocean.

Poor lion-bull, go back to your hard labour, follow the plough, wield the hammer! Have not three ministers and one non-minister, one duke, one professor of medicine, and one pious lord testified to the public in the House of Peers and in the Lower House, in the journals and in the drawing-rooms, that the strong man whom you saw yesterday is sick, and so sick that he must be sent the length of the Atlantic and across the Mediterranean . . . ? 'Whom do you prefer to believe, my ass or myself?' said the offended miller in the old fable to his sceptical friend who doubted whether the ass was out when he heard him braying. . . .

And are they not the friends of the people—more than its friends, its guardians, its parents? . . . The newspapers are full of detailed descriptions of fêtes and banquets, speeches and swords, addresses and concerts, Chiswick and Guildhall. Ballets and spectacles, pantomimes and harlequinades, depicting this 'Midspring Night's Dream,' have been described enough. I do not intend to enter into competition with them, but simply want to give a few of the snapshots I have taken with my little camera from the modest corner from which I looked on. In them, as is always the case in photographs, much that is accidental is seized and retained, awkward draperies, awkward poses, overprominent details, with the lines of events left untouched and lines of faces unsoftened. . . .

This is my gift to you, my absent children (it is partly for you that it is written), and once more I deeply, deeply regret that you were not here with us on April the 17th.

1

At Brooke House

Garibaldi arrived at Southampton on the evening of the 3rd of April. I wanted to see him before he was caught up, whirled off, and exhausted.

I wanted to do so for many reasons: in the first place, simply because I loved him and had not seen him for about ten years. I had followed his great career step by step since 1848; by 1854 he had become in my eyes a character taken straight out of Cornelius Nepos or Plutarch . . . since then he had outstripped half those characters, had become the Uncrowned King of the Peoples, their enthusiastic hope, their living legend, their holy man—and this from the Ukraine and Serbia to Andalusia and Scotland, from South America to the northern of the United States. Since then with a handful of men he had conquered an army, set free a whole country, and been dismissed from it as a cabman is dismissed when he has driven you to the station. Since then he had been deceived and defeated; and just as he had gained nothing for himself by victory, he had lost nothing by defeat, but his power among the people had been doubled. The wound dealt him by his own countrymen had cemented him with blood to the common people. To the greatness of the hero was added the crown of a martyr. I longed to see whether he was still the same simple-hearted sailor who had brought *The Commonwealth* from Boston to the India Docks, dreaming of a floating brotherhood of exiles that should sail over the ocean, and regaling me with Nice Bellet brought from America.

In the second place, I wanted to tell him a little about the intrigues and absurdities here, about the good people who with one hand were setting up a pedestal for him and with the other putting Mazzini in the pillory. I wanted to tell him about the harrying of Stansfeld, and about the Liberals of mean understanding who joined in the baying of the reactionary packs without seeing that the latter had at least an object—to trip up the piebald and characterless Ministry over Stansfeld, and to replace them, together with their gout, their musty relics and their faded heraldic rags.

In Southampton I did not find Garibaldi. He had

just gone off to the Isle of Wight. In the streets there were still signs left of his triumphal reception—flags, groups of people, crowds of foreigners. . . .

Without stopping at Southampton, I set off for Cowes. On the steamer and in the hotels every one was talking of Garibaldi, of his reception. Anecdotes were told: how he had come out on deck leaning on the arm of the Duke of Sutherland; how, when going from the steamer into Cowes, Garibaldi had been on the point of bowing to the sailors, but had suddenly stopped, stepped up to them and shaken each by the hand instead of giving tips.

I reached Cowes at nine o'clock in the evening; I learnt that Brooke House was a long way off, ordered a carriage for the next day, and walked along the seafront. It was the first warm evening of 1864. The sea was perfectly calm, dancing in languid ripples; here and there a phosphorescent light gleamed and vanished; I drank in with delight the moist salt smell of the sea, which I love like the fragrance of hay. In the distance was the sound of dance-music from some club or casino, everything was bright and festive.

But next morning when I opened my window at six o'clock England was herself again; instead of sea and sky, earth and distance, there was one thick mass in tints of grey from which a fine steady rain was falling with that British persistence which tells one plainly: 'If you imagine that I am going to stop, you are wrong. I am not.' At seven o'clock I drove off to Brooke House in this shower-bath. Wishing to avoid long explanations with English servants, who are slow-witted and lacking in courtesy, I sent in a note to Garibaldi's secretary, Guerzoni. Guerzoni led me into his room and went to tell Garibaldi. Then I heard the tapping of a stick, and a voice saying, 'Where is he, where is he?' I went out into the corridor. Garibaldi stood before me, looking me straight in the face with his candid, gentle expression; then he held out both hands to me, and saying, 'Very, very glad, you are full of strength and health; you will do more work yet,' embraced me. 'Where would you like to be? This is Guerzoni's room; would you rather come to mine or rather stay here?' he asked, and sat down.

It was now my turn to look at him.

He was dressed as you know him from innumerable photographs, pictures and statuettes; he had a red woollen shirt, and over it a cloak buttoned in a peculiar way over the chest; he had a kerchief, not on his neck but on his shoulders, as sailors wear it, tied in a knot over the chest. All this suited him marvellously, especially his cloak.

He had changed much less in those ten years than I had expected. None of the portraits or photographs of him are good enough, all of them make him look older, darker, and, above all, fail to give the expression of his face. And it is just in the expression that the whole secret is revealed, not only of his face but of himself, of his power—of that magnetic and generous force by means of which he invariably dominated the circle around him whatever it might be, great or small: a handful of fishermen at Nice, a crew of sailors on the ocean, a *drappello* of guerillas at Monte Video, an army of volunteers in Italy, the masses of the people of all lands, whole quarters of the terrestrial globe. Every feature of his face, which is very irregular and more suggestive of the Slavonic type than the Italian, is full of life and of boundless good-nature, loving-kindness, and what is called *bienveillance* (I use the French word because our benevolence has been so cheapened in our Government offices and antechambers that its meaning is distorted and vulgarised). There is the same quality in his glance, the same quality in his voice, and it is all so simple, so straight from the heart, that unless a man has some ulterior motive, is in the pay of some Government, or deliberately determined against it, he is bound to love him.

But neither his character nor the expression of his face is made up of goodness alone; side by side with his kindness and attractiveness one feels the presence of unflinching moral firmness and a sort of return upon himself, reflective and mournful. I had not observed this melancholy, gloomy characteristic in him before.

At moments the conversation broke off: thoughts flitted over his face like clouds over the sea. Was it horror at the destinies that rested on his shoulders, at his *consecration* by the people—which he could not now refuse? Was it doubt aroused by all the downfalls, all the treacheries, all the weaknesses of men that he had seen? Was it the temptation of greatness? That last I do not think; his personality had long ago passed into his work. . . .

I am certain that similar traces of anguish at their vocation were to be seen in the face of the Maid of Orleans, in the face of John of Leyden. They belonged to the people, and the elemental feelings or rather presentiments extinct in us are stronger in the common people. There was fatalism in their faith, and fatalism in itself is infinitely sad. 'Thy will be done,' says the Sistine Madonna in every feature of her face. 'Thy will be done,' says her Son, the Man of the people and the Saviour, as He sorrowfully prays on the Mount of Olives.

Garibaldi recalled various details of his visit to London in 1854, how he had spent the night with me when he had been too late to return to the India Docks; I reminded him how he had gone for a walk with my son and had his photograph taken for me at Caldesi's, how we had dined at the American Consul's with Buchanan,[1]

---

[1] Probably James Buchanan, then President of the United States, is meant.—(*Translator's Note*.)

which made so much talk at the time though it was really of no importance.

'I must confess that I have not hastened to see you without an object,' I said at last; 'I was afraid that the atmosphere with which you are surrounded would be too English, that is, too foggy for you to see clearly the strings behind the scenes working the drama which is being successfully played out now in Parliament . . . the further you go the thicker the fog will be. Do you want to hear me?'

'Tell me, tell me—we are old friends.'

I told him of the debates, of the wailing in the newspapers, of the grotesqueness of the manœuvres against Mazzini, the ordeal to which Stansfeld[1] was being subjected. 'Observe,' I added, 'that in Stansfeld the Tories and their supporters are persecuting not only the revolution which they mix up with Mazzini, not only the Ministry of Palmerston, but, in addition to all that, a man who by his personal qualities, his industry and his intelligence, has obtained at a comparatively early age the post of a Lord of the Admiralty, a man of no family or connections in the aristocracy. They will not dare to attack you directly at this moment, but just see how unceremoniously they are treating you. I bought the latest *Standard* yesterday at Cowes; I have read it driving here; just look at this: "We are convinced that Garibaldi will understand the obligations laid upon him by the hospitality of England, that he will have nothing to do with his former comrade, but will have too much tact to visit at 35 Thurloe Square." Then follows the sentence passed upon you

[1] Stansfeld, The Rt. Hon. James, born 1820, was, 1859, returned to Parliament for Halifax as an advanced Liberal. He was a Lord of the Admiralty from 1863 to 1864, when he resigned. In 1886 he was President of the Local Government Board, with a seat in the Cabinet. He was a close friend of Mazzini.—(*Translator's Note.*)

par anticipation if you do not act in accordance with this hint.'

'I have heard something of this intrigue,' said Garibaldi. '*Of course one of my first visits will be to Stansfeld.*'

'You know better than I what to do. I only wanted to show you clearly the ugly outlines of this intrigue.'

Garibaldi stood up. I thought that he meant to put an end to the interview, and began taking leave.

'No, no, let us go to my room now,' he said, and he went off. He limps badly, but his constitution has emerged triumphantly from every sort of injury and operation, moral or surgical.

His dress, I say once more, is wonderfully becoming to him and wonderfully elegant; there is nothing suggestive of the professional soldier, nothing bourgeois about it, it is very simple and very convenient. The ease, the absence of all affectation with which he wears it, checks the tattle and sly mockery of the drawing-rooms; there can hardly be another European who could wear the red shirt successfully in the halls and palaces of England.

Moreover, his dress is of the greatest significance; in the red shirt the common people recognise one of themselves, and their man. The aristocracy imagine that, having clutched his horse by the bridle, they may lead him where they like, and above all, away from the people; but the people look at the red shirt and are delighted that dukes, marquises and lords have turned stable-boys and grooms to the revolutionary leader, have taken on the duties of major-domos, pages and couriers to the great plebeian in his plebeian dress.

Conservative newspapers saw what was wrong, and, to soften the immorality and unseemliness of Garibaldi's dress, invented the tale that he was wearing the uniform of a Monte Video volunteer. But since those days the rank of general had been bestowed on Garibaldi by the king upon whom he had bestowed two kingdoms;

why then should he wear the uniform of a Monte Video volunteer?

And indeed, in what way is his dress a uniform?

With the uniform is associated some deadly weapon, some symbol of authority or of bloody remembrance. Garibaldi goes about unarmed, he fears no one and seeks to be feared by no one; there is as little of the military man about Garibaldi as there is of the aristocrat or the petty bourgeois.

'I am not a soldier,' he said at the Crystal Palace to the Italians who presented him with a sword, 'and I do not like the soldier's trade. I saw my father's house filled with robbers and snatched up a weapon to drive them out.' 'I am a workman, I have come from working people, and I am proud of it,' he said in another place.

With that it must be noted that Garibaldi has not one grain of plebeian roughness or affectation of democracy. His manner is soft as a woman's. A man and an Italian, he stands at the pinnacle of the civilised world, not only as a son of the people faithful to his origin but as an Italian faithful to the aesthetic instinct of his race.

His cloak, buttoned over the chest, is not so much a military cape as the robe of the martial high priest, the prophet. When he lifts his hand one expects words of greeting and blessing, not words of military command.

Garibaldi began talking of the Polish position. He wondered at the daring of the Poles. 'With no organisation, no arms, no men, no open frontier, no support of any kind—to stand up against a strong military autocracy and to hold their ground for over a year—there has never been anything like it in history; it would be well if other nations would imitate them. Such heroism must not, cannot perish in vain. I suppose that Galicia is on the point of rising?'

I said nothing.

'And Hungary too—you do not believe it?'

'No, it is not that. I simply do not know.'

'Well, may we expect any movement in Russia?'

'None whatever. Nothing has changed since I wrote to you in November. The Government, conscious of public support for all their crimes in Poland, goes its headlong way, caring not a straw for Europe, while the educated class sinks lower and lower. The people are dumb. The Polish question is not their question; we have one common enemy, but the question is differently presented. Besides, we have plenty of time before us while they have none.'

So the conversation continued for a few minutes longer, when typically English countenances began to appear at the door, there was a rustle of ladies' dresses. I stood up.

'Why are you in such a hurry?' said Garibaldi.

'I won't steal you longer from England.'

'We shall meet in London, shan't we? '

'I will certainly come to see you. Is it true that you are staying at the Duke of Sutherland's?'

'Yes,' said Garibaldi, and added as though apologising, 'I could not get out of it.'

'Then I shall come to see you with my head powdered so that the flunkeys at Stafford House may think you have a powdered servant.'

At that moment the poet-laureate, Tennyson, appeared with his wife. This was too many laurels for me, and through the same unceasing downpour I returned to Cowes.

The scene was changed, but the same play continued. The steamer from Cowes to Southampton had just left, but another set off three hours later, so I went to a restaurant hard by, ordered dinner and took up *The Times*, At the first sentence I was dumbfounded. The seventy-year-old Abraham who had two months before been condemned for intrigues with a new Hagar had finally sacrificed his Isaac from Halifax. Stansfeld's resignation had been accepted. And this at the very minute when Garibaldi was beginning his triumphal progress through England! I had no idea of this when speaking with Garibaldi.

That Stansfeld should for a second time have sent in his resignation, seeing that the attacks upon him persisted, was perfectly natural. He ought from the very first to have taken his own stand and to have flung up his post in the Admiralty. Stansfeld had done what he ought, but what were Palmerston and his colleagues doing? And what was Palmerston babbling in his speech afterwards? . . . With what cringing flattery he spoke of their magnanimous ally, of their fervent desire for his long life and continual blessings upon him. As though any one took *au sérieux* this police farce of Greco Trabucco and Company.

This was Magenta.[1]

I asked for paper and wrote a letter to Guerzoni. I wrote it in all the first flush of my annoyance and begged him to read *The Times* to Garibaldi; I wrote of the ugliness of this apotheosis of Garibaldi side by side with the insults paid to Mazzini. 'I am fifty-two,' I wrote, 'but I must own that tears come into my eyes at the thought of this injustice.'

A few days before my visit to Garibaldi I had been to see Mazzini, The man has endured much and can endure much; he is an old fighter who cannot be cast down nor worn out; but this time I found him bitterly mortified just because he had been chosen as the means by which his friend was to be brought low. As I was writing the letter to Guerzoni the noble emaciated figure of the old man with his flashing eyes rose before me.

[1] A village in the province of Milan where the French defeated the Austrians in 1859.—(*Translator's Note.*)

A DEPUTATION

When I had finished and the waiter had brought my dinner, I noticed that I was not alone—a short, fair-haired young man with moustaches, wearing the dark blue reefer-coat of a sailor, was sitting by the fire *à l'Américain*, his legs skilfully raised to the level of his ears. His rapid manner of speech and provincial accent, which made his words incomprehensible to me, convinced me that this was some seaman carousing on shore. I left off paying attention to him—he was not speaking to me but to the waiter. Our acquaintance was limited to my passing him the salt and his shaking his head in response.

Soon he was joined by a dark elderly gentleman all in black and buttoned to the chin, with that peculiar air of insanity people acquire from a close acquaintance with heaven and an affected religious exaltation which has become natural from long perseverance.

It seemed that he was well acquainted with the sailor and had come to see him. After three or four words he left off *speaking* and began *preaching*. 'I have seen,' he said, 'Maccabeus . . . Gideon . . . the weapon in the hands of Providence, His sword, His sling . . . and the more I gazed upon him the more deeply was I moved and with tears I repeated "The sword of the Lord! the sword of the Lord!" He hath chosen the weak David to vanquish Goliath. Wherefore the English people, the chosen people, go forth to greet him as to the bride of Lebanon . . . the heart of the people is in the hands of the Lord, it tells them that this is the sword of the Lord, the weapon of Providence—Gideon.'

The doors were flung wide open and there walked in not the bride of Lebanon but a dozen important-looking Britons, among them Lord Shaftesbury and Lord Lindsay. They all sat down to the table and asked for something to eat, announcing that they were going on at once to Brooke House. It was the official deputation from London with an invitation to Garibaldi. The preacher subsided, but the sailor rose in my esteem; he looked with such unmistakable aversion at the deputation that it struck me, remembering his friend's sermon, that he might be taking these people, if not for the swords and bucklers of Satan, at least for his penknives and lancets.

I asked him how I ought to address a letter to Brooke House, whether it was sufficient to put the name of the house or whether I ought to add that of the nearest town. He told me there was no need to add anything.

One of the deputation, a stout, grey-headed old gentleman, asked me to whom I was sending a letter in Brooke House.

'To Guerzoni.'

'He is Garibaldi's secretary, isn't he?'

'Yes.'

'You need not trouble then. We are going there directly. I shall be pleased to take the letter.'

I took out my card and handed it him with the letter. Could anything like that have happened on the Continent? Imagine in France any one asking you in a hotel to whom you were writing, and, on learning that it was to Garibaldi's secretary, undertaking to give him the letter!

The letter was delivered, and next morning I had an answer in London.

The editor of the foreign news column of the *Morning Star* recognised me; inquiries followed as to how I had found Garibaldi, how he was. After talking to him for a few minutes I went off into the smoking-room. There my fair-haired sailor and his swarthy theological friend were sitting over pale ale and pipes.

'Well,' he said to me, 'have you had a good stare at those people? . . . That is jolly fine, Lord Shaftesbury and Lord Lindsay going as deputies to invite Garibaldi. What a farce! As though they knew what Garibaldi is!'

'The weapon of Providence, a sword in the hands of the Lord, His buckler . . . to that end He hath raised him up and hath kept him in his holy simplicity.'

'That is all very fine, but what have these gentry come for? I'd like to ask every one of them how much money they have in the *Alabama*[1] . . . let Garibaldi come to Newcastle-on-Tyne or Glasgow, there he will see the people closer, there he won't be hindered by lords and dukes.'

He was not a seaman, but a shipwright. He had lived for some years in America, had a thorough knowledge of the relations of South and North, and spoke of the hopelessness of the war there, to which the consolatory theologian observed: 'If the Lord hath divided that people and set brother against brother, He hath His own designs, and if we comprehend them not, we must submit to His Providence even when it chastises us.'

It was under these circumstances and in this form that I heard for the last time a commentary on the celebrated Hegelian motto: 'All that is real is rational.' Shaking hands in a friendly way with the sailor and his chaplain, I departed for Southampton.

On the steamer I met the Radical journalist Holyoake; he had seen Garibaldi a little later than I had. Garibaldi had sent through him an invitation to Mazzini, and had already telegraphed to the latter to come to Southampton, where Holyoake intended to wait for

[1] The *Alabama* was a vessel built by a British firm in a British port for the Southern States in the American Civil War. It did great damage to the shipping of the Northern States, capturing sixty-five ships. Feeling on the subject ran so high that at one time there seemed a danger of England's taking part in the war on the side of the South.—(*Translator's Note*.)

him with Menotti Garibaldi and his brother. Holyoake very much wanted to get two letters to London by that evening (they could not reach by post before the morning). I offered my services.

I arrived in London at eleven o'clock in the evening, ordered a room at the York Hotel near Waterloo Station, and drove off with the letters, surprised to find that the rain had not yet managed to stop. At one o'clock or a little later I reached the hotel again. It was locked up. I knocked and knocked. . . . A drunken individual who was finishing his festive evening near the railing of a tavern said: 'Don't knock there, there is a night-bell round the corner.' I went to look for the night-bell, found it and set to ringing. A sleepy-looking head was poked out of some basement and the porter asked me rudely without opening the door: 'What do you want?'

'A room.'

'There is not one.'

'I engaged one myself at eleven o'clock.'

'I tell you there is not one,' and he slammed the door of the netherworld without even waiting for me to swear at him, which I did indeed to no purpose, since he could not hear me.

It was an unpleasant position; to find a room in London at two o'clock at night, especially in that quarter of the town, is not easy. I remembered a little French restaurant and made my way there.

'Have you a room?' I asked the man who kept it.

'Yes, but not a very nice one.'

'Show it me.'

He had told the truth indeed. The room was more than not very nice, it was very nasty. But I had no choice. I opened the window and went down to the bar for a minute. There were still Frenchmen drinking, shouting, playing cards and dominoes there. A German of colossal height whom I had seen before came up to me and asked whether I had time for a word with him in private, as he had something of special importance to tell me.

'Of course I have; let us go into the next room, there is no one there.'

The German sat down opposite me and began telling me tragically how his *patron*, a Frenchman, had cheated him, how he had been exploiting him for three years past, making him do the work of three and beguiling him with the hope that he would take him into partnership, and now, all of a sudden, without saying a disagreeable word, he had gone off to Paris and there taken a partner. On the strength of this, the German had told him that he should leave the place, but the *patron* had not returned. . . .

'But why did you trust him without any agreement?'

'*Weil ich ein dummer Deutscher bin.*'

'Well, that is another matter.'

'I want to close the establishment and go away.'

'You had better look out, he will bring an action against you; do you know the law here?'

The German shook his head.

'I should like to pay him out. . . . I suppose you have been to see Garibaldi?'

'Yes.'

'Well, how is he? *Ein famoser Kerl*—but you know, if he had not promised it me for the last three years I should have been doing something else. I could not expect it, I could not . . . and how is his wound?'

'I think it is all right.'

'The beast, he kept it all quiet and the last day says "I have a partner already." I am afraid I am boring you?'

'Not at all, only I am a little tired and sleepy. I got up at six and now it is a little past two.'

'But what am I to do? I was awfully pleased when

you came in, *ich habe so bei mir gedacht, der wird Rat schaffen*. So I am not to close the establishment?'

'No. But as he is so in love with Paris, you write to him to-morrow: "I have shut up the place. When will you be pleased to come and take charge of it?" You will see the effect; he will leave his wife and his gambling on the Bourse, come here post-haste and see that it is not shut up.'

'*Saperlot! das ist eine Idee—ausgezeichnet*, I will go and write the letter.'

'And I will go to bed. *Gute Nacht!*'

'*Schlafen Sie wohl.*'

I asked for a candle. The restaurant-keeper brought it with his own hand and announced that he wanted a word with me. It was as though I had turned father confessor.

'What is it? It is a little late, but I am ready to hear.'

'Only a word or two. I wanted to ask you: What do you think if I were to put up a bust of Garibaldi to-morrow—you know, with flowers and a laurel wreath; wouldn't it be very nice? I have been wondering about an inscription in letters of three colours: Garibaldi—*Libérateur*?'

'To be sure you might! Only the French embassy will forbid the French to come to your restaurant, and they are here from morning till night.'

'That is so . . . but you know one would rake in a lot of money exhibiting the bust, and they will forget about it afterwards. . . .'

'Mind,' I observed, resolutely getting up to go, 'you don't tell any one. Some one will steal the original idea from you.'

'Not a word, not a word to any one. What we have said will remain, I hope, I beg, between us.'

'Have no doubt about that,' and I went off to his dirty bedroom.

Such was the sequel to my first interview with Garibaldi in 1864.

2

At Stafford House

On the day of Garibaldi's arrival in London I did not see him, but I saw the sea of people, the streams of people, the streets flooded with them for several miles, the crowded squares; everywhere where there was a coping, a balcony, a window, people were perched, and they were all waiting, in some places waiting for six hours. Garibaldi arrived at the station of Nine Elms at half-past two, and only at half-past eight reached Stafford House, where the Duke of Sutherland and his wife were awaiting him on the steps.

The English crowd is coarse; no large gatherings take place without fights, without drunken men, without all sorts of revolting scenes, and without thieving organised on a vast scale. On this occasion the order was wonderful; the people understood that this was *their* holiday, that they were doing honour to one of *themselves*, that they were more than spectators. And only look in the police columns of the papers at the number of thefts on the day of the arrival of the Prince of Wales' bride and the number[1] on the day of Garibaldi's triumphal march, though the police were far less numerous. What had become of the pickpockets?

At Westminster Bridge near the Houses of Parliament the people were so closely packed that the carriage, moving at a walking pace, stopped, and the procession, three-quarters of a mile long, moved on with its standards,

[1] I remember one case of a stolen watch and two or three of fights with Irishmen,—(*Author's Note*.)

its band and so on. With shouts of 'Hurrah!' the people clung to the carriage, all who could push forward shook hands, kissed the edge of Garibaldi's cloak, shouted 'Welcome!' Adoring the great plebeian with delirious enthusiasm, the people wanted to unharness horses and to draw the carriage themselves, but they were dissuaded. No one noticed the dukes and lords who surrounded him; they had dropped into the modest position of grooms and attendants. This ovation lasted about an hour, he was passed from one living wave to the next while the carriage moved on a step or two and stood still again.

The resentment and exasperation of the continental Conservatives was perfectly natural. Garibaldi's reception was not only an insult to the system of graces and ranks, to the livery of flunkeys, but was extremely dangerous as a precedent. And the fury of the personages who had been in the service of three emperors and one 'imperial' reaction surpassed all bounds, the bounds of courtesy to begin with. They felt faint and dizzy; the England of palaces, the England of coffers, forgetful of all decorum, was going hand in hand with the England of the workshops to greet an *'aventurier*,' a rebel, who would have been hanged if he had not succeeded in freeing Sicily. 'Why,' *la France* asked naïvely, 'why has England never so welcomed Marshal Pélissier, whose fame is so untarnished? 'In spite of the fact, she forgot to add, that he had burnt hundreds of Arabs with their wives and children, just as we burn out black-beetles.

It is a pity that Garibaldi accepted the hospitality of the Duke of Sutherland. The small consequence and the political insignificance of the fireman duke made Stafford House to a certain extent Garibaldi's hotel; still, the surroundings were inappropriate and the intrigue hatched before his arrival in London found a

THE DUKE'S HOSPITALITY

propitious background in the palace. Its object was to keep Garibaldi away from the people, that is, away from the working classes, and to cut him off from those of his friends and acquaintances who had remained true to the old flag, most of all, of course, from Mazzini. A good half of these barriers were blown down by the nobility and simplicity of Garibaldi's character, but the other half—to wit, the impossibility of speaking to him except in the presence of witnesses—remained. If Garibaldi had not got up at five and received visitors at six, it would have completely succeeded; but luckily the zeal of the intriguers could not get them up before half-past eight in the morning; only on the day of his departure ladies began the invasion of his bedroom an hour earlier. On one occasion Mordini, who had not succeeded in getting in a word with Garibaldi in the course of an hour, said to me, laughing: 'No man in the world could be easier to see than Garibaldi, but no one could be more difficult to speak to.'

The duke's hospitality was entirely lacking in that liberality which at one time reconciled men to aristocratic luxury. He only assigned one room to Garibaldi and one to the young man who bandaged his foot, but would have hired rooms for the others, namely Garibaldi's sons, Guerzoni, and Basilio. They, of course, refused to accept this, and lodged at their own expense in the Bath Hotel. To appreciate the oddity of this, one must understand what sort of place Stafford House is. One could easily without inconveniencing the owners have lodged in it all the peasant families turned homeless into the world by the duke's father—and there are very many of them.

The English are poor actors, and that does them the greatest credit. The first time I went to see Garibaldi in Stafford House I saw at once the intrigue going on around him. Figaros and factotums of all sorts, servants and observers, were in and out continually. An Italian was made police-master, master of the ceremonies, major-domo, stage-manager, butler, *Souffleur*. And, indeed, who would not take such a job for the honour of sitting with dukes and lords, and with them taking steps to prevent and circumvent all intercourse between the people and Garibaldi, and assisting duchesses in weaving the spider's web to catch the Italian leader, though the lame general broke it every day without seeing it?

Garibaldi, for instance, had gone to see Mazzini. What was to be done? How was it to be concealed? At once stage-managers and factotums were on the scene, a means was found. Next morning all London read: 'Yesterday at such an hour Garibaldi visited John France in Onslow Terrace.' You will think that this was an invented name; no, it was the name of the landlord of Mazzini's lodging.

Garibaldi had no thought of breaking with Mazzini, but he might easily have left this vortex without meeting him before witnesses and without proclaiming it publicly. Mazzini refused to visit Garibaldi while he was at Stafford House. They might have met on a few occasions, but no one took the initiative. After considering this, I wrote a note to Mazzini and asked him whether Garibaldi would accept an invitation to go as far as Teddington; that if he would not, I would not invite him and that would be an end of the matter; if he would come, I should be very glad to invite them both. Mazzini wrote to me next day that Garibaldi would be delighted, and that, if nothing prevented him, they would come on Sunday at one o'clock. Mazzini added in conclusion that Garibaldi would be very glad to see Ledru-Rollin at my house.

On Saturday morning I went to Garibaldi, and not finding him at home, remained with Saffi, Guerzoni and the others to wait for him. When he returned, the crowd of visitors waiting for him in the anteroom and corridor fell upon him; one dauntless Briton snatched the stick out of his hand and thrust another in it, repeating in a sort of frenzy, 'General, it is a better one, take it, allow me, it is a better one.' 'But what for?' asked Garibaldi, smiling. 'I am used to my own stick.' But, seeing the Englishman would not relinquish the stick without a struggle, he gave a faint shrug of his shoulders and walked on.

In the drawing-room a weighty conversation was taking place behind my back. I should have paid no attention to it if I had not caught the words loudly repeated: '*Capite*, Teddington is only two or three steps from Hampton Court. Upon my word, but it is impossible. . . . Two or three steps from Hampton Court! It is sixteen to eighteen miles.' I turned round, and seeing a man who was a complete stranger to me taking the distance from London to Teddington so much to heart, I said to him: 'Twelve or thirteen miles.'

The argumentative gentleman turned at once to me: 'Even thirteen miles is a terrible distance. The General has to be in London at three o'clock. . . . Teddington must be postponed in any case.'

Guerzoni repeated to him that Garibaldi wanted to go and was going.

The Italian guardian was joined by an Englishman, who felt that to accept an invitation to such a distance would be a fatal precedent. . . . Wishing to suggest to them the indelicacy of debating the question in my presence, I observed: 'Gentlemen, allow me to put an end to your discussion,' and going up to Garibaldi on the spot said to him: 'A visit from you is infinitely precious to me, and now more than ever, at an epoch so black for Russia, your visit will have a special significance; your visit will be not to me alone but to our friends, fettered in prison and banished to penal servitude. Knowing your many engagements, I was afraid to invite you. But at a word from a common friend you sent word to me that you would come. That is even more precious to me. I believe that you want to come, but I do not insist (*je n'insiste pas*) if there are such insuperable obstacles in the way as this gentleman, with whom I am unacquainted, tells me.' I indicated him with my finger.

'What is the difficulty?' asked Garibaldi.

The impresario ran up and hurriedly laid before him all the considerations which made driving at eleven o'clock the next day to Teddington and returning by three out of the question.

'That is very simple,' said Garibaldi, 'I must start at ten then instead of eleven. That is clear, isn't it?' The impresario vanished.

'In that case,' I said, 'to avoid loss of time, worries or fresh difficulties, allow me to come and fetch you between nine and ten and we will go together.'

'I shall be delighted. I will expect you.'

From Garibaldi I went off to see Ledru-Rollin. I had not seen him for two years. It was not because there had been any misunderstanding between us but because we had very little in common. Moreover, London, and especially suburban life, makes people drift apart imperceptibly. He had of late years led a quiet and solitary existence, though he believed with the same intensity as he had done on the 14th of June 1849 in the approaching revolution in France. I had disbelieved in it almost as long, and I too was unshaken in my conviction.

With the greatest courtesy to me Ledru-Rollin refused my invitation. He said that he would have been truly glad to meet Garibaldi again, and would of course have

LEDRU-ROLLIN

been pleased to come and see me, but that, as the representative of the French Republic, as one who had suffered for Rome (on 13th of June 1849), he could not see Garibaldi for the first time anywhere but in his own house. 'If,' he said, 'Garibaldi's political views do not permit him to show officially his sympathy for the French Republic—whether in my person, in the person of Louis Blanc, or of some other one of us I do not care—I shall not complain. But I should decline an interview with him wherever that might be. As a private man I should like to see him, though I have no particular reason for doing so; the French Republic is not a *courtisane* to give assignations half in secret. Forget for a moment that you are inviting me, and tell me candidly, do you not agree with my contention?'

'I think that you are right, and I hope that you have nothing against my repeating our conversation to Garibaldi.'

'Quite the contrary.'

With that we changed the subject. The revolution of February and the year 1848 rose again from the tomb and stood before me once more in the same figure of the tribune of that day with a few wrinkles and a few more grey hairs. Language, thoughts, turns of phrase, and above all hopes, were the same. 'Things are going magnificently. The Empire does not know what to do. *Elle est débordée*. Only to-day I have had news of an incredible advance in public opinion. And indeed it is high time; who could have supposed that so grotesque a state of things could have lasted till 1864?'

I did not contradict him, and we parted pleased with each other.

On reaching London next day I began by hiring a carriage with a pair of sturdy horses and driving to Stafford House. When I went up to Garibaldi's room he was not in it, but the zealous Italian was already desperately expounding the utter impossibility of driving to Teddington.

'Can you suppose,' he was saying to Guerzoni, 'that the duke's horses can take him for twelve or thirteen miles there and then back again? Why, they simply would not let him have them for such a journey.'

'There is no need, I have a carriage.'

'But what horses will bring him back? The same?'

'Don't be anxious; if the horses are tired they can put in fresh ones.'

Guerzoni said to me with fury: 'Where will it end? This is slavery; every wretched little cur gives orders and intrigues.'

'I don't know whether you are referring to me,' the Italian shouted, pale with rage, 'I sir, will not allow myself to be treated like a flunkey,' and he snatched up a pencil on the table, broke it and threw it away. 'If that is how it is, I will give it all up and will leave you at once.'

'That is just what we ask you to do.'

The zealous Italian strode rapidly towards the door, but Garibaldi appeared in the doorway, looked calmly at them and at me, and then said: 'Isn't it time to start? I am at your disposal, only please bring me back to London by half-past two or three o'clock; and now, allow me to receive an old friend who has only just arrived. Perhaps you are acquainted with him—Mordini?'

'More than acquainted, we are friends. If you have nothing against it, I will invite him too.'

'We will take him with us.'

Mordini came up; I moved away to the window with Saffi. All at once the factotum, changing his mind, ran up to me and boldly asked me: 'Excuse me, I don't understand. You have a carriage and your party is— reckon up: the General, you, Menotti, Guerzoni, Saffi and Mordini. . . . How will you sit?'

'If necessary, we will have another carriage—two . . .'

'But is there time to get them . . . ?'

I looked at him, and turning to Mordini said to him: 'Mordini, I want to ask Saffi and you to do something. Take a hansom and drive at once to Waterloo Station. You will catch the train there, for this gentleman is afraid that there won't be room for us all and that there is no time to send for another carriage. Had I known yesterday that there would have been these difficulties I would have asked Garibaldi to come by train, but now that won't do, because I can't answer for our finding a cab or a carriage at Teddington Station. And I don't want to make him walk to my house.'

'Delighted; we will go at once,' answered Saffi and Mordini.

'Let us go too,' said Garibaldi, getting up.

We went out; a dense crowd had already gathered before Stafford House, and a loud, prolonged 'Hurrah!' greeted and accompanied our carriage.

Menotti could not come with us, he was going with his brother to Windsor. I was told that the Queen, who was longing to see Garibaldi, but who alone in all Great Britain had not the right to do so, desired an *accidental* meeting with his sons. In this division the lion's share certainly was not the Queen's.

3

At Home

That day was wonderfully successful and was one of the brightest, loveliest and most cloudless days of the last fifteen years. There was a wonderful serenity and fulness about it, an aesthetic proportion and completeness such as very rarely comes. One day later, and our festive day would not have had that character. One more—not an Italian—of our party, and the tone would have been different; at any rate, there would have been an uneasy fear that it would be spoilt. Such days stand out like mountain-tops . . . as with notes fully sung, as with flowers fully opened; there is nothing further, nothing higher, nothing beyond.

From the moment when the steps of Stafford House with the Duke of Sutherland's lackeys, factotums and porter had vanished and the crowd received Garibaldi with its 'Hurrah,' our hearts grew light, everything was attuned to a free human key and so remained till the moment when Garibaldi, pressed and crowded by the people again, kissed on his shoulder and on the hem of his coat, got into the carriage and drove back to London.

On the way we talked of different things. Garibaldi wondered that the Germans did not understand that it was not their freedom, not their unity, that was victorious in Denmark, but the two armies of two despotic states which they would not be able to control later.[1] 'If Denmark had been supported in her struggle,' he said, 'the forces of Austria and Prussia would have been diverted and a line of action on the opposite coast would have been thrown open to us.'

I observed that the Germans were terrible nationalists, that they were labelled as cosmopolitan because they were only known from books. They were just as patriotic as the French, but the French were calmer in their patriotism, knowing that they were feared. The Germans knew the poor opinion in which they were held by other peoples and strained themselves to the utmost to keep up their reputation. 'Do you imagine,' I added, 'that there are Germans who want to give

[1] Is it not strange that Garibaldi was at one with Karl Vogt in his estimate of the Schleswig-Holstein question?—(*Author's Note.*)

up Venice and the Quadrilateral?[1] Perhaps Venice they would: that question is too conspicuous, the injustice of that is obvious, the aristocratic name has an effect on them; but you should just talk to them about Trieste, which they need for trade, or Galicia or Posen, which they need in order to civilise them.'

Among other things I repeated to Garibaldi my conversation with Ledru-Rollin, and added that in my opinion Ledru-Rollin was right.

'Undoubtedly,' said Garibaldi, 'perfectly right. I had not thought of it. To-morrow I will go to him and to Louis Blanc. Couldn't we go now?' he added.

We were in the Wandsworth Road and Ledru-Rollin was in St. John's Wood, that is eight miles away. I had à l'imprésario to tell him that it was utterly impossible.

And again at moments Garibaldi sank into thought and was silent, and again his face expressed that great sadness of which I have spoken. He looked away into the distance as though seeking something on the horizon. I did not interrupt him, but gazed and thought: 'Whether he is a sword in the hands of Providence or not, he is certainly not a military leader by profession, he is not a general. He told the holy truth when he said he was not a soldier but simply a man who had taken up arms to defend his outraged hearth, an apostle-warrior ready to preach a crusade and go at the head of it, ready to lay down his soul and his children's for his people, to give and receive terrible blows, to shake the life out of his enemy, to scatter his ashes to the winds . . . and then, forgetting his victory, to fling his blood-stained sword together with its sheath no the depths of the sea. . . .'

All that, and precisely that, was fully understood by

[1] The region including the four towns of Verona, Legnago, Peschiera and Mantua is meant.—(*Translator's Note.*)

the people, by the masses, by the ignorant mob, with that clearness of vision, that insight with which in other days the slaves of Rome understood the incomprehensible mystery of the coming of Christ and crowds of the weary and heavy-laden, women and old men, prayed at the cross of the crucified. For them understanding meant believing, believing meant worship, prayer.

That was why all the poorer classes of Teddington had crowded round the railings of our house waiting from early morning for Garibaldi. When we drove up, the crowd rushed to greet him in a sort of ecstasy, pressed his hands, shouted 'God bless you, Garibaldi!' Women caught at his hand and kissed it, kissed the hem of his cloak—I saw with my own eyes—lifted their children up to him, shed tears. . . . He, smiling as though among his own family, shook their hands, bowed, and could scarcely make his way to the door. When he had gone in the shouts were redoubled; Garibaldi came out again, and laying both hands on his breast bowed in all directions. The people grew quieter, but they remained standing there all the time till Garibaldi went away.

It is hard for people who have seen nothing like it, men who have grown up in offices, barracks and the anterooms of courts, to understand such manifestations —'a filibuster,' the son of a sailor from Nice, a seaman, a rebel . . . and this royal reception! What had he done for the English people? . . . And worthy men rack their brains for an explanation and look for some secret wires by which it was worked: 'It is wonderful with what astuteness the *Government* in England can get up demonstrations . . . you won't take us in—*wir wissen was wir wissen*—we have read Gneist ourselves!'

I daresay, and perhaps the Neapolitan boatman who used to declare that the medallion of Garibaldi, like the medallion of the Madonna, was a charm against shipwreck had been bought by the party of Sicardi and the ministry of Venosta!

Though it is doubtful whether the journalistic Vidocqs,[1] particularly our Moscow ones, could detect the play of such masters as Palmerston, Gladstone and Company so clearly, yet they would through the sympathy of the tiny spider for the immense tarantula understand it more readily than the secret of Garibaldi's reception. And that is a good thing for them—if they did understand *that* secret there would be nothing left for them but to hang themselves on the nearest aspen-tree. Bugs can only live happily so long as they have no suspicion of their smell. Woe to the bug who develops a human sense of smell!

Mazzini arrived immediately after Garibaldi; we all went out to meet him at the gate. The crowd, hearing who it was, gave him a loud welcome; the common people have nothing against him. The old-womanish terror of a conspirator is only to be found at the level of shopkeepers, small property-owners and so on.

The few words said by Mazzini and Garibaldi are familiar to readers of the *Bell*, we do not think it necessary to repeat them.[2]

[1] Chief agent of the French police before 1827 and author of famous Memoirs. The name has been wrongly transliterated as 'Vidok' in Volume II.—(*Translator's Note*.)

[2] This refers to the following passage, which appeared in the *Bell*, Number 184, May 1, 1864:—

April 17, 1864.

'To *young* Russia suffering and struggling for the new Russia which, when once it has vanquished the Russian Tsardom, will undoubtedly in its development have immense significance for the destinies of the world!'
From the health proposed by Garibaldi.

'Your words will reach our friends, they will reach into the fortresses and mines. . . .' *From the reply to it.*

We promised an article describing Garibaldi's visit to England; now that it has so *unexpectedly* come to an end we are convinced of

... All were so touched by Garibaldi's words about Mazzini, by the sincere voice in which they were its historical significance, but that article is to come. For the moment we would only give our friends some details concerning Garibaldi's visit to us, and those details, indeed, will consist of the brief speeches of Mazzini and Garibaldi. The English newspapers have been so overloaded with descriptions of receptions, welcomes, dishes, garlands, and so on, that we are as little anxious to enter into competition with them as we are capable of equalling the aristocratic Balthazar feasts in honour of the revolutionary leader.

Our banquet was a modest one, there were not twenty invited guests to it (among them, not counting Garibaldi and Mazzini, there were several of their nearest friends: Saffi, who was one of the Triumvirate in Rome, Mordini, the Dictator of Sicily, Guerzoni, et cetera. Mrs. Stansfeld was among the ladies). In the *Daily News*, in the *Morning Star*, in Prince Dolgoruky's *Listok*, there have been descriptions of the crowds of people before the garden railings, the shouts of 'Hurrah!' (as Garibaldi walked in he was almost carried off his feet, the ladies kissed his hands and the hem of his cloak) and so on—as it has been at every house which the uncrowned king has visited.

At lunch Mazzini stood up, and raising his glass spoke as follows:—

'In the toast proposed by me I unite all that we love, all for which we are struggling—

> To the freedom of the Peoples;
> To the union of the Peoples;
> To the man who in our day stands as the living incarnation of these great ideas,
> To Giuseppe Garibaldi;
> To unhappy, holy, heroic Poland, whose sons for more than a year have been fighting in silence and dying for freedom;
> To young Russia, which under the standard of Zemlya i Volya (Land and Freedom) will soon hold out the hand of brotherhood to Poland, will recognise her equality, her independence, and efface the memory of imperial Russia;
> To those Russians who following our friend Herzen are working their utmost for the development of that Russia;
> To the religion of duty which gives us the strength to struggle and die for these ideas!'

Then Garibaldi got up, and with a glass of Marsala in his hand said:—

'I want to-day to do a duty which I ought to have done long ago. Among us here is a man who has performed the greatest services

THE TOASTS 65

uttered, the depth of feeling which resounded in them, the impressiveness given them by the series of pre-
both to my native land and to freedom in general. When I was a lad and was full of vague longings I sought a man to be my guide, the counsellor of my youth, I sought him as a thirsty man seeks water. . . . I found him. He alone was awake when all around were slumbering, he became my friend and has remained my friend for ever; in him the holy fire of love for fatherland and freedom has never dimmed; that man is Giuseppe Mazzini—I drink to him, to my friend, to my teacher!'

In the voice, in the expression of face with which these words were uttered, there was so much that gripped and thrilled the heart that they were received not with applause but with tears.

After a momentary silence Garibaldi continued with the words:—

'Mazzini has said a few words of unhappy Poland with which I am in complete sympathy.

'To Poland the home of martyrs, to Poland facing death for independence and setting a grand example to the peoples!

'Now let us drink to young Russia, who is suffering and struggling as we are, and like us will be victorious; to the new people which, vanquishing the Russian Tsardom and winning its freedom, is evidently destined to play a great part in the future of Europe.

'And finally to England, the land of freedom and independence, the land which for its hospitality and sympathy with the persecuted deserves our fullest gratitude; to England, which gives us the possibility of a friendly gathering like this. . . .'

After Garibaldi's departure I wrote him the following letter:—

'I was so excited yesterday that I did not say all I wanted, but confined myself to a mere expression of gratitude in the name of *coming* Russia, no less persecuted than Poland; in the name of the Russia that is dying in the fortresses and mines and living in the consciousness of the awakening people with their ideal of the indissoluble connection of Land and Freedom, and in the minority that is persecuted for having given expression to this instinct of the people.

'Our far-away friends will hear with joy your words of sympathy; they need them; rarely are garlands flung upon their agonies; the shadow of the crimes that are being committed in Poland falls upon us all.

'In reality I do not regret that I added nothing to my words of gratitude. What could I add? A toast to Italy? But was not our whole gathering in honour of Italy? What I was feeling could hardly have been put into such a speech. I looked at you both, listened to you with a youthful feeling of devotion no longer appropriate to my age, and seeing how you, the two great leaders of the ceding incidents, that no one answered, only Mazzini held out his hand and twice repeated: 'It is too much.' I did not see one face, even among the servants, which did not wear a *recueilli* look and was not stirred by the sense that grand words had just been uttered and that the moment was passing into history. . . . I went up to Garibaldi with my glass when he spoke of Russia and told him that his words would reach our friends in the fortresses and mines, that I thanked him in their name.

We went into the other room. Various persons had gathered in the corridor; all at once an old Italian, an exile of days long gone by, a poor fellow who sold ice-cream, caught Garibaldi by the shirt of his coat, stopped him, and bursting into tears said: 'Well, now I can die. I have seen him, I have seen him!' Garibaldi embraced and kissed the old man. Then in stumbling and halting phrases, with the terrible rapidity of a peasant's Italian, the old man began telling Garibaldi his adventures, and wound up his speech with an amazing flower of Southern eloquence: 'Now I shall die content, but you—God bless you—live long, live for our country, live for us, live till I rise again from the dead!' He clutched his hand, covered it with kisses, and went out sobbing.

Accustomed as Garibaldi must have been to all this, he was obviously agitated as he sat down on a little sofa. The ladies surrounded him; I stood near the sofa. A cloud of painful thoughts seemed to swoop down upon

peoples, greeted the rise of dawning Russia, I blessed you under our modest roof.

'I owe to you the best day of my winter, a day of untroubled serenity, and for that I embrace you once more with ardent gratitude, with deep love, and boundless respect.

'*April* 18, 1864,
 'Elmfield House,
  'Teddington.'

him—and this time he could not refrain from saying: 'It sometimes seems dreadful and so overwhelming that I am afraid of losing my head . . . it is too much happiness. I remember when I came back an exile from America to Nice—when I saw my father's house again, found my family, my relations, found the old familiar places, the people I knew—I was crushed with happiness. . . . You know,' he added, turning to me, 'what happened afterwards, what a succession of calamities it was. The welcome of the English people has surpassed my expectation. . . . What is to come? What is before us?'

I had not one word of comfort to give him. I inwardly shuddered at the question, What is to come, what is before us?

It was time for him to go. Garibaldi got up, warmly embraced me, took a friendly leave of us all—and again there were shouts, again hurrahs, again two stout policemen together with us, smiling and pleading, made our way through the crowd, again cries of 'God bless you!' 'Garibaldi for ever!' and the carriage rolled away. We all remained in an exalted, quietly solemn state of mind, as after a festival service, after a christening or the departure of the bride; our hearts were full, and we were inwardly going over every detail and brooding upon that sinister unanswered 'What is to come?'

Prince P. V. Dolgoruky was the first to take up a sheet of paper and write down both the speeches. He wrote them down faithfully while others supplied details. We showed the result to Mazzini and the rest, and so made up the text (with slight and insignificant alterations) which flew like an electric shock over Europe, evoking a shout of enthusiasm and a howl of indignation. Then Mazzini went away; the other visitors went too. We were left alone with two or three intimate friends, and twilight slowly fell. How deeply and truly sorry I was, children, that you were not with me on that day! It is good to remember such days for long years; they refresh the soul and reconcile it to the seamy side of life. They are very few. . . .

4

26 Prince's Gate

'What is to come?' . . . The immediate future did not keep us long waiting. As in the old epic poems while the hero is calmly resting on his laurels, feasting or sleeping, Malice, Vengeance and Envy assemble in their gala dress on storm-clouds of some sort; Vengeance and Envy brew a poison and temper daggers, while Malice blows the bellows and whets the blades: so it happened now in a form decorously adapted to our mild and peaceful manners. In our day all this is done simply by men and not by allegorical figures; they meet together in brightly lighted drawing-rooms instead of in 'the darkness of night,' and are attended by powdered flunkeys instead of by dishevelled Furies; the horrors and scenery of classical poems and children's pantomimes are replaced by simple peaceful playing with marked cards, and magic is superseded by the every-day tricks of commerce with which the honest shop-keeper selling some black-currant juice mixed with spirits swears that it is port, and old port xxx, too, knowing that though no one believes him, no one will take proceedings, or if any one does, he will only fare the worse for it.

At the very time when Garibaldi called Mazzini his friend and teacher, called him the first sower who had stood alone on the field when all were sleeping about him, who, pointing out the way, had shown it to the young warrior yearning to do battle for his country, and had

THE ENGLISH GOVERNMENT

become the leader of the Italian people; at the very time when, surrounded by friends, he looked at the weeping old Italian exile who repeated his 'Lord, now lettest Thou Thy servant . . . ' and himself almost wept with him; at the time when he confided to us his secret dread of the future, conspirators were resolving at all costs to get rid of the awkward guest; and although men grown old in diplomacy and intrigue, grey and decrepit in subterfuge and hypocrisy, took part in the conspiracy, they played their game no worse than the shopkeeper who sells his black-currant juice for old port xxx on his word of honour.

The English Government never had invited nor sent for Garibaldi; that is all nonsense invented by the ingenious journalists on the Continent. The Englishmen who invited Garibaldi had nothing in common with the Ministry; the assumption of a Government plan is as absurd as the subtle observation of our *crétins* that Palmerston gave Stansfeld a post in the Admiralty just because the latter was a friend of Mazzini. Note that in the most furious onslaughts upon Stansfeld and Palmerston there was no word suggesting this in Parliament or in the English newspapers.

Such silliness would have provoked as much mirth as Urquhart's accusation that Palmerston was in receipt of pay from Russia. Chambers and the others asked Palmerston whether Garibaldi's visit would be disagreeable to the Government. Palmerston answered, as was fitting for him to answer: that it could not be disagreeable to the Government for General Garibaldi to visit England, that the Government neither forbade his visit nor invited it.

Garibaldi agreed to come with the object of raising the Italian question in England once more and collecting enough money to begin a campaign in the Adriatic and to win Victor Emmanuel by the accomplished fact.

That was all.

That Garibaldi would be received with ovations was very well known to those who visited him and to all who desired him to come. But the aspect it assumed among the common people was not expected.

At the news that the man 'in the red shirt,' the hero wounded by an Italian bullet, was coming to visit them, the English people stirred and fluttered their wings, unaccustomed to flight and stiff with heavy and incessant toil. There was not only joy and love in this, there was complaint, a murmur, a moan; the apotheosis of one was the condemnation of others.

Remember my meeting with the shipwright from Newcastle. Remember that the working men of London were the first who in their address intentionally put the name of Mazzini side by side with that of Garibaldi.

At the present time the English aristocracy have nothing to fear from their powerful down-trodden and undeveloped working class; moreover, their vulnerable point is not in the direction of the European revolution. But yet the character which the reception was taking was extremely displeasing to them. What made the shepherds of the people most wince at the working men's peaceful agitation was that it was drawing them out of the fitting order, was distracting them from the excellent, moral, and, moreover, never-ending preoccupation with their daily bread, from the lifelong hard labour to which not they, the masters, had doomed them but our common Manufacturer, our Maker—the God of Shaftesbury, the God of Derby, the God of the Sutherlands and the Devonshires—in His incomprehensible wisdom and infinite mercy.

It never, of course, entered the heads of the real English aristocracy to turn Garibaldi out; on the contrary, they tried to draw him away to themselves,

THE ARISTOCRACY

to hide him from the people in a cloud of gold, as ox-eyed Hera was hidden whenever she sported with Zeus. They proposed to show him kindness, to overwhelm him with food and drink, not to let him come to himself nor to recover his senses nor to be one moment alone. Garibaldi wants money: could those condemned by the mercy of our 'Maker,' the Maker of Shaftesbury, Derby and Devonshire, to obscure and blessed poverty collect much for him? We, they said, will throw him half a million—a million—francs, half the betting on a horse at Epsom races, we will buy him—

> 'Estate and home and villa,
> A hundred thousand in pure silver.'

We will buy him the rest of Caprera, we will buy him a wonderful yacht, he is so fond of sailing about over the sea; and that he may not waste his money on nonsense (by *nonsense* understand the emancipation of Italy), we will entail the estate, we will let him enjoy the interest.[1] All these plans were carried out with the most brilliant scenery and setting, but had little success. Garibaldi, like the moon on a dull night, however the clouds were moved forward, hastened or changed, shone out clear and bright and shed light on us below.

The aristocracy began to be a little embarrassed. The business men came to their aid. Their interests were too immediate for them to think about the moral consequences of the agitation; they wanted to control the moment; they fancied one Caesar had frowned, the other looked sulky and feared the Tories would

---

[1] As though Garibaldi had asked for money for himself! I need hardly say he refused the dowry given by the English aristocracy on such absurd conditions, to the extreme mortification of the police newspapers which had been reckoning up the shillings and pence he would be carrying away to Caprera.—(*Author's Note*.)

take advantage of it. The scandalous Stansfeld affair was bad enough already.

Fortunately, just at that time Clarendon had to make a pilgrimage to the Tuileries! His business was of no great importance, he returned immediately. Napoleon talked with him about Garibaldi and expressed his satisfaction that the English people honours great men. Dronyn de Lhuys[1] said—that is, he said nothing, but if he had, he would have stammered:—

> 'I was born near the Caucasus,[2]
> Civis Roman us sum.'

The Austrian Ambassador did not even rejoice at the reception of the *Umweltzungs* General. Everything was arranged satisfactorily. But there was an uneasy gnawing in some hearts.

The Ministers could not sleep at nights. The first whispered to the second, the second to a friend of Garibaldi's, a friend of Garibaldi's to a kinsman of Palmerston's, to Lord Shaftesbury, and to a still greater friend of his, Seeley; Seeley whispered to the surgeon Fergusson; Fergusson, who cared nothing for his neighbour, was alarmed and wrote letter after letter about Garibaldi's illness. After reading them, Gladstone was even more alarmed than the surgeon. Who could have imagined that so much love and sympathy lies sometimes hidden under the portfolio of the Ministry of Finance? . . .

The day after our festivity I went to London. At the railway station I picked up the evening paper and read in large letters Illness of General Garibaldi,' then the announcement that he was going in a day or two to Caprera *without visiting a single other city*. Not being

---

[1] French Minister for foreign affairs under Napoleon the Third.
[2] In Pushkin's poem 'The Fountain of Bahtchisaray' the lines occur:—
> 'I know how to use a dagger,
> I was born near the Caucasus.'—(*Translator's Notes*.)

so nervously sensitive as Shaftesbury, nor so anxious over the health of my friends as Gladstone, I was not in the least troubled by the announcement in the newspaper of the illness of a man whom I had seen the day before perfectly well. Of course there are illnesses that run a very rapid course—the Emperor Paul, for instance, was not long ill—but Garibaldi was a long way from an *apoplectic stroke*, and if anything had happened to him, one of our common friends would have let me know, and so it was easy to guess that it was a deliberate plan, *un coup monté*.

It was too late to go to Garibaldi. I went to Mazzini's and did not find him in, then to the house of a lady from whom I learnt the chief facts concerning the ministerial sympathy for the great man's illness. While I was there Mazzini arrived in a state such as I had never seen him in before; there were tears in his eyes and in his voice.

From the speech uttered at the second meeting on Primrose Hill by Shaen one can tell *en gros* how it was done. The 'conspirators' were named by him, and the circumstances described fairly accurately. Shaftesbury went to take counsel with Seeley; Seeley as a practical man at once said that they must have a letter from Fergusson; Fergusson was too polite a man to refuse the letter. Armed with it, the conspirators went on Sunday evening, the 17th of April, to Stafford House and deliberated what to do, close to the room where Garibaldi was quietly sitting, eating grapes, unaware that he was so ill, or that he was departing. At last the valiant Gladstone undertook the difficult task, and, accompanied by Shaftesbury and Seeley, went to Garibaldi's room. Gladstone used to talk over whole Parliaments, universities, corporations, deputations; it was easy for him to talk over Garibaldi. Moreover, he carried on the conversation in Italian, and did well, as in that way he talked without witnesses, though there were four in the room. Garibaldi answered first that he was quite well, but the Minister of Finance could not accept the chance fact of his good health as an answer, and pointed out that according to Fergusson he was ill, and confirmed this by the document in his hand. At last Garibaldi, perceiving that something else was hidden under this tender sympathy, asked Gladstone, Did all this mean that they wanted him to go? Gladstone did not conceal from him that his presence added to the complications of their already difficult position. 'In that case I will go,' said Garibaldi.

Gladstone, softened, was alarmed at a too *conspicuous* success and suggested he should visit two or three towns and then depart for Caprera.

'I cannot choose between the towns,' answered Garibaldi, wounded, 'and I give you my word that within two days I shall be gone.'

On Monday there was a question asked in Parliament. The feather-headed old Palmerston in one House and the fleet-footed pilgrim Clarendon in the other explained everything with perfect candour. Clarendon assured the peers that Napoleon had not asked for Garibaldi to be turned out. Palmerston for his part was not at all desirous for his departure. He was only anxious about his health . . . and thereupon he entered into all the details which a loving wife, or a doctor sent by an insurance society, goes into—the hours of sleep and of dinner, the consequences of his wound, his diet, the effects of excitement, his age. The sitting of the House of Commons was turned into a consultation of physicians. The Minister had recourse not to Chatham and Campbell but to therapeutics and Fergusson, who had been so helpful in this difficult operation.

The legislative assembly decided that Garibaldi was ill. Towns and villages, counties and banks are left entirely to self-government in England. The Government, which jealously guards itself from every suspicion of interference, which allows men to die of hunger every day through fear of limiting the self-government of workhouses, which permits whole populations to be worked to death and turned into *crétins*, was suddenly transformed into a hospital-nurse. These statesmen abandoned the helm of the great ship and babbled in hushed voices of the health of a man who had not asked for their sympathy, and, uninvited, prescribed for him the Atlantic Ocean and Sutherland's Undine; the Minister of Finance forgot his budget, his income-tax, his debit and credit, and turned consulting physician. The Prime Minister laid this pathological case before Parliament. But is self-government in the case of a man's legs and stomach less sacred than the freedom of charitable establishments whose task is to lead men to the graveyard?

Not long before this Stansfeld had had to pay for not thinking himself bound to quarrel with Mazzini because he was serving the Queen. And now were not the most securely placed Ministers writing, not addresses, but prescriptions and worrying themselves to prolong the days of another revolutionary like Mazzini?

Garibaldi *ought* to have been suspicious of the desire of the Government expressed to him by over-ardent friends and to have remained. Could any one have doubted the truth of the words of the Prime Minister, uttered to the representatives of England? All his friends advised him to remain. 'Palmerston's words cannot relieve me of my promise,' answered Garibaldi, and told them to pack up.

This was Solferino.[1]

Byelinsky observed long ago that the secret of the

[1] An Italian village where in 1859 the Austrians were defeated by the French and Piedmontese,—(*Translator's Note*.)

success of diplomatists lies in the fact that they treat us as though we were diplomatists, while we treat diplomatists as though they were men.

Now you understand why our festive gathering and Garibaldi's speech, his words about Mazzini, would have had a different character had they come one day later.

Next day I went to Stafford House and learnt that Garibaldi had moved to Seeley's, 26 Prince's Gate, near Kensington Gardens. I went to Prince's Gate; there was no possibility of talking to Garibaldi, he was not allowed out of sight; some twenty visitors were walking about, sitting silent, or talking in the drawing-room and the study.

'You are going?' I said, and took him by the hand. Garibaldi pressed my hand and answered in a mournful voice: 'I bow to the necessities (*je me plie aux nécessités*).'

He was going off somewhere. I left him and went downstairs; there I found Saffi, Guerzoni, Mordini and Richardson; all were beside themselves with anger at Garibaldi's departure. Mrs. Seeley came in, followed by a thin, elderly, lively Frenchwoman who addressed herself with excessive eloquence to the lady of the house, speaking of her happiness in making the acquaintance of such a *personne distinguée*. Mrs. Seeley turned to Stansfeld, asking him to translate. The Frenchwoman went on: 'Ah my God, how delighted I am! Of course that is your son, allow me to introduce myself.' Stansfeld disabused the Frenchwoman, who had not observed that Mrs. Seeley was about his age, and asked her to tell him what it was she wanted. She flung a glance at me (Saffi and the others had gone out) and said: 'We are not alone.' Stansfeld mentioned my name. She immediately turned and harangued me, begging me to remain, but I preferred to leave her to a *tête-à-tête* with

Stansfeld and went upstairs again. A minute later Stansfeld came up with some sort of hook or rivet. The Frenchwoman's husband had invented it and she wanted Garibaldi's approval.

The last two days were full of confusion and gloom. Garibaldi avoided talking about his departure and said not a word about his health. . . . In all his friends he met a look of sorrowful reproach. He was sick at heart, but he said nothing.

At two o'clock on the day before his departure I was sitting with him when they came to tell him that there was already a crowd in the reception-room. On that day the members of Parliament with their families and all sorts of nobility and gentry, numbering two thousand people according to *The Times*, were presented to him. It was a *grand lever*, a regal reception, but such a one as no king of Würtemberg or even of Prussia could ever have attracted without calling in professors and lower ranks of officers.

Garibaldi got up and asked: 'Is it really time?' Stansfeld, who happened to be there, looked at his watch and said: 'There is still five minutes before the time fixed.' Garibaldi heaved a sigh of relief and sat down cheerfully. But then a factotum ran in and began arranging where the sofa was to stand, by which door people were to come in, by which to go out.

'I am going,' I said to Garibaldi.

'Why? Do stay.'

'What am I going to do?'

'Surely,' he said, smiling, 'I can keep one man I know, since I am receiving so many I don't.'

The doors were opened; in the doorway stood an improvised master of the ceremonies with a sheet of paper in his hand from which he began reading aloud as from a directory: the Right Honourable So-and-so— the Honourable So-and-so—Esquire—Lady—Esquire

—Lordship—Mrs.—Esquire—M.P., M.P., without end. At every name there burst in at the doorway and sailed into the room old and young crinolines, grey heads and bald heads, tiny little old men and stout sturdy little old men, and thin giraffes with no hind legs, who drew themselves up to such a height that it looked as though the upper part of their head was propped on huge yellow teeth, and tried to draw themselves higher still. Each one of them had three, four or five ladies, and this was very fortunate, since they occupied the space of fifty men, and in that way saved us from a crush. They all came up to Garibaldi in turn. The men shook his hand with the vigour with which a man shakes his own when he has put his finger in boiling water; some said something as they did so, the majority grunted, remained dumb and bowed as they turned away. The ladies too were mute, but they gazed so long and so passionately at Garibaldi that there will certainly be a crop of children born this year in London with his features; and as the children even now are going about in red shirts like his, there will be nothing left to imitate but his cloak.

Those who had paid their respects sailed towards the opposite door, which opened into the drawing-room, and descended the stairs; the bolder among them were in no haste to go, but tried to remain in the room.

At first Garibaldi stood up, then he kept sitting down and getting up again, finally he simply remained sitting; his leg did not allow him to remain standing for long. The end of the reception was beyond hoping for: carriages kept driving up, the master of the ceremonies kept reading out titles.

The band of the Horse Guards struck up. I stood about and stood about, and at last went out into the drawing-room, and there, with a stream of surging crinolines, reached the cascade, and with it was carried to the doors of the room where Saffi and Mordini usually sat. There was no one in it. I had a feeling of confusion and disgust in my heart; what a farce it all was, this gilded dismissal, and with it this comedy of a royal reception! Tired out, I threw myself on the sofa; the band was playing from 'Lucrezia,' and playing very well. I listened.—Yes, yes, *'Non curiamo l'incerto domani.'*

From the window could be seen rows of carriages; these had not yet driven up; here one moved up, after it a second and a third, again there was a pause; and I fancied how Garibaldi with his bruised hand was sitting tired and gloomy, how that dark cloud was coming over his face and no one noticing it, while still the crinolines float up and still the Right Honourables come—grey-headed, bald, broad-faced, giraffes. . . .

The band played on, the carriages drove up. I don't know how it happened, but I fell asleep. Some one opened the door and woke me . . . . The music was still playing, the carriages still driving up. There was no end in sight. . . . They really will kill him!

I went home.

Next day, that is on the day of his departure, I went to see Garibaldi at seven o'clock in the morning, and slept the night before in London on purpose to do so. He was gloomy and abrupt. For the first time one could see that he was accustomed to command, that he was an iron leader on the field of battle and on the sea.

He was caught by some gentleman who had brought with him a bootmaker, the inventor of a boot with an iron contrivance for Garibaldi. With self-sacrificing resignation Garibaldi sat down in a low chair; the shoemaker in the sweat of his brow forced his irons on him, then made him stamp and walk a step; it seemed all right. 'What must we pay him?' asked Garibaldi.

'Upon my soul!' answered the gentleman; 'why, you will make him happy if you accept it.' They withdrew.

'It will be put up over his shop in a day or two,' some one observed, while Garibaldi said with a supplicating expression to the young man who waited upon him: 'For God's sake get this contrivance off me; I can't stand it, it hurts.' It was frightfully funny.

Then the aristocratic ladies made their appearance; those of less consequence were waiting in a crowd in the drawing-room.

Ogaryov and I went up to him. 'Good-bye,' I said. 'Good-bye till we meet in Caprera.' He embraced me, sat down, stretched out both hands to us, and, in a voice which cut us to the heart, said: 'Forgive me, forgive me, my head is going round. Come to Caprera' and once more he embraced us.

After the reception Garibaldi had to go for an interview with the Prince of Wales at Stafford House.

We went out of the gate and separated. Ogaryov went to Mazzini, I went to Rothschild. There was no one yet at Rothschild's bank. I went to St. Paul's tavern, and there was no one there either. I asked for a rump-steak, and, sitting down quite alone, went over the details of this Midspring Night's Dream.

Go, great child, great force, great fanatic and great simplicity! Go to your rock, peasant in the red shirt! Go, King Lear! Goneril drives you out; leave her, you have poor Cordelia. She will not cease to love you, and she will not die!

The fourth act was over!

What is to come in the fifth?

May 15, 1864.

APOGEE AND PERIGEE

OUR acquaintances, and the Russian ones especially, used to meet at our house on Sunday evenings. In 1862 the number of the latter greatly increased: merchants and tourists, journalists and officials of all the departments, and of the Third Section[1] in particular, were arriving for the Exhibition. It was impossible to make a strict selection; we warned our more intimate friends to come on another day. The respectable boredom of a London Sunday was too much for their discretion, and these Sundays did to some extent lead to disaster. But before I tell the story of that, I must describe two or three samples of our native fauna who made their appearance in the modest drawing-room of Orsett House. Our gallery of living curiosities from Russia was, beyond all doubt, more interesting than the Russian Section at the Great Exhibition.

In 1860 I received from a hotel in the Haymarket a Russian letter in which some unknown persons informed me that they were Russians and were in the service of Prince Yury Nikolayevitch Golitsyn, who had secretly left Russia: 'The prince himself has gone to Constantinople, but has sent us by another route. The prince bade us wait for him and gave us money enough for a few days. More than a fortnight has passed; there is no news of the prince; our money is spent, the hotel-keeper is angry. We don't know what to do. Not one of us speaks English.' Finding themselves in this helpless position, they asked me to get them out of it. I went to them and arranged things. The hotel-keeper knew me, and consented to wait another week.

Five days later a sumptuous carriage with a pair of dapple-grey horses drove up to my front-door. However often I explained to my servants that no one was to be

[1] That is, of the Secret Police—(*Translator's Note.*)

admitted in the morning—even though he should arrive in a four-in-hand and should be called a duke—I could never overcome their respect for an aristocratic turn-out and title.

On this occasion both these temptations to transgression were present, and so a moment later an immense man, stout and with the handsome face of an Assyrian bull-god, was embracing me and thanking me for my visit to his servants.

This was Prince Yury Nikolayevitch Golitsyn. It was a long time since I had seen so solid and characteristic a specimen of old Russia, so choice a flower of our fatherland.

He at once began telling me some incredible story, which afterwards turned out to be true, of how he had given a Cantonist an article from the *Kolokol* to copy, and how he had parted from his wife; how the Cantonist had given the police information against him, and how his wife did not send him money; how the Tsar had sent him into perpetual banishment to Kozlov, in consequence of which he had made up his mind to escape abroad, and had carried off with him over the Moldavian frontier some young lady, a governess, a steward, a 'regent' and a maid-servant.

At Galatz he had picked up also a valet who spoke five languages after a fashion, and seemed to him to be a spy. Then he explained to me that he was an enthusiastic musician and was going to give concerts in London; and that therefore he wanted to make the acquaintance of Ogaryov.

'They d-do make you p-pay here in England at the C-customs,' he said with a slight stammer, as he completed his course of universal history.

'For goods, perhaps, they do,' I observed, 'but the Customs-house is very lenient to travellers.'

'I should not say so. I paid fifteen shillings for a crocodile.'

'Why, what do you mean?'

'What do I mean? Why, simply a crocodile.'

I opened my eyes wide and asked him: 'But what is the meaning of this, prince? Do you take a crocodile about with you instead of a passport to frighten the police on the frontier?'

'It happened like this. I was taking a walk in Alexandria, and I saw a little Arab selling a crocodile. I liked it, so I bought it.'

'Oh, did you buy the little Arab too?'

'Ha-ha!—no.'

A week later the prince was already installed in Porchester Terrace, that is, in a large house in a very expensive part of the town. He began by ordering his gates to be for ever wide open, which is not the English custom, and a pair of dapple-grey horses to be for ever waiting in readiness at the door. He lived in London as though he were in Kozlov or in Tambov.

He had, of course, no money, that is, he had a few thousand francs, enough to pay for the advertisement and title-page of a London life; they were spent at once; but he made a sensation, and succeeded for a few months in living free from care, thanks to the stupid trustfulness of the English, of which the foreigners from all parts of the Continent have not yet been able to cure them.

But the prince did have his fling. The concerts began. London was impressed by the prince's title on the placards, and at the second concert the room (St. James's Hall, Piccadilly) was full. The concert was magnificent. How Golitsyn had succeeded in training the chorus and the orchestra is only known to himself, but the concert was absolutely first-rate. Russian songs and prayers, the Kamarinsky and the Mass, fragments from Glinka's opera and from the Gospel (Our Father)—it was all splendid. The ladies could not sufficiently admire the colossal fleshy contours of the handsome Assyrian god, so majestically and gracefully wielding his ivory sceptre; the old ladies recalled the athletic figure of the Emperor Nicholas, who had conquered the hearts of the London fair most of all by the tight doeskin *collants*, white as the Russian snows, of his Horse Guard uniform.

Golitsyn found the means of making this success his ruin. Intoxicated by the applause, he sent at the end of the first half of the concert for a basket of bouquets (remember the London prices), and before the beginning of the second part of the programme he appeared on the platform; two liveried servants carried the basket, and the prince, thanking the singers and chorus, presented each with a bouquet. The audience received this act of gallantry on the part of the aristocratic conductor with a storm of applause. My prince, towering to his full height and beaming all over, invited all the musicians to supper at the end of the concert.

At this point not only London prices but also London habits must be considered. Without sending previous notice in the morning, there is no place where one can give a supper to fifty persons at eleven o'clock at night. The Assyrian chief walked valiantly along Regent Street at the head of his musical army, knocking at the doors of various restaurants; and at last he knocked successfully. A restaurant-keeper, grasping the situation, rose to the occasion—cold meats and ardent beverages.

Then followed a series of concerts with every possible variation, even with political tendencies. At each of them the orchestra struck up Herzen waltzes, an Ogaryov quadrille, and then the Emancipation Symphony . . . compositions with which the prince is very likely even now enchanting Moscow audiences, and which have probably lost nothing in moving from Albion, except their names; they could easily be altered to Potapoff waltzes, Mina waltzes, and Komissaroff's *Partitur*.

With all this glory there was no money, he had nothing to pay with. His purveyors began to murmur. And little by little there was actually something like the slave revolt of Spartacus....

One morning the prince's factotum, that is, his steward who styled himself his secretary, together with the 'regent,' that is, not the father of Philippe of Orleans, but a fair-haired, curly-headed Russian lad of two-and-twenty who led the singers, came to me.

'We have come to see you, Alexandr Ivanovitch, sir.'

'What has happened?'

'Why, Yury Nikolayevitch is treating us very badly. We want to go back to Russia, and we ask him to settle our account—do not fail in your gracious kindness, defend us.'

I felt myself instantly surrounded by the atmosphere of 'Home,' which seemed to rise up like steam in a bath-house.

'Why do you come to me with this complaint? If you have serious grounds for complaining of the prince, there is a Court of Justice here for every one, which will not turn aside in favour of any prince or any count.'

'We have heard of that indeed, but *why go to law*? You had much better go into it.'

'What good will it be to you if I do go into it? The prince will tell me to mind my own business; I shall look like a fool. If you do not want to go to law, go to the ambassador; the Russians in London are in his care, not in mine....'

'But where should we be then? As soon as Russian gentlemen sit together, what chance can there be of settling with the prince? But you see, you are on the side of the people; so that is why we have come to you. Do be gracious, and take up our cause.'

'What fellows you are! But the prince won't accept my decision; what will you gain by it?'

'Allow We to lay before you,' the secretary retorted eagerly, 'he will not venture on that, sir, as he has a very great respect for you; besides, he would be afraid. He would not be pleased to get into the *Kolokol*—he is ambitious.'

'Well, listen, to waste no more time; here is my decision. If the prince will consent to accept my mediation, I will undertake the matter; if not, you must go to law; and as you know neither the language nor the mode of proceeding here, if the prince really is treating you unfairly, I will send you a man who knows English and English ways and speaks Russian.'

'Allow me,' the secretary was beginning.

'No, I won't allow you, my dear fellow. Good-bye.'

I will say a word about them too.

The 'regent' was in no way distinguished except by his musical abilities; he was a well-fed, soft, stupidly handsome, rosy servant-boy; his manner of speaking with a slight burr and his rather sleepy eyes called up before me a whole series, as when you see one reflection behind another in the looking-glass, of Sashkas, Senkas, Alyoshkas, and Miroshkas.

The secretary, too, was a purely Russian product, but a more striking specimen of his type. He was a man over forty, with an unshaven chin and battered face, in a greasy coat, unclean and soiled inwardly and outwardly, with small crafty eyes and that peculiar smell of Russian drunkards, made up of the ever-persistent aroma of vodka fumes mixed with a flavour of onion and cloves to conceal it. Every feature of his face approved and abetted every evil suggestion; it would doubtless have found response and appreciation in his heart, and would if profitable have received his aid. He was the prototype of the Russian petty official, the Russian shark, the Russian sharper. When I asked him whether he was pleased at the approaching emancipation of the peasants, he answered '' To be sure—most certainly,' and added with a sigh:: 'Good Lord, the lawsuits and the cases there will be! And the prince has brought me here as though to spite me at a time like this.'

Before Golitsyn arrived, this man had said to me with a show of genuine feeling: 'Don't you believe what people will tell you about the prince oppressing the peasants, or how he meant to set them free for a big redemption money without any land. That is all a story spread by his enemies. It is true he is hasty-tempered and extravagant, but he has a good heart and has been a father to his peasants.'

As soon as he had quarrelled with the prince he cursed his lot and lamented that he had trusted such a swindler. 'Why, he has done nothing all his life but squander money in debauchery and ruin his peasants; you know he is just keeping up a pretence before you now—but he is really a beast, a robber. . . .'

'When were you telling lies: now, or when you praised him?' I asked him, smiling.

The secretary was overcome with confusion. I turned on my heel and went away. Had this man not been born in the servants' hall of the Prince Golitsyn, had he not been the son of some village constable, he would long ago, with his abilities, have been a minister— a Valuev, or I don't know what.

An hour later the 'regent' and his mentor appeared with a note from Golitsyn. He asked me, with apologies, whether I could go and see him to put an end to these wretched difficulties. The prince promised beforehand to accept my decision without dispute.

There was no getting out of it; I went.

Everything in the house betrayed an extraordinary excitement; the French servant Picot hurriedly opened the door to me, and, with the solemn fussiness with which doctors are conducted to a consultation at the bedside of a dying man, led me into the drawing-room. There I found Golitsyn's second wife, flustered and irritated. Golitsyn himself, with no cravat, his heroic chest bare, was pacing up and down the room with huge strides. He was furious, and so stammered twice as much as usual; his whole face betrayed his suffering from the blows, kicks and punches that were surging inwardly but could have no outlet in the actual world, though they would have been his answer to the insurgents in the Tambov province.

'For G-G-God's sake, forgive me for t-t-troubling you about these b-b-blackguards.'

'What is the matter?'

'P-p-please ask them yourself; I will merely listen.'

He summoned the 'regent,' and the following conversation took place between us:—

'Are you dissatisfied in any way?'

'Yes, very much dissatisfied; that is why I want to go to Russia.'

The prince, who had a voice as strong as Lablache's, emitted a leonine moan: another five blows in the face had to be stifled within him.

'The prince cannot keep you; so tell us what it is you are dissatisfied with.'

'Everything, Alexandr Ivanovitch.'

'Well, do speak more definitely.'

'What can I say? Ever since I came away from Russia I have been run off my legs with work, and had only two pounds of pay, and what the prince gave me the third time, in the evening, was more by way of a present.'

'And how much ought you to have received?'

'That I can't say, sir. . . .'

'Have you a definite agreement?'

'No indeed, sir. The prince, when he was graciously pleased to run away' (this was said without the slightest malicious intention), 'said to me: "If you like to come with me, I 'll make your future," says he, "and if I have luck, I 'll give you a good salary; but if not, then you must be satisfied with a little"; so I took, and came.'

He had come from Tambov to London on such terms. Oh, Russia!

'Well, and what do you think? has the prince been lucky or not?'

'Lucky? no, indeed! Though to be sure, he might . . .'

'That is a different question. If he is not lucky, then you ought to be satisfied with a small salary.'

'But the prince himself has told me that for my duties and my abilities, according to the rate of pay here, I ought not to get less than four pounds a month.'

'Prince, are you willing to pay him four pounds a month?'

'I shall be d-d-delighted.'

'That is capital; what more?'

'The prince promised that if I wanted to go back he would pay my return fare to Petersburg.'

The prince nodded and added: 'Yes, but only if I were pleased with him!'

'Are you displeased with him?'

Then the pent-up torrent burst out; the prince leapt up. In a tragic bass, which gained weight from the quiver on some vowels and the little pauses before some of the consonants, he delivered the following speech: 'Could I be p-p-pleased with that m-milksop, that p-p-pup? What enrages me is the foul ingratitude of the beggar. I took him into my service from the very poorest family of peasants, barefoot, devoured by lice; I trained the rascal. I have made a m-m-man of him, a m-musician, a "regent"; I have trained the scoundrel's voice so that he could get a hundred roubles a month in Russia in the season.'

'That is all very true, Yury Nikolayevitch, but I don't share your view of it. Neither he nor his family asked you to make a Ronconi of him; so you can't expect any special gratitude on his part. You have trained him as one trains a nightingale, and you have done a good thing, but that is the end of it. Besides, that is not the point.'

'You are right; but I meant to say, see what I have to put up with, see what I have done for the rascal . . .'

'So you consent to pay his fare?'

'The devil take him. For your sake, simply, for your sake, I will . . . '

'Well, the matter is settled, then: and do you know what the fare is?'

'I am told it is twenty pounds.'

'No, that is too much. A hundred roubles from here to Petersburg is enough. Will you give that?'

'Yes, I will.'

I worked out the sum on paper and handed it to Golitsyn; the latter glanced at the total . . . it amounted, if I remember rightly, to just over thirty pounds. He handed me the money on the spot.

'You can read and write, of course?' I asked the young man.

'Of course, sir.'

I wrote out a receipt for him in some such form as this: I have received from Prince Yury Nikolayevitch Golitsyn thirty odd pounds (so much in Russian money), being salary owing to me and my fare from London to Petersburg. With that I am satisfied, and have no other claims against him.

'Read it for yourself, and sign it.'

The young man read it, and made no movement to sign it.

'What is the matter?'
'I can't, sir.'
'Why can't you?'
'I am not satisfied.'

A restrained leonine roar—and, indeed, I was on the point of crying out myself.

'What the devil is the matter? You said yourself what you claimed. The prince has paid you everything to the last farthing. Why are you dissatisfied?'

'Why, upon my word, sir, and the straits I have been put to ever since I have been here.'

It was clear that the ease with which he had obtained the money had whetted his appetite.

'For instance, sir, I ought to have something more for copying music'

'You liar!' Golitsyn boomed, as Lablache can never have boomed; the piano responded with a timid echo; Picot's pale face appeared at the crack of the door and vanished with the speed of a frightened lizard . . . . 'Wasn't copying music a part of your definite duty? Why, what else had you to do all the time when there were no concerts?'

The prince was right, though he need not have frightened Picot by his *contrabombardo* voice.

The 'regent,' being accustomed to notes of all sorts, did not give way, but, dropping the music-copying, turned to me with the following absurdity: 'And then, too, there is something for clothes. I am quite threadbare.'

'But do you mean to tell me that Yury Nikolayevitch undertook to clothe you, as well as to give you about fifty pounds a year salary?'

'No, sir; but in old days the prince did sometimes give me things, but now, I am ashamed to say so, I have come to going about without socks.'

'I am going about without s-s-socks myself,' roared

the prince, and, folding his arms across his chest, he looked haughtily and contemptuously across at the 'regent.' This outburst I had not expected, and I looked into his face with surprise; but, seeing that he was about to continue, I said very gravely to the precious singer: 'You came to me this morning to ask for my mediation: so you trusted me?'

'We know you very well, we have no doubt of you at all, you will not let us be wronged.'

'Very good. Well, this is how I settle the matter: sign the receipt at once or give me back the money, and I will give it back to the prince and decline to meddle any further.'

The 'regent' had no inclination to hand the money to the prince; he signed the receipt and thanked me. I will spare you the description of his reckoning it in roubles. I could not din into him that the rouble was not the same in the exchange as it was when he left Russia.

'If you imagine that I am trying to cheat you of thirty shillings, this is what you had better do: go to our priest and ask him to reckon it for you.' He agreed to do so.

It seemed as though all were over, and Golitsyn's breast no longer heaved with such stormy menace; but as fate would have it, the sequel recalled our fatherland as the beginning had.

The 'regent' hesitated and hesitated, and suddenly, as though nothing had happened between them, turned to Golitsyn with the words: 'Your Excellency, as the steamer does not go from Hull for five days, be so gracious—allow me to remain with you for the while.' My Lablache will give it him, I thought, devotedly preparing myself for the shock of the sound.

'Of course you can stay. Where the devil would you go?'

The 'regent' thanked the prince and went away.

Golitsyn by way of explanation said to me: 'You see he is a very good fellow; it is that b-b-blackguard, that thief, that unclean Yuss leads him astray.'

Let Savigny and Mittermeyer do their best to formulate and classify the ideas of justice developed in our orthodox fatherland between the stable where they flog the house-serfs and the master's study where they fleece the peasants.

The second *cause célèbre*, that is, the one with the aforesaid Yuss, was not so successful. Golitsyn came in, and he suddenly shouted so loud, and the secretary shouted so loud that there was nothing left but to come to blows with each other, and then the prince of course would have smashed the mangy sharper. But as everything in that household followed the laws of a peculiar logic, it was not the prince who fought with the secretary, but the secretary who fought with the door. Brimming over with spite and invigorated by an extra glass of gin, he aimed a blow with his fist at the big glass window in the door, and broke it to bits.

'Police!' roared Golitsyn. 'Burglary! Police!' and going into the drawing-room he fell exhausted on the sofa. When he had recovered a little, he explained to me among other things how great was the ingratitude of the secretary. The man had been his brother's trusted agent and had swindled him—I do not remember how—and was on the point of being brought to trial. Golitsyn was sorry for him; he entered so thoroughly into his position that he pawned his only watch to buy him off. And so having the fullest proof that he was a rogue, he took him into his service as a steward!

There could be no doubt whatever that he had cheated Golitsyn at every turn.

I went away. A man who could smash a glass door with his fist could find justice and protection for himself. Moreover, he told me afterwards himself when he asked me to get him a passport to return to Russia, that he had proudly offered Golitsyn a pistol and suggested casting lots which should fire.

If this was so, the pistol was certainly not loaded.

The prince spent his last penny in pacifying the Servile Revolt, and none the less ended, as might have been expected, by being imprisoned for debt. Any one else would have been clapped in prison, and that would have been the end of it; but even that could not happen to Golitsyn simply in the common way.

A policeman used to conduct him between seven and eight o'clock every evening to Cremona Gardens; there he used to conduct a concert for the edification of the *lorettes* of all London, and with the last wave of his ivory sceptre a policeman, till then unobserved, would spring up as though out of the earth and escort the prince to the cab which took the captive in the black swallow-tail and white gloves to prison. There were tears in his eyes as he said 'Good-bye' to me in the Gardens. Poor prince! Another man might have laughed at it, but he took his captivity to heart. His relations redeemed him at last; then the Government permitted him to return to Russia, and banished him at first to Yaroslavl, where he could conduct religious concerts together with Felinski, the Bishop of Warsaw. The Government was kinder to him than his father; as free a liver as his son, he advised the latter to go into a monastery. The father knew the son well; and yet he was himself so good a musician that Beethoven dedicated a symphony to him.

Following the exuberant figure of the Assyrian god, of the fleshy ox-Apollo, a series of other Russian curiosities must not be forgotten.

I am not speaking of flitting shades like the 'colonel russe,' but of those who, stranded by fate and various adventures, have remained a long time in London; such as the clerk in the War Office who, having got into a mess with his accounts and debts, threw himself into the Neva, was drowned . . . and popped up in London, an *exile*, in a fur cap and a fur-lined coat, which he never abandoned, regardless of the muggy warmth of a London winter.

Or such as my friend Ivan Ivanovitch S., who, with antecedents and future and all, with raw skin on his head where there should have been hair, clamours for a place in my gallery of curiosities. A retired officer of the bodyguard of the Pavlov regiment, he lived in comfort in foreign parts, and so continued up to the revolution of February. Then he took fright, and began to look on himself as a criminal. Not that his conscience troubled him; what troubled him was the thought of the gendarmes who would meet him at the frontier, the thought of dungeons, of a troika, of the snow, and he resolved to postpone his return. All at once the news reached him that his brother had been arrested in connection with Shevtchenko's case. There really was some risk for him, and he at once resolved to return. It was at that time that I made his acquaintance at Nice. S. was setting off, having bought a minute phial of poison for the journey, which he intended as he crossed the frontier to insert in a hollow tooth and to swallow if he were arrested.

As he approached his native land his panic grew greater and greater, and by the time he arrived at Berlin it had become a suffocating anguish. However, S. mastered himself and took his seat in the train. He remained there for the first five stations; further than that he could not bear it. The engine stopped to take in water; on a different pretext he left the train. The engine whistled, the train moved off without S.; and that was just what he wanted. Leaving his trunk to the caprice of destiny, by the first train going in the opposite direction he returned to Berlin. Thence he sent a telegram concerning his luggage, and went to get a *visa* for his passport to Hamburg. 'Yesterday you were going to Russia, and to-day you are going to Hamburg,' remarked the policeman, without refusing the *visa*. The panic-stricken S. said: 'Letters—I have had letters,' and probably his expression as he said it was such that the Prussian official ought to be dismissed the service for not arresting him. Thereupon S., like Louis-Philippe, escaping though pursued by no one, arrived in London. In London a hard life began for him, as for thousands of others; for years he maintained an honest and resolute struggle with poverty. But for him, too, destiny provided a comic trimming to all his tragic adventures. He made up his mind to give lessons in mathematics, drawing and even French (for English people). After consulting various advisers, he saw that it could not be done without an advertisement or cards. 'But the trouble is this: how will the Russian Government look at it? I thought and thought about it, and I have had anonymous cards printed.'

It was a long time before I could get over my delight at this grand invention: it had never occurred to me that it was possible to have a visiting-card without a name on it. With the help of his anonymous cards, and with great perseverance (he used to live for days together on nothing but bread and potatoes), he succeeded in getting afloat, was employed in selling things on commission, and his fortunes began to mend.

And this was precisely at the date when the fortunes of another officer of the Pavlov bodyguard failed completely; defeated, robbed, deceived, cheated, and deluded, the commander-in-chief of the Pavlov regiment departed into eternity. Pardons, amnesties, followed; S. too wished to take advantage of the Imperial mercies, and so he writes a letter to Brunov and asks whether he comes under the amnesty.

A month later S. was summoned to the Embassy. 'My case is not so simple,' he thought; 'they have been thinking it over for a month.'

'We have received an answer,' the senior secretary said to him; 'you have inadvertently put the Ministry in a difficult position; they have nothing against you. They have applied to the Ministry of Home Affairs, and they can find nothing relating to you either. Tell us plainly what it was; it could not have been anything of great consequence?'

'Why, in 1849 my brother was arrested and afterwards exiled.'

'Well?'

'That was all.'

'No,' thought the official, 'he is joking'; and he told S. if that was the case the Ministry would make further inquiries.

Two months passed. I can imagine what went on during these two months in Petersburg: references, reports, confidential inquiries, secret questions passed from the Ministry to the Third Section, from the Third Section to the Ministry, the report of X. . . . of the Governor-General . . . reprimands, observations . . . but S.'s case could not be found.

The Ministry reported to that effect to London.

Brunov himself sent for S. 'Here,' he said—' look —is the answer: there is nothing anywhere concerning you.—Tell me, what case was it you were mixed up in?'

'My brother . . .'

'I have heard all that, but with what case were you yourself connected?'

'There was nothing else.'

Brunov, who had never been surprised at anything from his birth up, was surprised.

'Then why do you ask for a pardon since you have done nothing?'

'I thought that it was better, anyway.'

'So the fact is you don't need a pardon, but a passport,' and Brunov ordered a passport to be given him.

In high delight S. dashed off to us.

After describing in detail the whole story of how he had obtained a pardon, he took Ogaryov by the arm and led him away into the garden. 'For God's sake, give me advice,' he said to him, 'Alexandr Ivanovitch always laughs at me—that is his way; but you have a kind heart. Tell me candidly: do you think I can safely go through Vienna?' Ogaryov did not justify this good opinion; he burst out laughing. But not only Ogaryov —I can imagine how the faces of Brunov and his secretary for two minutes lost the wrinkles traced by weighty affairs of State and grinned when S., amnestied, walked out of their office.

But with all his eccentricities, S. was an honest man.

The other Russians who rose to the surface, God knows whence, strayed for a month or two about London, called on us with their own letters of introduction and vanished God knows whither, were by no means so harmless.

The melancholy case which I am going to describe took place in the summer of 1862. The reaction was at that time in its incubation stage, and the internal hidden rottenness had not yet shown itself externally. No one was afraid to come and see us; no one was afraid to take copies of the *Kolokol* and our other publications away with him; many people boasted of the clever way they conveyed them over the frontier. When we advised them to be careful they laughed at us. We hardly ever wrote letters to Russia: we had nothing to say to our old friends, we were drifting further and further away from them; with our new unknown friends we corresponded through the *Kolokol*.

In the spring Kelsiev returned from Moscow and

A SUBSCRIPTION-SUPPER

Petersburg. His journey is undoubtedly one of the most remarkable episodes of that period. The man who had slipped under the noses of the police, scarcely concealing himself, who had been present at conversations of raskolniks and drinking parties of comrades, with an absurd Turkish passport in his pocket, and had returned safe and sound to London, had grown reckless.

He took it into his head to get up a subscription-supper in our honour on the fifth anniversary of the *Kolokol* at a restaurant. I begged him to put off the celebration to another happier time. He would not. The supper was not a success, there was no *entrain* about it, and there could not be. There were too many outsiders taking part in it.

Talking of one thing and the other between toasts and anecdotes, it was mentioned as the simplest thing in the world that Vyetoshnikov, Kelsiev's friend, was going to Petersburg and was ready to take anything with him. The party broke up late. Many people said that they would be with us on Sunday. There was indeed a regular crowd among whom were people whom we knew very little, and unfortunately Vyetoshnikov himself; he came up to me and said that he was going next morning, and asked me whether I had any letters or commissions. Bakunin had already given him two or three letters. Ogaryov went downstairs to his own room and wrote a few words of friendly greeting to Nikolay Serno-Solovyevitch; to them I added a word of greeting and asked the latter to call the attention of Tchernyshevsky (to whom I had never written) to our proposal in the *Kolokol* to print the *Sovremennik* in London at our expense.

The party began to break up about twelve o'clock. Two or three guests remained. Vyetoshnikov came into my study and took the letter. It is very possible that even that might have remained unnoticed. But this is what happened. By way of thanking those who had taken part in the supper, I asked them to choose any one of our publications or a big photograph of myself as a souvenir from me. Lyev Vyetoshnikov took the photograph; I advised him to cut off the margin and roll it up; he would not, but said he should put it at the bottom of his trunk, and so wrapped it in a sheet of *The Times* and went off. That could not escape notice.

Saying good-bye to him, the last of the party, I quietly went off to bed—so great is one's blindness at times—and of course never dreamed how dearly that minute would cost me and what sleepless nights it would bring me. It was all stupid and careless in the extreme. We might have delayed Vyetoshnikov until Tuesday, he might have been sent off on Saturday; why had he not come in the morning? . . . and indeed why had he come himself at all? . . . and, indeed, why did we write the letters?

We were told that one of our guests telegraphed at once to Petersburg.

Vyetoshnikov was arrested on the steamer; the rest is well known.

To conclude this gloomy narrative, I will speak of a man whom I have casually mentioned and whom I must not pass over. I mean Kelsiev.

BEHIND THE SCENES

(1863 TO 1864)

WE were left alone without faith listening to the far-away thunder of cannon, the far-away moan of the wounded. Early in April the news came that Potebnya had been killed in battle at the Pyeskov Rock. In May Padlewski was shot at Plotsk, and so it went on and on.

It was a hard, unbearably hard, time! And, to add to all the gloom, one was the involuntary spectator of the stupidity, the senselessness of men, the cursed recklessness destroying every force about one.

V. I. KELSIEV

The name of V. Kelsiev has gained a mournful notoriety of late: the rapidity of his inward and the haste of his outward transformation, the success of his penitence, the urgent craving for a public confession and its strange scantiness, the tactlessness of his story, its inappropriate jocosity together with the easy levity so unseemly in the penitent and forgiven—all this, among people so unaccustomed as we are to abrupt and public conversions, set the better part of our journalists in arms against him. Kelsiev wanted at all costs to occupy the public attention; he made himself a target at which every one flings a stone without sparing. I am far from condemning the intolerance displayed in that case by our slumbering journalism. This indignation proves that there is still much that is uncorrupted and vigorous left among us, in spite of the black period of moral sloppiness and immoral talk. The indignation poured upon Kelsiev was the same as that which was unsparing of Pushkin for one or two poems and turned against Gogol for his 'Correspondence with Friends.'

To cast a stone at Kelsiev is superfluous; a whole pavement has been thrown at him already. I want to tell others and to remind him what he was like when he came to us in London, and what he was like when for the second time he went away to Turkey.

Let him compare the bitterest moments of his life then with the sweetest of his present career.

These pages were written before his penitence and conversion, before his metempsychosis and metamorphosis. I have changed nothing and added nothing but extracts from letters. In my hasty sketch Kelsiev is presented as he remained in my memory until his arrival on a boat at the Skulyany[1] Customs in the character of prohibited goods asking to be confiscated and to be treated according to the law.

In 1859 I received the first letter from him.

The letter came from Plymouth. Kelsiev had arrived there on the steamer of a North American company, and was going on to a job in the Aleutian Islands. After spending a little time in Plymouth he gave up the idea of going to the Aleutian Islands, and wrote to me asking whether he could gain a livelihood in London. He had already succeeded in making the acquaintance of some theological gentlemen in Plymouth, and told me that they had called his attention to remarkable interpretations of prophecy. I warned him off the English clergymen, and invited him to London 'if he really wanted to work.' A fortnight later he made his appearance.

A rather tall, thin, sickly-looking young man with a rectangular skull and a thick crop of hair on his head, he reminded me—not by his hair (for the other was

[1] A Russian town on the Roumanian frontier.—(*Translator's Note.*)

bald) but by his whole character—of Engelson, and he really was like him in very many ways. From the first glance one could discern in him much that was inharmonious and unstable, but nothing that was vulgar. It was evident that he had escaped from every form of bondage and authority but had not yet enrolled himself in the service of any cause or party: he had no definite object. He was much younger than Engelson, but yet he did belong to the latest section of the Petrashev group, and had some of their virtues and all of their defects, had studied everything in the world and learnt nothing thoroughly, read everything of every sort, and worried his brains rather uselessly over it all. Through continual criticism of every accepted idea, Kelsiev had shaken all his moral conceptions without discovering any guiding principle of conduct.

What was particularly original about Kelsiev was that in all his sceptical questioning there remained an element of fantastic mysticism: he was a Nihilist with the ways and manners of the religious, a Nihilist in the robes of a deacon. The flavour of the Church, its manner of speech and imagery, were retained in his deportment, his language, his style,[1] and gave his whole life a peculiar character, a peculiar unity, made by the welding together of opposing metals.

Kelsiev was passing through that stage of revaluation so familiar to us which almost every truly awakened Russian accomplishes within himself, and of which the Western European through practical preoccupations and lack of leisure never dreams at all, drawn as he is by his specialised knowledge into other tasks. Our elder brothers never verify their elementary assumptions, and that is how it is that their generations succeed each

---

[1] Extremely hard-working young men often end by becoming followers of Petrashev; they might be described as the top class of our historical development in education.—(*Author's Note*.)

other, building and destroying, rewarding and punishing, bestowing crowns and fetters, always firmly convinced that it is the right thing and that they are doing their job. Kelsiev, on the contrary, doubted everything and refused to accept on hearsay that good was good or that evil was evil. This haughty spirit that denies all previous morality and accepted truths was particularly strong in the *mi-carême* of our Lent under Nicholas, and found striking expression as soon as the yoke that weighed on our brains was lifted one inch. This analysis, so full of life and vigour, was fiercely attacked by the conservative literary movement—conserving God knows what—and after it by the Government.

At the time of our awakening in the din of the Sevastopol cannon, many of our clever fellows kept repeating the words they had heard from others, that Western European conservatism was the right thing for us, that we had been hurriedly thrust into European culture, not that we might share their hereditary diseases and out-of-date prejudices, but that we might compare ourselves with our elder brothers, so that it might be possible to advance in step with them. But as soon as in actual fact we see that in awakening thought, that in mature speech there is no firm principle, 'nothing sacred,' nothing but questions and problems, that thought is seeking, that speech is denying, that the most certain good is tottering together with what is bad, and that the spirit of doubt and experiment is dragging everything indiscriminately into an abyss, from which all safeguards have been removed—then a cry of consternation and horror bursts from the lips, and the first-class passengers close their eyes that they may not see the train leaving the rails while the drivers try to put on the brakes and stop the engine.

In reality there was no cause to be afraid: the rising force was too weak to change the course of sixty millions materially. But it had a programme, perhaps a prophecy.

Kelsiev had developed under the first influence of the period of which we are speaking. He was far from having attained clarity or reached any equilibrium; his moral property was in complete liquidation. All that was old he denied, all that was solid he had dissolved, he had shoved off from the shore and was drifting recklessly into the open sea; with equal suspicion and mistrustfulness he regarded belief and disbelief, Russian methods and the methods of Western Europe. The one thing that had sent deep roots into his heart was a passionate and profound recognition of the economic injustice of the present political order, a hatred for it and an intense but vague passion for the social theories in which he saw a solution.

Apart from all understanding of it, he had an undeniable right to this sense of injustice and this hatred of it.

In London he settled in one of the remotest parts of the town, in a blind alley of Fulham, inhabited by pale, smutty Irish and emaciated workmen of all sorts. In these damp, stony, unroofed corridors, it is fearfully still, there is almost no sound nor light nor colour: people, flower-pots and houses, all are faded and shrunk. Smoke and soot have wrapped all outlines in a shroud of mourning. No tradesmen's carts rattle down them with provisions, no cabmen drive that way, no hawkers cry their wares, no dogs bark (there is absolutely nothing to feed the latter on); only from time to time a thin, dishevelled-looking, smutty cat emerges, clambers on to the roof and goes up to the chimney to get warm, arching her spine and betraying unmistakably how chilled she has been indoors.

The first time I visited Kelsiev I did not find him at home. A very young, very plain woman—thin, lymphatic, with tear-stained eyes—was sitting on the floor by a mattress, on which a baby of a year or a year and a half was tossing in a high fever, suffering and dying.

I looked at its face, and thought of the face of another baby on the point of death: it was the same expression. A few days later it died, and another was born.

No poverty could have been more complete. The young frail woman, or rather married child, endured it heroically and with extraordinary simplicity.

No one looking at her sickly, scrofulous, feeble appearance could have imagined what energy, what force of devotion, resided in that frail body. She might have served as a bitter lesson for our popular novelists. She was, or rather wanted to be, what was afterwards called a *Nihilist*: did her hair queerly, was careless in her dress, smoked a great deal, and was not afraid either of bold thoughts or bold words; she was not enthusiastic over the domestic virtues, did not talk of the sacredness of duty and the sweetness of the sacrifice she made daily, or of the lightness of the burden that weighed on her young shoulders. There was no pose or affectation about her struggle with poverty; and she did everything —sewed, washed, suckled her baby, cooked the meat and scrubbed the room. She was a resolute comrade to her husband, and like a great martyr laid down her life in the distant East, following her husband's restless, wandering flight and losing her two last children in succession.

At first I struggled with Kelsiev, trying to persuade him not to cut himself off from the path of return before he knew what the life of an exile was like.

I had told him that he ought first to learn what poverty in a strange land meant, poverty in England, particularly in London; I told him that every vigorous man was precious now in Russia.

'What are you going to do here?' I asked him.

Kelsiev proposed to study everything and to write about everything; most of all, he wanted to write about the Woman Question and the reorganisation of the family.

'Write first,' I told him, 'about the necessity that the peasants should have the land when they are emancipated. That is the first question that confronts us.'

But Kelsiev was not attracted in that direction. He did, as a fact, bring me an article on the Woman Question. It was incredibly poor. Kelsiev was angry with me for not publishing it, though he thanked me for it two years later.

He did not want to go back. Work had to be found for him at all costs. We did our best to find it. His theological eccentricities assisted us in doing so. We obtained for him the job of correcting the proofs of the Russian edition of the Scriptures published by the London Bible Society, and then handed over to him a heap of papers we had received at various times relating to the Old Believers. Kelsiev undertook the task of arranging and editing them with enthusiasm. What he had been groping for and dreaming of lay revealed before him: he discovered in the dissenters a coarsely naïve socialism in a gospel setting. This was the best period in Kelsiev's life. He worked passionately, and used to run in to see me in the evening to tell me of some socialistic idea of the Duhobors or the Molokans, or some communistic doctrine of the Fedoseyevtsy. He was delighted with their wanderings in the forests, and found an ideal for his life in wandering among them and becoming the founder of a socialist Christian sect in Belaya-Krinitsa,[1] or Russia.

And indeed Kelsiev was a 'vagrant' soul, a vagrant morally and in practice: he was tormented by unstable

[1] A district in Bukovina settled by Russian raskolniks.—(*Translator's Note.*)

thoughts, by depression. He could not remain in one spot. He had found work, occupation, a livelihood free from want, but he did not find work which would completely absorb his restless temperament; he was ready to go anywhere to seek it, even to become a monk, to accept the holy calling without faith in it.

A typical Russian, Kelsiev made a new programme of work every month, thought of new schemes and took up a new task without finishing the old one. He worked by bouts, and by bouts did nothing. He grasped things easily, but was at once satisfied and cloyed; he plucked at once all the essence out of a thing, to the last deduction, sometimes even more than was in it.

The book about the raskolniks came off successfully; he published six parts, which were quickly distributed. The Government, seeing this, allowed the publication of the facts concerning the Old Believers. The same thing happened with the translation of the Bible. The translation from the Hebrew was not successful. Kelsiev tried to perform a *tour de force* and to translate it word for word, regardless of the fact that the grammatical forms of the Semitic tongues do not correspond with those of the Slavonic. Nevertheless, the books that were issued were instantly sold, and the Holy Synod, alarmed at the success of the foreign edition, gave its blessing to the publication of the Old Testament in Russian. These back-handed victories were never put down to the credit of our press by any one.

At the end of 1862 Kelsiev went to Moscow with the object of establishing permanent relations with the raskolniks. This expedition he ought one day to describe himself. It was incredible, impossible, but it actually took place. The daring of this trip borders on insanity; its recklessness was almost criminal; but of course it is not for me to blame him for that. Incautious chatter at the frontier might have done a great deal of harm, but that is not the point, and has nothing to do with the estimate of the expedition itself.

On his return to London he undertook the suggestion of Trübner to compile a Russian grammar for Englishmen, and to translate some financial book. He did not complete either of these tasks: his travels had ruined his *Sitzfleisch*. He was bored by work, sank into hypochondria and depression, while work was necessary, for again they had not a penny. Moreover, a new craze began to fret him. The success of this expedition, the daring he had incontestably displayed, the mysterious negotiations, the triumph over dangers—all this fanned the flame of vanity that was already strong in his heart; unlike Caesar, Don Carlos, and Vadim Passek, Kelsiev, passing his hands through his thick hair, would say, shaking his head mournfully: 'Not yet thirty, and such immense responsibilities undertaken!' From all this it might readily be deduced that he would not finish the grammar but would go away. And he did go. He went to Turkey with the firm intention of there getting into closer touch with the raskolniks, forming new ties and if possible remaining there, and beginning to preach the free church and communistic life. I wrote him a long letter, trying to persuade him not to go, but to stick to his work. The passion for wandering, the desire to do great deeds and to have a grand destiny, which haunted him, were too strong, and he went. He and Martyanov disappeared almost at the same time— one, after passing through a series of trials and misfortunes, to bury his dear ones and be lost between Jassy and Galatz, the other to bury himself in penal servitude, to which he was sent by the incredible stupidity of the Tsar and the incredible spite of the revengeful landowning senators.

After them men of a different stamp appear upon the

scene. Our social metamorphosis, having no great depth and affecting only a thin layer, rapidly wears out and changes its forms and colours.

A whole stratum lay between Engelson and Kelsiev, just as between us and Engelson. Engelson was a man injured and broken by his whole environment; the foul atmosphere which he had breathed from childhood had distorted him. A ray of light gleamed upon him and warmed him for three years before his death, but by then the sickness that was consuming him could not be arrested. Kelsiev, who was also damaged and injured by his environment, was yet free from despair and fatigue; he was not merely seeking peace abroad, but had simply run away from oppression; without looking behind him, he was going *somewhere*. Where? That he did not know (and therein lay the most prominent characteristic of his group), he had no definite aim; he was seeking it, and meanwhile looking about him and setting in order, and maybe in disorder, a whole mass of ideas caught up at school from books and from life. Within him that destructive process of which we have spoken was going on, and it was for him the essential question in which he lived, while waiting either for a cause which should absorb him or a thought to which he could devote himself.

After making his way to Turkey, Kelsiev decided to settle in Tulcea; there he meant to form a centre for his propaganda among the raskolniks, to found a school for Cossack children and to make the experiment of a communal life, in which profit and loss was to fall equally upon all, and the work, skilled or unskilled, light or heavy, should be divided among all. The cheapness of dwelling and of food made the experiment possible. He made the acquaintance of Gonchar, the old ataman of the Nekrassovtsys, and at first praised him up to the skies.

In the summer of 1863 his younger brother Ivan, a fine and gifted youth, joined him. He had been exiled from Moscow to Perm in connection with the students' rising; there he came into collision with a wretch of a governor, who oppressed him. Then he was sent again to Moscow on account of some investigation; he was in danger of being exiled to some place more remote than Perm. He escaped from custody and made his way through Constantinople to Tulcea. His elder brother was extremely glad to see him. He was looking for comrades, and in the end sent for his wife, who was eager to go to him, and had been living under our protection in Teddington. While we were fitting her out, Gonchar himself arrived in London.

The crafty old man, who scented the approach of war and disturbance, had come out of his hole to sniff what was in the air and to see what he had to expect, and from which quarter; that is, with whom and against whom to ally himself. Knowing no single word of any language but Turkish and Russian, he set off for Marseilles, and from there reached Paris. In Paris he saw Czartorysczki and Zamoisky; I was even told that he had been taken to Napoleon, but I did not hear that from himself. His negotiations led to nothing, and the old Cossack, shaking his grizzled head and screwing up his cunning eyes, wrote in the scrawl of the seventeenth century, and, addressing me as Count, asked if he could come and see us and how he could reach us. We were then living in Teddington; it was not easy to find us without a word of English, and I went to London to meet him at the station. An old Russian peasant of the more prosperous sort, rather thin, but sturdy, muscular, fairly tall and sunburnt, with a big Russian beard, stepped out of the carriage, wearing a grey kaftan and carrying a bundle tied up in a coloured handkerchief.

'You are Osip Semyonovitch?' I asked him.

'I am, my good sir, I am'; he gave me his hand. His kaftan flew open and I saw on his jerkin a big star— of course a Turkish one; Russian stars are not given to peasants. The jerkin was dark blue and was bordered with a wide coloured braid; I had not seen one like it in Russia.

'I am Alexandr Ivanovitch Herzen. I have come to meet you and to take you to us.'

'What did you put yourself out for, Your Excellency? . . . Why . . . you might have sent some one or something. . . .'

'Evidently because I am not an Excellency. What put it into your head, Osip Semyonovitch, to call me Count?'

'Well, Christ only knows how to address you; surely you are the head-man in your line. Well, I am an ignorant man, you see, so, says I, he is a Count, that is an Excellency, that is the chief.' Not only Gonchar's turn of speech, but even his accent was that of a Great Russian peasant. How have these men preserved their language so splendidly in the wilds, surrounded by natives of another race? It would be hard to explain it apart from the compact solidarity of the Old Believers. Their sect has divided them off so strictly that no foreign influence has crossed its barrier.

Gonchar spent three days with us. For the first two days he ate nothing but dry bread which he had brought with him and he drank nothing but water. The third day was Sunday, and he allowed himself a glass of milk, some boiled fish and, if I am not mistaken, a glass of sherry. Russian circumspection, Oriental cunning, the caution of a hunter, the reserve of a man accustomed from childhood to being entirely without rights and in close contact with powerful enemies, a long life spent in struggle, in unceasing toil among dangers—all this was apparent behind the seemingly simple features and simple words of the grey-headed Cossack. He was continually qualifying what he said, using evasive phrases, quoting texts from Scripture; he assumed a modest air while he very consciously described his successes, and if he was sometimes carried away in his stories of the past and said a good deal, he certainly never let drop a word concerning anything of which he meant to be silent.

This stamp of man scarcely exists in Western Europe. It is not needed there, as Damascus steel is not needed for the blade of a penknife.

In Europe everything is done wholesale, in the mass; the individual man does not need so much strength and caution.

He had no faith now in the success of the Polish rebellion, and spoke of his interviews in Paris, shaking his head. 'It is not for us, of course, to judge: we are little, ignorant people, while they, look you, are grand gentlemen as is only right; but there, they are a bit light in their ways. "Don't you doubt, Gonchar," they say. "This is how we'll manage, we will do this and that for you. . . . Do you understand? . . . It will all be satisfactory." . . . To be sure, they are good-natured gentlemen, but look you here, when will they manage it . . . with politics like that . . .?' He wanted to find out what connections we had with the raskolniks and what support in his country; he wanted to make certain whether there could be any practical benefit for the Old Believers in connection with us. In reality, it was all one to him; he would as readily have allied himself with Poland or with Austria, with us or with the Greeks, with Russia or with Turkey, if only it had been profitable for his Nekrassovtsy. He shook his head as he left us, too. He wrote two or three letters afterwards, in which, among other things, he complained of Kelsiev and, contrary to our advice, sent an appeal to the Tsar.

At the beginning of 1864 two Russian officers, both exiles, Krasnopyevtsev and V., went to Tulcea. At first the little colony set to work zealously. They taught the children and salted cucumbers, patched their clothes and dug in the kitchen-garden. Kelsiev's wife cooked the dinner and made their clothes. Kelsiev was pleased with the beginning, pleased with the Cossacks and with the raskolniks, pleased with his comrades and with the Turks.[1]

Kelsiev was still writing us his humorous descriptions of their installation, but the dark hand of destiny was already menacing the little band of Tulcea Communists. In June 1864, just a year after his arrival, Ivan Kelsiev died of malignant typhus in his brother's arms. He was only three-and-twenty. His death was a fearful blow for his brother; the latter fell ill himself, but somehow survived. His letters of that period are terrible reading. The spirit which had sustained the recluses drooped, they were overcome by gloomy depression; crimes and quarrels followed. Gonchar wrote that Kelsiev was drinking heavily. Krasnopyevtsev shot himself. V. went away. Kelsiev, too, could stand it no longer; he took his wife and his children (he had another by then), and without means or aim set off first for Constantinople, then for the Balkan States. Completely cut off from every one, for the time even cut off from us, it was then that he broke off all relations with the Polish exiles in Turkey. In vain he tried to earn a crust of bread, with despair he looked at the wan faces

[1] And this was the awful Tulcea agency with connections with the revolution all over the world, inciting the villages with money from Mazzini's funds, a menacing danger two years after it had ceased to exist, and even now flourishing in the literature of the detectives and of Katkov's Police News!—(*Author's Note.*)

of his poor wife and children. The money we sent him now and then could not be sufficient. 'It happened at times that we had no bread at all,' his wife wrote not long before her death. At last, after long efforts, Kelsiev obtained in Galatz a job as 'overseer of work on the high-roads.' He was consumed, devoured by boredom. He could not but blame himself for the position of his family. The ignorance of the barbarous Eastern world oppressed him. He pined in it and longed to get away. He had lost his faith in the raskolniks; he had lost his faith in Poland; his faith in men, in science, in revolution, was growing more and more unsteady, and it was easy to predict when it too would collapse. He dreamt of nothing but at all costs struggling back again into the world and coming to us, and saw with horror that he could not leave his family. 'If I were alone,' he wrote several times, 'I would set off at hazard with a daguerrotype machine, or a barrel-organ, and, wandering over the world, would reach Geneva on foot.'

Help was at hand.

Malusha (so they called the elder girl) went to bed quite well, but woke up in the night ill. Towards morning she died of cholera. A few days later the younger child died; the mother was taken to the hospital, she was found to be suffering from galloping consumption.

'Do you remember,' she said to him, 'you promised once to tell me when I was going to die, that it was death? Is this death?'

'It is death, my dear, it is.'

And she smiled once more, sank into forgetfulness and died.

Extract from a Letter

They write to us in Petersburg that the other day the official in charge of the Skulyany Customs House received a letter signed V. Kelsiev informing him that the passenger who would have to present himself at that Customs House with a regular Turkish passport bearing the name of Ivan Zheludkov was no other than himself, Kelsiev, and that, wishing to give himself up to the Russian Government, he begged the said official to arrest him and send him to Petersburg.

THE COMMON FUND

KELSIEV had hardly passed out of our door when fresh people, driven out by the chill blasts of 1863, were knocking at it. These came not from the training-schools of the coming upheaval but from the devastated stage on which they had already played their parts. They were taking refuge from the storm without and seeking nothing within; all they needed was a temporary haven until the weather improved, until a chance presented itself to return to the fray. These men, while still very young, had done with ideas, with culture; theoretical questions did not interest them, partly because they had not yet arisen among them, partly because they were concerned with putting them into practice. Though they had been defeated, they had given proofs of their reckless daring. They had furled their flag, and their task was to preserve its honour. Hence their dry, *cassant, raide*, abrupt and rather elevated tone. Hence their martial, impatient aversion for prolonged deliberation, for criticism, their somewhat elaborate contempt for all intellectual superfluities, among which they put Art in the foreground. What need of music? What need of poetry? 'The fatherland is in danger, *aux armes, citoyens!*' In certain cases they were theoretically right, but they did not take into account the complex, intricate process of balancing the ideal with the actual, and, I need hardly say, assumed that their views and theories were the views and theories of all Russia. To blame our young pilots of the coming storm for this would be unjust. It is the common characteristic of youth; a year ago a Frenchman, a follower of Comte, assured me that Catholicism no longer existed in France, that it had *complètement perdu le terrain*, and pointed to the medical profession, to the professors and students who were not merely not Catholics but not even

Deists. 'Well, but that part of France,' I observed, 'which neither gives nor hears medical lectures?'

'It, of course, keeps to religion and its rites—but more from habit and ignorance.'

'Very true, but what will you do with it?'

'What did they do in 1792?'

'A little: at first the Revolution closed the churches, but afterwards opened them again. Do you remember Augereau's answer to Napoleon when they were celebrating the Concordat? "Do you like the ceremony?" the consul asked as they came out of Notre-Dame. The Jacobin general answered: "Very much. I am only sorry that the two hundred thousand men who have gone to their graves to abolish such ceremonies are not present!"'

'*Ah bah*, we have grown wiser, and we shall not open the church doors—or rather we shall not close them at all, but shall turn the temples of idolatry into schools.'

'*L'infâme sera écrasée*,' I wound up, laughing.

'Yes, no doubt of it; that is certain!'

'But that you and I will not see it—that is even more certain.'

It is to this looking at the surrounding world through a prism coloured by personal sympathies that half the revolutionary failures are due. The life of young people, spent as a rule in a noisy and limited seclusion of a sort, remote from the everyday and wholesale struggle for personal interests, though it grasps universal truths clearly, is almost always doomed to a false understanding of their application to the needs of the day.

At first our new visitors cheered us with accounts of the movement in Petersburg, of the wild pranks of the full-fledged reaction, of the trials and persecutions, of university and literary parties. Then, when all this had been told with the rapidity with which in such cases men hasten to tell all they know, a pause, a hiatus would follow; our conversations became dull and monotonous.

'Can this really be,' I thought, 'old age divorcing two generations? Is it the chill induced by years, by weariness, by experience?'

Whatever it might be due to, I felt that our horizon was not widened, but narrowed, by the arrival of these new men. The scope of our conversations was more limited. Sometimes we had nothing to say to one another. They were occupied with the details of their circles, beyond which nothing interested them. Having once related everything of interest about them, there was nothing to do but to repeat it, and they did repeat it. They took little interest in learning or in public affairs; they even read little, and did not follow the newspapers regularly. Absorbed in memories and anticipations, they did not care to step forth into other spheres; while we had not air to breathe in that exhausted atmosphere. We, spoiled by wider horizons, were stifled.

Moreover, even if they did know a certain section of Petersburg, they did not know Russia at all, and, though sincerely desirous of coming into contact with the people, they only approached them bookishly and theoretically.

What we had in common was too general. Advance together, *serve*, as the French say, take action together we might, but it was hard to stand still with hands folded and live together. It was useless to dream of a serious influence on them. A morbid and very unceremonious vanity had long ago got the upper hand.[1] Sometimes, it is true, they did ask for a programme, for

---

[1] Their vanity was not so great as it was touchy and irritable, and above all, unrestrained in words. They could conceal neither their envy nor a special kind of irritable insistence on respectful recognition of the position they ascribed to themselves, at the same time that they looked down on everything and were perpetually jeering at one another—which was why their friendships never lasted more than a month.—(*Author's Note.*)

guidance, but for all their sincerity there was no reality about that. They expected us to formulate their own opinions, and only assented when what we said did not contradict them in the least. They looked upon us as respectable veterans, as something past and over, and were naively surprised that we were not yet so very much behind themselves.

I have always and in everything dreaded 'above all sorrows' *mésalliances*; I have always endured them, partly through humanity, partly through carelessness, and have always suffered from them.

It was not hard to foresee that our new connections would not last long, that sooner or later they would be broken, and that, considering the churlish character of our new friends, this rupture would not come off without disagreeable consequences.

The subject upon which our unstable relations came to grief was that old subject upon which acquaintances tacked together with rotten threads usually come to grief. I mean money. Knowing absolutely nothing of my resources nor of my sacrifices, they made demands upon me which I did not think it right to satisfy. That I had been able through bad times without the slightest assistance to maintain the Russian propaganda for fifteen years was only because I had put a careful limit to my other expenses. My new acquaintances considered that all I was doing was not enough, and looked with indignation at a man who pretended to be a Socialist and did not distribute his property in equal shares among people who wanted money without working. Obviously they had not advanced beyond the impractical point of view of Christian charity and voluntary poverty, and mistook that for practical Socialism.

The efforts to collect a 'Common Fund' yielded no results of importance, Russians are not fond of giving money to any common cause, unless it includes the building of a church, and a banquet, a drinking-party, and the approval of the higher authorities.

When the impecuniosity of the exiles was at its height, a rumour circulated among them that I had a sum of money entrusted to me for purposes of propaganda.

It seemed perfectly right to the young people to relieve me of it.

To make the position clear, I must describe a strange incident that occurred in the year 1858. One morning I received a very brief note from an unknown Russian; he wrote to me that he 'urgently desired to see me,' and asked me to fix an hour.

I happened to be going to London at the time, and so instead of answering I went myself to the Sablonnière Hotel and inquired for him. He was at home. He was a young man who looked like a cadet, shy, very depressed, and with the peculiar rather rough-hewn appearance of the seventh or eighth son of a Steppe landowner. Very uncommunicative, he was almost completely silent; it was evident that he had something on his mind, but he could not come to the point of putting it into words.

I went away, inviting him to dinner two or three days later. Before that date I met him in the street. 'May I walk with you?' he asked.

'Of course; there is no risk for me in being seen with you, though there is for you in being seen with me. But London is a big place.'

'I am not afraid'—and then all at once, taking the bit between his teeth, he hurriedly burst out: 'I shall never go back to Russia—no, no, I shall certainly never go back to Russia. . . .'

'Upon my word, and you so young?'

'I love Russia—I love her dearly; but there the people . . . I cannot live there. I want to found a colony on completely socialistic principles; I have thought it all over, and now I am going straight there.'

'Straight where?'

'To the Marquesas Islands.'

I looked at him in dumb amazement.

'Yes, yes; it is all settled. I am sailing by the next steamer, and so I am very glad that I have met you to-day—may I put an indiscreet question to you?'

'As many as you like.'

'Do you make any profit out of your publications?'

'Profit! I am glad to say that now the press pays its way.'

'Well, but what if it should not?'

'I shall make it up.'

'So that no sort of commercial aim enters into your propaganda?' said the young man.

I laughed heartily.

'Well, but how are you going to pay all the expenses alone? And your propaganda is essential. You must forgive me, I am not asking out of curiosity: when I left Russia for ever, I had the thought in my mind of doing something useful for her, and I made up my mind to leave a small sum of money with you. Should your printing-press need it, or the Russian propaganda generally, then you must make use of it.'

Again I could do nothing but look at him with amazement.

'Neither the printing-press nor Russian propaganda nor I are in need of money; on the contrary, things are going swimmingly. Why should I take your money? But though I refuse to take it, allow me to thank you from the bottom of my heart for your kind intention.'

'No, it is all settled. I have fifty thousand francs. I shall take thirty thousand with me to the Islands, and I shall leave twenty with you for propaganda.'

'What am I to do with it?'

'Well, if you don't need the money you can give it back to me if I return; but if I don't return within ten years, or if I die—use it for the benefit of your propaganda. Only,' he added, after a moment's thought, 'do anything you like . . . but don't give anything to my heirs. Are you free to-morrow morning?'

'Certainly, if you like.'

'Do me the favour to take me to the bank and to Rothschild; I know nothing about it, I can't speak English, and speak French very badly. I want to make haste to get rid of the twenty thousand and be off.'

'Very well, I will take the money—but on these conditions: I will give you a receipt.'

'I don't want a receipt.'

'No, but I want to give you one—I won't take your money without it. Listen. In the first place, it shall be stated in the receipt that your money is entrusted not to me alone, but to me and to Ogaryov. In the second, since you may get sick of the Marquesas Islands and begin to pine for your native country . . .' (he shook his head). 'How can one tell of what one does not know? . . . There is no need to specify the object with which you give us the capital, we will only say that the money is put at the complete disposal of Ogaryov and myself; should we make no other use of it, we will invest the whole sum for you in securities at five per cent, or thereabouts, guaranteed by the English Government. Then I give you my word that we will not touch your money except in case of extreme necessity for propaganda purposes; you may reckon upon it in any case, except that of bankruptcy in England.'

'If you insist on taking so much trouble, do so. And let us go to-morrow for the money!'

The following day was an extremely amusing and busy one. It began with the bank and with Rothschild. The money was paid in notes, B. at first announced the guileless intention of changing them into Spanish gold or silver. Rothschild's clerks looked at him in amazement, but when, as though suddenly awakening, he said in broken Franco-Russian: 'Well, then, a *lettre de crédit to* the *lie Marquise*,' Kessner, the manager, bent an alarmed and anxious look upon me, which said better than any words: 'He is not dangerous, is he?' Never before in Rothschild's bank had any one asked for a letter of credit to the Marquesas Islands.

We decided to take thirty thousand francs in gold and go home; on the way we went into a café. I wrote the receipt; B. for his part wrote for me that he put eight hundred pounds at the complete disposal of myself and Ogaryov; then he went home to get something and I went off to a bookshop to wait for him there; a quarter of an hour later he came in, pale as a sheet, and announced that of his thirty thousand francs two hundred and fifty, that is ten pounds, were missing.

He was utterly overwhelmed. How the loss of two hundred and fifty francs could so upset a man who had just given away twenty thousand without any secure guarantee is again a psychological riddle of human nature.

'Had not you a note too much?' he asked me.

'I have none of the money with me, I gave it to Rothschild, and here is the receipt, precisely eight hundred.' B., who had changed his French notes into pounds with no necessity to do so, scattered them on Tchorszewski's counter; he counted them and counted them over again; ten pounds were missing, and that was all about it. Seeing his despair, I said to Tchorszewski: 'I'll somehow take that damned ten pounds on myself; here he has done a good deed and is punished for it.'

'It is no use grieving and discussing it,' I said to him. 'I propose going straight to Rothschild's.'

We drove there. It was by now after four and the bank was closed, I went in with B., who was overwhelmed with confusion. Kessner looked at him, and, smiling, took a ten-pound note from the table and handed it to me. 'How did it happen?' 'Your friend when he changed the money gave me two ten-pound notes instead of two five-pound ones, and at first I did not notice it.' B. stared and stared at it, and commented: 'How stupid it is that ten-pound notes and five-pound notes are the same colour; who would notice the difference? You see what a good thing it is that I changed the money into gold.'

Comforted, he came to dine with me, and I promised to go and say good-bye to him next day. He was quite ready to start. A little shabby, battered trunk such as cadets or students carry, a greatcoat tied up in a strap, and . . . and . . . thirty thousand francs in gold tied up in a thick pocket-handkerchief, as people tie up a pound of gooseberries or nuts!

This was how the man was setting off for the Marquesas Islands.

'Upon my soul!' I said to him; 'why, you will be robbed and murdered before you are afloat, you had better put your money in your trunk.'

'It is full.'

'I will get you a bag.'

'No, I would not think of it.'

And so he went off.

At first I supposed that he would be killed for a certainty and I should incur the suspicion of having sent some one to kill him.

From that day no sign nor sound of him again. . . . I put his money in Consols with the firm intention of not touching it except in the case of the printing-press or propaganda being in the utmost straits.

For a long time no one in Russia knew of this incident; then there were vague rumours, for which we were indebted to two or three of our friends who had promised to say nothing about it. At last it was discovered that the money really existed and was in my keeping.

This news served as an apple of discord, as a chronic irritant and ferment. It appeared that every one needed the money—while I did not give it to them. They could not forgive me for not having lost the whole of my own property—and here I had a deposit given me for the propaganda; and who were 'the propaganda' if not they? The sum quickly grew from modest francs to silver roubles, and was still more tantalising for those who desired to consume it privately for the public benefit. They were indignant with B. for having entrusted the money to me and not to some one else; the boldest among them declared that it was an error on his part; that he really meant to give it not to me but to a Petersburg political circle, and that, not knowing how to do this, he had given it to me in London. The audacity of these opinions was the more remarkable since no one knew B.'s surname or had heard of his existence, and since he had not spoken to any one of his intention before his departure, nor had any one spoken with him since then.

One man needed the money to send emissaries; another for establishing centres on the Volga; a third for the publication of a journal. They were dissatisfied with the *Kolokol*, and did not readily respond to our invitation to work on it.

I resolutely refused to give the money; and let those who demanded it tell me what would have become of it if I had.

'B. may return without a farthing,' I said; 'it is not easy to make a fortune by founding a socialist colony in the Marquesas Islands.'

'He is sure to be dead.'

'But what if to spite you he is living?'

'Well, but he gave you the money for the propaganda.'

'So far I do not need it.'
'But we do.'
'What for precisely?'
'We must send some one to the Volga and some one to Odessa....'
'I don't think that is very necessary.'
'So you don't believe in the urgency of sending them?'
'I do not.'

'He is growing old and getting miserly,' the most determined and ferocious said about me in different variations.

'But why mind him? Just take the money from him and have done with it,' the still more resolute and ferocious added, 'and if he resists, we will show him up in the papers and teach him to keep other people's money.'

I did not give them the money.

They did not show me up in the papers. I was abused in the press much later, and that was about money too....

These more ferocious ones of whom I have spoken were the extreme examples, the angular and uncouth representatives of the 'New Generation,' who may be called the Sobakevitches and Nozdryovs of Nihilism.

However superfluous it may be to make a reservation, yet I will do so, knowing the logic and the manners of our opponents. I have not the slightest desire in what I am saying to fling a stone at the younger generation or at Nihilism. Of the latter I have written many times. Our Sobakevitches of Nihilism are not its fullest expression, but only represent its exaggerated extremes.[1]

---

[1] At that very time in Petersburg and Moscow, and even in Kazan and Harkov, there were circles being formed among the university youth who devoted themselves in earnest to the study of science, especially among the medical students. They worked honestly and conscientiously, but, Cut off from active participation in the questions of the day, they were not forced to leave Russia and we scarcely knew anything of them.—(*Author's Note.*)

Who would judge of Christianity from the Flagellants, or of the Revolution from the September butchers, or the *tricoteuses* of Robespierre?

The conceited lads of whom I am speaking are worth studying, because they are the expression of a temporary type, very definitely marked and very frequently repeated, a transitional form of the sickness of our development from our old stagnation.

For the most part, they were lacking in the polish given by breeding, and the persistence given by scientific studies. In the first heat of emancipation they were in a hurry to cast off all the conventional forms and to push away all the rubber buffers which avert rough collisions. This made the simplest relations with them difficult.

Flinging off everything to the last rag, our *enfants terribles* proudly appeared as their mothers bore them, and their mothers had not borne them well, not as simple comely lads but as heirs of the evil and unhealthy life of our lower classes in Petersburg. Instead of athletic muscles and youthful nakedness, they displayed the melancholy traces of hereditary anaemia, the traces of old scars and fetters and manacles of all sorts. There were few among them who had come up from the people. The servants' hall, the barrack-room, the seminary, the petty proprietor's farm survived in their blood and their brains, and lost none of their characteristic features though twisted in an opposite direction. So far as I know, this fact has attracted no serious attention.

On the one hand, the reaction against the old narrow oppressive world was bound to throw the younger generation into antagonism and opposition to their hostile surroundings; it was useless to expect moderation or justice in them. On the contrary, everything was done in defiance, everything was done in resentment. You have been hypocrites, we will be cynics; you have been moral in words, we will be wicked in words; you have been polite to your superiors and rude to your inferiors, we will be rude to every one; you have bowed down to those you did not respect, we will shove others aside without apologising; your feeling of personal dignity consisted in nothing but decorum and external honour, we make it our point of honour to trample on every decorum and to scorn every *point d'honneur*.

But on the other hand, though disowning all the ordinary forms of social life, their character was full of its own hereditary failings and deformities. Casting off, as we have said, all veils, the most desperate played the dandy in the costume of Gogol's Pyetuh[1] and did not preserve the pose of the Venus of Medici. Their nakedness did not conceal, but revealed, what they were. It revealed that their systematic roughness, their rude and insolent talk, had nothing in common with the inoffensive and simple-hearted coarseness of the peasant, but a great deal in common with the manners of the low-class pettifogger, the shop-boy and the flunkey. The peasants no more considered such a Nihilist as one of themselves than they did a Slavophil in a *murmolka*. To the peasantry these men remain strangers, the lowest class of the enemies' camp, inferior young masters, scribblers out of a job, Germans among Russians.

To be completely free, one must forget one's freedom and that from which one has been set free, and cast off the habits of the environment one has outgrown. Until men have done this we cannot help being conscious of the servants' hall, the barrack-room, the government-office or the seminary in every gesture they make and every word they utter.

To hit a man in the face at the first objection he advances—if not with a fist with a word of abuse—to call Stuart Mill a sneak, forgetting all the service he has

---

[1] A character in Gogol's *Dead Souls*.—(*Translator's Note*.)

done, is not that the same as the Russian master's way of 'punching old Gavrilo in the face for a crumpled cravat'? In this and similar rudeness, do we not recognise the policeman, the police officer, the village constable dragging the peasant by his grey beard? Do we not, in the insolent arrogance of their manners and answers, clearly recognise the insolence of the officers of the days of Nicholas? Do we not see in men who talk haughtily and disdainfully of Shakespeare and Pushkin, grandsons of Skalozub, reared in the house of their grandsire who wanted 'to make a Voltaire of his corporal'?

The very curse of bribery has survived in the extortion of money by violence, by intimidation and threats on the pretext of a common cause, in the efforts to be kept at the expense of the service and to revenge a refusal by slanders and libels.

All this will be transformed and come right with time. But there is no blinking the fact that a strange subsoil has been prepared by the Tsar's paternal Government and Imperial civilisation in our kingdom of darkness. It is a soil on which seedlings that promised much have grown, on the one hand, into the followers of the Muravyovs and the Katkovs, and, on the other, into the bullies of Nihilism and the lawless gang of Bazarovs.

Our black earth needs a good deal of drainage!

BAKUNIN AND THE CAUSE OF POLAND

AT the end of November we received from Bakunin the following letter:—

'SAN FRANCISCO, *October* 15, 1861.

'FRIENDS,—I have succeeded in escaping from Siberia, and after long wanderings on the Amur, on the shores of the sea of Tartary and across Japan, I am to-day in San Francisco.

'Friends, I long to come to you with my whole heart, and as soon as I arrive I will set to work, I will take a job under you on the Polish Slavonic cause, which has been my *idée fixe* since 1846 and was in practice my speciality in 1848 and 1849.

'The destruction, the complete destruction, of the Austrian empire will be my last word; I don't say deed——that would be too ambitious; to promote it, I am ready to become a drummer-boy or even a rascal, and if I should succeed in advancing it by one hair's-breadth I shall be satisfied. And after that will come the glorious free Slav federation, the one way out for Russia, the Ukraine, Poland, and the Slavonic peoples generally.'

We had known of his intention of escaping from Siberia some months before. By the New Year Bakunin in his own exuberant person was clasped in our arms.

A new element, or rather an old element, the shadow of the'forties, and most of all of 1848, risen up from the dead, came into our work, into our league that consisted of two. Bakunin was just the same; he had grown older in body only, his spirit was as young and enthusiastic as in the days of the all-night arguments with Homyakov in Moscow. He was just as devoted to one idea, just as capable of being carried away by it, and of seeing in everything the fulfilment of his desires and ideals, and even more ready for every effort, every sacrifice, feeling that he had not so much life before him, and consequently he must make haste and not let slip a single chance. He fretted against prolonged study, the weighing of pros and cons, and, as confident and theoretical as ever, longed for any action if only it were in the midst of the turmoil of revolution, in the midst of upheavals and menacing danger. Now, too, as in the articles signed Jules Elizard,[1] he repeated: '*Die Lust der Zerstörung ist eine schaffende Lust.*' The fantasies and ideals with which he was imprisoned in Königstein in 1849 he had preserved complete and carried across Japan and California in 1861. Even his language recalled the finer articles of *La Réforme* and *La vraie République*, the striking speeches of *La Constituante* and Blanqui's Club. The spirit of the parties of that period, their exclusiveness, their personal sympathies and antipathies, above all, their faith in the second coming of the revolution—it was all there.

Strong characters, if not at once ruined by prison and exile, are preserved in an extraordinary way by it; they come out of it as though from out of a swoon and go on with what they were about when they lost consciousness. The Decembrists came back from being buried in the snows of Siberia more youthful than the crushed and trampled young people who met them. While two generations of Frenchmen changed backwards and forwards several times, turned red and turned white, advancing with the flow and borne back by the ebb tide, Barbès and Blanqui remained steady beacons, recalling from behind prison bars and distant foreign lands the old ideals in all their purity.

'The Polish Slavonic cause . . . the destruction of

[1] Under this pseudonym Bakunin published articles on the Reaction in Germany in the *Jahrbücher* of 1842, which were brought out under the editorship of Ruge.—(*Translator's Note.*)

the Austrian empire . . . the glorious free Slav Federation . . .' and all this is to happen straight off as soon as he arrives in London! And he writes from San Francisco with one foot on the ship!

The European reaction did not exist for Bakunin, the bitter years from 1848 to 1858 did not exist for him either; of them he had but a brief, far-away, faint knowledge. He *read through* them, read through them in Siberia, just as he had read in Kaidanov's history of the Punic Wars and of the Fall of the Roman Empire. Like a man who has returned after a plague, he heard of those who were dead and heaved a sigh for them; but he had not sat by the bedside of the dying, had not hoped to save them, had not followed them to the grave. The events of 1848, on the contrary, were all about him, near to his heart; detailed and eager conversations with Caussidière, the speeches of the Slavs at the Prague Conference, discussions with Arago or Ruge—all these were affairs of yesterday to Bakunin; they were all still ringing in his ears and hovering before his eyes.

Though, indeed, it is no wonder that it was so, even apart from prison.

The first days after the February revolution were the happiest days in the life of Bakunin. Returning from Belgium, to which he had been driven by Guizot for his speech on the Polish anniversary of the 29th of November 1847, he plunged, head over ears, into all the depths and shallows of the revolutionary sea. He never left the barracks of the Montagnards, slept with them, ate with them and preached, preached continually, communism and *l'égalité du salaire*, levelling-down in the name of equality, the emancipation of all the Slavs, the destruction of all the Austrias, the revolution *en permanence*, war to the extinction of the last foe. Caussidière, the prefect from the barricades engaged in bringing 'order into chaos,' did not know how to get rid of the precious orator, and plotted with Flocon to send him off to the Slavs in earnest, with a brotherly *accolade* and a conviction that there he would break his neck and be no more trouble. '*Quel homme! quel homme!*' Caussidière used to say of Bakunin: 'On the first day of the revolution he is simply a treasure, but on the day after he ought to be shot!'[1]

When I arrived in Paris from Rome at the beginning of May 1848, Bakunin was already holding forth in Bohemia, surrounded by Old-believing monks, Czechs, Croats and democrats, and he continued haranguing them until Prince Windischgrätz put an end to his eloquence with cannon (and seized the opportunity to shoot his own wife by accident). Disappearing from Prague, Bakunin appeared again as military commander of Dresden; the former artillery officer taught the art of war to the professors, musicians and chemists who had taken up arms, and advised them to hang Raphael's Madonna and Murillo's pictures on the city walls and so guard them from the Prussians, who were *zu Klassisch gebildet* to dare to fire on Raphael.

Artillery was always his stumbling-block. On the way from Paris to Prague he came somewhere in Germany upon a revolt of peasants; they were shouting and making an uproar before the castle, not knowing what to do. Bakunin got out of his conveyance, and, without wasting time on finding out what was the subject of dispute, formed the peasants into ranks and so skilfully instructed them that by the time he resumed his seat to continue his journey the castle was burning on all four sides.

[1] 'Tell Caussidière,' I said in jest to his friends, 'that the difference between Bakunin and him is that Caussidière, too, is a splendid fellow, but it would be better to shoot him the day before the revolution.' Later on in London, in the year 1854, I reminded him of this. The prefect in exile merely smote with his huge fist upon his mighty chest with the force with which piles are driven into the earth, and said: 'I carry Bakunin's image here, here.'—(*Author's Note*.)

Bakunin will some day conquer his sloth and keep his promise; some day he will tell the long tale of the martyrdom that began for him after the taking of Dresden. I recall here only the chief points. Bakunin was sentenced to the scaffold. The Saxon king commuted the axe to imprisonment for life; and afterwards, with no ground for doing so, handed him over to Austria. The Austrian police thought they would find out from him something concerning the plans of the Slavs. They imprisoned Bakunin in Gratchin, and getting nothing out of him they sent him to Olmütz. Bakunin was taken in fetters with a strong escort of dragoons; the officer who got into the conveyance with him loaded his pistol.

'What is that for?' asked Bakunin. 'Surely you don't imagine that I can escape under these conditions?'

'No, but your friends may try to rescue you; the Government has heard rumours to that effect, and in that case...'

'What then?'

'I have orders to put a bullet through your brains...'

And the party galloped off.

In Olmütz Bakunin was chained to the wall, and in that position he spent six months. At last Austria got tired of keeping a foreign criminal for nothing; she offered to give him up to Russia. Nicholas did not want Bakunin at all, but he had not the strength of mind to refuse. On the Russian frontier Bakunin's fetters were removed. Of that act of mercy I have heard many times; the fetters were indeed taken off, but those who tell the tale forget to add that others much heavier were put on. The Austrian officer who handed over the convict insisted on the return of the fetters as Crown property.

Nicholas commended Bakunin's valiant conduct at Dresden, and clapped him into the Alexeyevsky Ravelin.

There he sent Orlov to him with orders to tell him that he (Nicholas) desired from him an account of the German and Slav movement (the monarch was not aware that every detail of the same had been published in the newspapers). This account he asked for not as his Tsar, but as his spiritual father. Bakunin asked Orlov in what sense the Tsar understood the words 'spiritual father': did it imply that everything told in confession was bound to be kept a holy secret? Orlov did not know what to say: these people are more accustomed to ask questions than to answer them. Bakunin wrote a newspaper 'leading article.' Nicholas was satisfied with that. 'He is a good and intelligent fellow, but a dangerous man; he must be kept shut up,' and for *three whole years* after this approval from the Most High, Bakunin was buried in the Alexeyevsky Ravelin. The treatment must have been thorough, too, since even that giant was brought so low that he tried to take his own life. In 1854 Bakunin was transferred to the Schlüsselburg. Nicholas was afraid that Sir Charles Napier would rescue him; but Sir Charles Napier and company did not rescue Bakunin from the Ravelin, but Russia from Nicholas. Alexander II., in spite of his fit of mercy and magnanimity, left Bakunin in confinement till 1857, then sent him to live in Eastern Siberia. In Irkutsk he found himself free after nine years of imprisonment. Fortunately for him, the governor of that region was an original person—a democrat and a Tatar, a liberal and a despot, a relative of Mihail Bakunin's and of Mihail Muravyov's, himself a Muravyov, not yet nicknamed 'of the Amur.' He let Bakunin have a respite, the chance of living like a human being, of reading the newspapers and magazines, and even shared his dreams of future upheavals and wars. In gratitude to Muravyov, Bakunin in his own mind appointed him Commander-in-Chief of the future citizen army, with which he proposed to annihilate Austria and found the Slav league.

In 1860 Bakunin's mother petitioned the Tsar for her son's return to Russia; the monarch replied that Bakunin would never be brought back from Siberia in his lifetime, but, that she might not be denied all comfort and royal mercy, he permitted her son to enter the Government service as a copying clerk. Then Bakunin, taking into consideration that the Tsar was only forty and that his cheeks were ruddy with health, made up his mind to escape; I completely approve of this decision. The last years have shown better than anything else could have done that he had nothing to expect in Siberia. Nine years of imprisonment and several years of exile were enough. The political exiles were not, as was said, the worse off because of his escape, but because times had grown worse, men had grown worse. What influence had Bakunin's escape on the infamous persecution and death of Mihailov? And as for the reprimand of a man like Korsakov—that is not worth talking about. It is a pity he incurred nothing worse.

Bakunin's escape is remarkable owing to the space covered; it is the very longest escape in a geographical sense. After making his way to the Amur, on the pretext of commercial business, he succeeded in persuading an American skipper to take him to the shores of Japan. At Hako-date another American captain undertook to convey him to San Francisco. Bakunin went on board his ship and found the sea-captain busily preparing for a dinner; he was expecting some honoured guest, and invited Bakunin to join them. Bakunin accepted the invitation, and only when the visitor arrived, discovered that it was the Russian Consul.

It was too late, too absurd to conceal himself: he entered at once into conversation with him and said that he had obtained leave for a pleasure-trip. A small

Russian squadron under the command, if I remember right, of Admiral Popov was riding at anchor about to sail for Nikolayev: 'You are not returning with our men?' inquired the Consul. 'I have only just arrived,' said Bakunin, 'and I want to see a little more of the country.' After dining together they parted *en bons amis*. Next day he passed the Russian squadron in the American steamer: there were no more dangers to be feared, apart from those of the ocean. As soon as Bakunin had looked about him and settled down in London, that is, had made the acquaintance of all the Poles and Russians there, he set to work. To a passion for propaganda, for agitation, for demagogy, to incessant activity in founding, organising plots and conspiracies, and establishing relations, to a belief in their immense significance, Bakunin added a readiness to be the first to carry out his ideas, a readiness to risk his life, and reckless daring in facing all the consequences.

His was an heroic nature, deprived of complete achievement by the course of events. He sometimes wasted his strength on what was useless, as a lion wastes his strength pacing up and down in the cage, always imagining that he will escape from it. But Bakunin was not a mere rhetorician, afraid to act upon his own words, or trying to evade carrying his theories into practice. . . .

Bakunin had many weak points. But his weak points were small while his strong qualities were great. . . . Is it not in itself a sign of greatness that wherever he was flung by destiny, as soon as he had grasped two or three characteristics of his surroundings, he discerned the revolutionary forces and at once set to work to carry them on further, to fan the fire, to make of it the burning question of life?

It is said that Turgenev meant to draw Bakunin's portrait in Rudin; but Rudin barely suggests certain features of Bakunin. Turgenev, following the biblical example of the Almighty, created Rudin in his own image and semblance: though Turgenev's Rudin, saturated in the jargon of philosophy, is like Bakunin in his youth.

In London he first of all set to revolutionising the *Kolokol*, and in 1862 advanced against us almost all that in 1847 he had advanced against Byelinsky. Propaganda was not enough; there ought to be immediate action, centres and committees ought to be organised; to have people closely and remotely associated with us was not enough, we ought to have 'initiated and half-initiated brethren,' organisations on the spot—Slavonic organisations, Polish organisations. Bakunin thought us too moderate, unable to take advantage of the position at the moment, and not sufficiently inclined to resolute measures. He did not lose heart, however, but was convinced that in a short time he would set us on the right path. While awaiting our conversion, Bakunin gathered about him a regular circle of Slavs. Among them there were Czechs, from the writer Fritsch to a musician who was called Naperstok[1]; Serbs who were simply called after their father's names Ivanovic, Danilovic, Petrovic; there were Wallachians who did duty for Slavs, with the everlasting 'esko' at the end of their names; there was actually a Bulgarian who had been an officer in the Turkish army, and there were Poles of every shade—Bonapartist, Miroslavist, Czartorysczkist: democrats free from socialistic ideas but of a military tinge; socialists, catholics, anarchists, aristocrats, and men who were simply soldiers, ready to fight anywhere in the northern or in the southern states of America, but by preference in Poland.

With them Bakunin made up for his nine years' silence and solitude. He argued, lectured, made

[1] The word means 'thimble' in Russian.—(*Translator's Note.*)

arrangements, shouted, gave orders, and decided questions, organised and encouraged all day long, all night long, for days and nights together. In the brief minutes he had left, he rushed to his writing-table, cleared a little space from cigarette-ash, and set to work to write five, ten, fifteen letters to Semipalatinsk and Arad, to Belgrade and to Constantinople, to Bessarabia, Moldavia and Byelaya-Krinitsa. In the middle of a letter he would fling aside the pen and bring up to date the views of some old-fashioned Dalmatian, then, without finishing his exhortations, snatch up the pen and go on writing. This, however, was made easier for him by the fact that he was writing and talking about one and the same thing. His activity, his laziness, his appetite, his titanic stature and the everlasting perspiration he was in, everything about him, in fact, was on a superhuman scale. He was a giant himself with his leonine head and the mane that stood up round it. At fifty he was exactly the same vagrant student, the same homeless *Bohémien* from the *rue de Bourgogne*, with no thought for the morrow, careless of money, flinging it away when he had it, borrowing it indiscriminately, right and left, when he had not, as simply as children take from their parents, careless of repayment; as simply as he himself would give his last shilling to any one, only keeping what he needed for cigarettes and tea. This manner of life did not worry him; he was born to be a great vagrant, a great nomad. If any one had asked him point-blank what he thought of the rights of property, he might have answered as Lalande answered Napoleon about God: 'Sire, in my pursuits I have not come upon any necessity for these rights!' There was something childlike, simple and free from malice about him, and this gave him an extraordinary charm and attracted both the weak and the strong, repelling none but stiff petty-bourgeois. His striking personality, the eccentric and powerful appearance he made everywhere, in the circle of the young of Moscow, in the lecture-room of the Berlin University, among Weitling's Communists and Caussidière's Montagnards, his speeches in Prague, his leadership in Dresden, his trial, imprisonment, sentence to death, tortures in Austria and surrender to Russia—where he vanished behind the terrible walls of the Alexeyevsky Ravelin— make of him one of those original figures which neither the contemporary world nor history can pass by.

When carried away in argument, Bakunin poured on his opponent's head a noisy storm of abuse for which no one else would have been forgiven; every one forgave Bakunin, and I among the first. Martyanov would sometimes say: 'He is only a grown-up Lisa,[1] Alexandr Ivanovitch, a child; you can't be angry with him!'

That he ever came to get married, I can only put down to the boredom of Siberia. He preserved intact all the habits and customs of his fatherland, that is of student-life in Moscow; heaps of tobacco lay on his table like stores of forage, cigar-ash covered his papers, together with half-finished glasses of tea; from morning onwards, clouds of smoke hung about the room from a regular chorus of smokers, who smoked as though against time, hurriedly blowing it out and drawing it in—as only Russians and Slavs do smoke, in fact. Many a time I enjoyed the amazement, accompanied by a certain horror and embarrassment, of the landlady's servant, Grace, when at dead of night she brought boiling water and a fifth basin of sugar into this hotbed of Slav emancipation.

Long after Bakunin had left London, tales were told at No. 10 Paddington Green of the way he went on, which upset all the accepted notions and religiously

[1] Herzen's daughter by Madame Tutchkov-Ogaryov, born 1858. —(*Translator's Note*.)

observed forms and habits of English middle-class life. Note at the same time that both the maid and the landlady were passionately devoted to him.

'Yesterday,' one of his friends told Bakunin, 'So-and-so arrived from Russia; he is a very fine man, formerly an officer.'

'I have heard about him; he is very well spoken of.'

'May I bring him?'

'Certainly; but why bring him, where is he? I'll go and see him. I'll go at once.'

'He seems to be rather a constitutionalist.'

'Perhaps, but . . .'

'But I know he is a courageous and noble man.'

'And trustworthy?'

'He is much respected at Orsett House.'

'Let us go to him.'

'Why? He meant to come to you, that was what we agreed, I will bring him.'

Bakunin rushes to his writing; he writes and blots out something, copies it out, and seals up something addressed to Jassy; in suspense, he begins walking about the room with a tread which sets the whole house— No. 10 Paddington Green—moving with him.

The officer quietly and modestly makes his appearance. Bakunin *le met à l'aise*, talks like a comrade, like a young man, fascinates him, scolds him for his constitutionalism, and suddenly asks: 'I am sure you won't refuse to do something for the common cause.'

'Of course not.'

'There is nothing that detains you here?'

'Nothing; I have only just arrived, I . . .'

'Can you go to-morrow or next day with this letter to Jassy?'

Such a thing had not occurred to the officer either at the front in time of war or on the General's staff. However, accustomed to military obedience, he says, after a pause, in a voice that does not sound quite natural, 'Oh yes!'

'I knew you would. Here is the letter perfectly ready.'

'I am ready to set off at once . . .' (the officer is overcome with confusion). 'I had not at all reckoned on such a journey.'

'What? No money? Well, you should say so; that's of no consequence. I'll borrow it for you from Herzen, you can pay it back later on. Why, what is it? Some twenty pounds or so. I'll write to him at once. You will find money at Jassy. From there you can make your way to the Caucasus. We particularly need a trustworthy man there.'

The officer, amazed, dumbfounded, and his companion equally so, took their leave. A little girl whom Bakunin employed on great diplomatic occasions ran to me through the rain and sleet with a note. I used to keep chocolates expressly for her benefit, to comfort her for the climate and the country she lived in, and so I gave her a big handful and added: 'Tell the tall gentleman that I will talk it over with him personally.' The correspondence did in fact turn out to be superfluous. Bakunin arrived to dinner, that is an hour later.

'Why twenty pounds for X.?'

'Not for him, for the cause; and, I say, brother, isn't X. a splendid fellow?'

'I have known him for some years. He has stayed in London before.'

'It is such a chance, it would be a sin to let it slip. I am sending him to Jassy, and then he can have a look round in the Caucasus.'

'To Jassy? And from there to the Caucasus?'

'I see you are going to be funny,' said Bakunin. 'You won't prove anything by jokes.'

'But you know you don't want anything in Jassy.'

'How do you know?'

'I know, in the first place, because nobody wants anything in Jassy; and in the second place, if anything were wanted, you would have been telling me about it incessantly for the last week. You have simply come upon a shy young man who wants to prove his devotion, and so you have taken it into your head to send him to Jassy. He wants to see the Exhibition and you will show him Moldavia. Come, tell me what for?'

'What inquisitiveness! You never go into these things with me; what right have you to ask?'

'That is true: in fact, I imagine that it is a secret you will keep from all; anyway, I have not the slightest intention of giving money for messengers to Jassy and Bucharest.'

'But he will pay you back, he will have money.'

'Then let him make a wiser use of it; that is enough, you can send the letter by some Petresko-Manon-Lescaut; and now let's go and eat.'

And Bakunin, laughing himself, and shaking his head, which was always a little too heavy for him, set steadily and zealously to work upon dinner, after which he always said: 'Now comes the happy moment,' and lighted a cigarette.

He used to receive every one, at all times, everywhere. Often he would be asleep like Onyegin, or tossing on his bed, which creaked under him, while two or three Slavs would be in his bedroom smoking with desperate haste; he would get up heavily, souse himself with water, and at the same moment proceed to instruct them; he was never bored, never tired of them; he could talk without weariness, with the same freshness of mind, to the cleverest or the stupidest man.

This lack of discrimination sometimes led to very funny incidents.

Bakunin used to get up late; he could hardly have

done otherwise, since he spent the night talking and drinking tea.

One morning at eleven o'clock he heard some one stirring in his room. His bed stood curtained off in a large alcove.

'Who's there?' shouted Bakunin, waking.

'A Russian.'

'What is your name?'

'So-and-so.'

'Delighted to see you.'

'Why is it you get up so late and you a democrat?'

Silence: the sounds of splashing water, cascades.

'Mihail Alexandrovitch!'

'Well?'

'I wanted to ask you, were you married in church?'

'Yes.'

'You did wrong. What an example of inconsistency; and here is T. having his daughter legally married. You old men ought to set us an example.'

'What nonsense are you talking?'

'But tell me, did you marry for love?'

'What has that to do with you?'

'There was a rumour going about that you married because your bride was rich!'[1]

'Have you come here to cross-examine me? Go to the devil!'

'Well now, here you are angry, and I really meant no harm. Good-bye. But I shall come and see you again all the same.'

'All right, all right. Only be more sensible next time.'

Meanwhile the Polish storm was drawing nearer and nearer. In the autumn of 1862 Potyebnya arrived in London for a few days. Mournful, pure-hearted, completely devoted to the rebellion, he came to talk to

[1] Bakunin received no dowry with his wife.—(*Author's Note.*)

us for himself and his comrades, meaning in any case to go his own way. Poles began to arrive more and more frequently; their language was bolder and more definite. They were moving directly and consciously towards the outbreak. I felt with horror that they were going to inevitable ruin. 'I am terribly sorry for Potyebnya and his comrades,' I said to Bakunin, 'and the more so that I doubt whether their aims are the same as those of the Poles.'

'Oh yes they are, yes they are,' Bakunin retorted. 'We can't sit for ever with our hands folded, reflecting; we must take events as they come, or else one will always be too far behind or too far in front.'

Bakunin grew younger, he was in his element: he loved not only the uproar of the revolt and the noise of the club, the market-place and the barricade; he loved the preparatory agitation, also, the excited and at the same time restrained life, spent among conspiracies, consultations, sleepless nights, conferences, agreements, rectifications, invisible inks and cryptic signs. Any one who has taken part in rehearsals for private theatricals or in preparing a Christmas tree knows that the preparation is one of the nicest, most delightful parts of the entertainment. But though he was carried away by the preparations for the Christmas tree, I had a gnawing at my heart; I was continually arguing with him and reluctantly doing what I did not want to do.

Here I must stop to ask a sorrowful question. How, whence did I come by this readiness to give way with a murmur, this weak yielding after opposition and a protest? I had at the same time a conviction that I ought to act in one way and a readiness to act in quite another. This instability, this disharmony, *dieses Zögernde* has done me no end of harm in my life, and has not even left me the faint comfort of recognising that my mistake was involuntary, unconscious; I have made blunders *à contre-cœur*; I had all the arguments on the other side before my eyes. I have described already in one of my earlier chapters the part I took in the 13th of June 1849. That is typical of what I am describing. I did not for one instant believe in the success of the 13 th of June; I saw the absurdity of the movement and its impotence, the indifference of the people, the ferocity of the reaction, and the pettiness of the revolutionaries. (I had written about it already, and yet I went out into the square, though I laughed at the people who went.)

How many misfortunes, how many blows I should have been spared in my life, if at all the important crises in it I had had the strength to listen to myself alone. I have been reproached for being easily carried away; I have been carried away, too, but that is not what matters most. Though I might be carried away by my impressionable temper, I pulled myself up at once; thought, reflection and observation almost always gained the day in theory, but not in practice. That is just what is hard to explain: why I let myself be led *nolens volens*. . . .

My speedy surrender to persuasion was due to false shame, though sometimes to the better influences of love, friendship and indulgence; but why was all that too strong for my reason?

After the funeral of Worcell on the 5 th of February 1857, when all the mourners had dispersed to their homes and I, returning to my room, sat down sadly to my writing-table, a melancholy question came into my mind. Were not all our relations with the Polish exiles buried in the grave with that saint?

The gentle character of the old man, which was a conciliating element in the misunderstandings that were constantly arising, had gone for ever, but the misunderstandings remained. Privately, personally, we might love one or another among the Poles and be friendly with them, but there was little common understanding between us in general, and that made our relations strained and conscientiously reserved; we made concessions to one another, that is, weakened ourselves and decreased in each other what was almost the best and strongest in us. It was impossible to come to a common understanding by open talk. We started from different points, and our paths simply intersected in our common hatred for the autocracy of Petersburg. The ideal of the Poles was behind them, they strove towards their past, from which they had been cut off by violence and which was the only starting-point from which they could advance again. They had masses of holy relics, while we had empty cradles. In all their actions and in all their poetry there is as much of despair as there is of living faith.

They look for the resurrection of their dead, we long to bury ours as soon as possible. Our lines of thought, our forms of inspiration are different; our whole genius, our whole constitution has nothing in common with theirs. Our association with them seemed to them alternately a *mésalliance* and a marriage of prudence. On our side there was more sincerity, but not more depth: we were conscious of our indirect responsibility, we liked their reckless daring and respected their indomitable protest. What could they like, what could they respect in us? They did violence to themselves in making friends with us; they made an honourable exception for a few Russians.

In the dark prison-house of Nicholas's reign, sitting in bondage with our fellow-captives, we had more sympathy for each other than knowledge of each other. But as soon as the window was opened a little space, we divined that we were led by different paths and that we should go in different directions. After the Crimean War we heaved a sigh of relief, and our joy was an offence to them: the new atmosphere in Russia suggested to them not hopes but losses. For us the new times began with ambitious claims, we rushed forward ready to smash everything; with them it began with requiems and services for the dead. But for a second time the Government welded us together. At the sound of firing at priests and children, at crucifixes and women, the sound of firing above the chanting of hymns and prayers, all questions were silenced, all differences were wiped out. With tears and lamentations, I wrote then a series of articles which deeply touched the Poles.

From his deathbed, old Adam Czartorysczki sent me by his son a warm word of greeting; a deputation of Poles in Paris presented me with an address signed by four hundred exiles, to which signatures were sent from all parts of the world, even from Polish refugees living in Algiers and in America. It seemed as though in so much we were united; but one step further, and the difference, the vast difference, could not be overlooked.

One day Branicki, Hoetsky and one or two other Poles were sitting with me; they were all on a brief visit to London, and had come to shake hands with me for my articles. The talk fell on the shot fired at Constantine.

'That shot,' I said, 'will do you terrible damage. The Government might have made some concessions; now it will yield nothing, but will be twice as savage.'

'But that is just what we want!' one of the party observed with heat; 'there could be no worse misfortune for us than concessions. We want a breach, an open conflict.'

'I hope most earnestly that you may not regret it.'

He smiled ironically, and no one added a word. That was in the summer of 1861. And a year and a half later Padlewski said the same thing when he was on his way to Poland *via* Petersburg.

The die was cast! . . .

Bakunin believed in the possibility of a rising of the peasants and the army in Russia, and to some extent we believed in it too; and indeed the Government itself believed in it, as was shown later on by a series of measures, of officially inspired articles, and of punishments by special decree. That men's minds were working and in a ferment was beyond dispute, and no one saw at the time that the popular excitement would be turned to brutal patriotism.

Bakunin, not too much given to weighing every circumstance, looked only towards the ultimate goal, and took the second month of pregnancy for the ninth. He carried us away not by arguments but by his hopes. He longed to believe, and he believed, that Zhmud[1] and the regions of the Volga, the Don and the Ukraine would rise as one man when they heard of Warsaw; he believed that the Old Believers would take advantage of the Catholic movement to obtain a legal standing for dissent.

That the league among the officers of the troops stationed in Poland and Lithuania—the league to which Potyebnya belonged—was growing and gathering strength was beyond all doubt; but it was very far from possessing the strength which the Poles through design and Bakunin through simplicity ascribed to it.

One day towards the end of September Bakunin came to me, looking particularly preoccupied and somewhat solemn.

'The Warsaw Central Committee,' he said, 'have sent two members to negotiate with us. One of them you know—Padlewski; the other is G., a veteran

---

[1] The country between the lower Niemen and the Windau, the inhabitants of which are closely related to the Lithuanians, and from the fourteenth century were included in Lithuania.—(*Translator's Note.*)

RELATIONS DEFINED

warrior; he was sent from Poland in fetters to the mines, and as soon as he was back he set to work again. This evening I will bring them to see you, and to-morrow we will meet in my room. We want to *define our relations once for all*.'

My answer to the officers was being printed at that time.

'My programme is ready, I will read aloud my letter.'

'I agree with your letter, you know that; but I don't know whether they will altogether like it; in any case, I imagine that it won't be enough for them.'

In the evening Bakunin arrived with three visitors instead of two. I read my letter aloud. While we were talking and while I was reading, Bakunin sat looking anxious, as relations are at an examination, or as lawyers are when they tremble lest their client should make a slip and spoil the whole game of the defence that has been so well played, if not strictly in accordance with the whole truth, anyway to a successful finish.

I saw from their faces that Bakunin had guessed right, and that they were not particularly pleased by what I read them. 'First of all,' observed G., 'we will read the letter to you from the Central Committee.' M. read it; the document, with which readers of the *Kolokol* are familiar, was written *in Russian*, not quite correctly, but clearly. It has been said that I translated it from the French and altered the sense. That is *not true*. All three spoke Russian well.

The drift of the document was to tell the Russians through us that the provisional Polish Government agreed with us and adopted as its basis: '*The recognition of the right of the peasantry to the land tilled by them, and the complete independence of every people in the determination of its destiny.*'

This manifesto, M. said, bound me to soften the interrogative and hesitating form of my letter. I agreed to some changes, and suggested to them that they might accentuate and define more clearly the idea of the self-determination of provinces; they agreed. This dispute over words showed that our attitude towards the same questions was not identical.

Next day Bakunin was with me in the morning. He was displeased with me, thought I had been too cold, as though I did not trust them.

'Whatever more do you want? The Poles have never made such concessions. They express themselves in other words which are accepted among them as an article of faith; they can't possibly at the first step, as they hoist the national flag, wound the sensitive popular feeling.'

'I fancy, all the same, that they really care very little about the land for the peasants and far too much about the provinces.'

'My dear fellow, you will have a document in your hands corrected by you and signed in the presence of all of us; whatever more do you want?'

'I do want something else though!'

'How difficult every step is to you! You are not a practical man at all.'

'Sazonov used to say that before you said it.'

Bakunin waved his hand in despair and went off to Ogaryov's room. I looked mournfully after him. I saw that he was in the middle of his revolutionary debauch, and that there would be no bringing him to reason now. With his seven-league boots he was striding over seas and mountains, over years and generations. Beyond the insurrection in Warsaw he was already seeing his 'Glorious and Slav Federation'[1] of which the Poles spoke with something between horror and repulsion; he already saw the red flag of 'Land and Freedom' waving on the Urals and the Volga, in the Ukraine and the Caucasus, possibly on the Winter

[1] 'Slava' is the Russian for 'glory.'—(*Translator's Note.*)

Palace and the Peter-Paul fortress, and was in haste to smooth away all difficulties somehow, to blot out contradictions, not to fill up ravines but to fling a skeleton bridge across them.

'There is no freedom without land.'

'You are like a diplomat at the Congress of Vienna,' Bakunin repeated to me with vexation, when we were talking afterwards with the representatives of the Polish Committee in his room. 'You keep picking holes in words and expressions. This is not an article for a newspaper, it is not literature.'

'For my part,' observed G., 'I am not going to quarrel about words; change them as you like, so long as the main drift remains the same.'

'Bravo, G.,' cried Bakunin, gleefully.

'Well, that fellow,' I thought, 'has come prepared for every emergency; he will not yield an inch in fact, and that is why he so readily yields in words.'

The manifesto was corrected, the members of the Committee signed it. I sent it off to the printing-press.

G. and his companions were fully persuaded that we represented the centre of a whole organisation in Russia which depended upon us and would at our command join them or not join them. For them what was essential lay not in words nor in theoretical agreements; they could always tone down their *profession de foi* by interpretations which would dim its vivid colours and change them.

That the first nucleus of an organisation was being formed in Russia there could be no doubt. The first threads could be discerned with the naked eye; from these threads, these knots, a web on a vast scale might be woven, given time and tranquillity. All that was true, but it was not there yet, and every violent shock threatened to ruin the work for a whole generation and to tear asunder the first lacework of the spider's web.

That is just what, after sending the Committee's letter to the press, I said to G. and his companions, telling them of the prematureness of their rising. Padlewski knew Petersburg too well to be surprised by my words—though he did assure me that the vigour and number of branches of the League of Land and Freedom went much further than we imagined; but G. grew thoughtful. 'You thought,' I said to him, smiling, 'that we were stronger? You were right. We have great power and influence, but that power rests entirely on public opinion, that is, it may evaporate all in a minute; we are strong through the sympathy with us, through our harmony with our own people. There is no organisation to which we could say, "Turn to the right or turn to the left."'

'But, my dear fellow, all the same . . .' Bakunin was beginning, walking about the room in excitement.

'Why, *is* there?' I asked him.

'Well, that is as you like to call it; of course if you go by the external form, it is not at all in the Russian character, but you see . . .'

'Allow me to finish; I want to explain to G. why I have been so insistent about words. If people in Russia do not see on your standard "Land for the Peasants" and "Freedom for the Provinces," then our sympathy *will do you no good at all but will ruin us*; because all our strength rests on their hearts beating in unison with ours. Our hearts may beat more strongly and so be one second ahead of our friends; but they are bound to us by sympathy and not by duty!'

'You will be satisfied with us,' said G. and Padlewski.

Next day two of them went off to Warsaw, while the third went off to Paris.

The calm before the storm followed. It was a hard and gloomy time, in which it kept seeming as though the storm would pass over, while it drew nearer and nearer. Then came the decree tampering with the levying of recruits; this was the last straw; men who were still hesitating to take the final and irrevocable step dashed into the fray. Now even the *Whites* began to go over to the side of the rebellion.

Padlewski came again; the decree was not withdrawn. Padlewski went off to Poland.

Bakunin was going to Stockholm quite independently of Lapinski's expedition, of which no one dreamed at the time. Potyebnya turned up for a brief moment. A plenipotentiary from 'Land and Freedom' came from Petersburg *via* Warsaw at the same time as Potyebnya; he described with indignation how the Poles who had summoned him to Warsaw had done nothing. He was the first Russian who had seen the beginning of the rebellion; he told us about the murder of the soldiers, about the wounded officer who was a member of the society. The soldiers thought that this was treachery and began furiously beating the Poles. Padlewski, who was the chief leader in Kovno, tore his hair, but was afraid to act openly in opposition to his followers.

The plenipotentiary was full of the importance of his mission and invited us to become the *agents* of the League of Land and Freedom. I declined this, to the extreme surprise not only of Bakunin but even of Ogaryov. I said that I did not like this hackneyed French term. The plenipotentiary treated us as the Commissaires of the Convention of 1793 treated the generals in the distant armies. I did not like that either.

'And are there many of you?' I asked him.

'That is hard to say: some hundreds in Petersburg and three thousand in the provinces.'

'Do you believe it?' I asked Ogaryov afterwards. He did not answer. 'Do you believe it?' I asked Bakunin.

'Of course; but,' he added, *'well, if there are not as many now there soon will be!'* and he burst into a roar of laughter,

'That is another matter.'

'The whole point is to give support to what is beginning; if they were strong they would not need us,' observed Ogaryov, who was always displeased with my scepticism on these occasions.

'Then they ought to come to us frankly admitting their weakness and asking for friendly help instead of proposing the silly position of agents.'

That is youth,' Bakunin commented, and he went off to Sweden. And after him Potyebnya went off too. With heartfelt sorrow I said good-bye to him. I did not doubt for one second that he was going straight to his death.

A few days before Bakunin's departure Martyanov came in, paler than usual, gloomier than usual; he sat down in a corner and said nothing. He was pining for Russia and brooding over the thought of returning home. A discussion of the Polish rebellion sprang up. Martyanov listened in silence, then got up, preparing to go, and suddenly standing still, facing me, said gloomily:—

'You must not be angry with me, Alexandr Ivanovitch; that may be so or it may not, but anyway you have done for the *Kolokol*. What business had you to meddle in Polish affairs? The Poles may be in the right, but their cause is for their gentry, not for you. You have not spared us. God forgive you, Alexandr Ivanovitch; you will remember what I say, I shall not see it myself, I am going home. There is nothing for me to do here.'

'You are not going to Russia, and the *Kolokol* is not ruined,' I answered him.

He went out without another word, leaving me heavily weighed down by this second prediction and by a dim consciousness that a blunder had been made.

Martyanov did as he had said; he returned home in the spring of 1863 and went to die in penal servitude, exiled by his Liberal Tsar for his love for Russia and his trust in him.

Towards the end of 1863 the circulation of the *Kolokol* dropped from two thousand or two thousand five hundred to five hundred, and never again rose above one thousand copies. The Charlotte Corday from Orlov and the Daniel from the peasants had been right.

Written at Montreux and Lausanne
at the end of 1865.

LETTERS FROM OGARYOV AND BAKUNIN TO THE RUSSIAN OFFICERS WHO TOOK PART IN THE POLISH REBELLION.

'FRIENDS,—With deep love and deep sorrow we bid farewell to this comrade as he sets off to join you; only the secret hope that this rebellion will be postponed brings us some comfort as regards your future and the fate of the whole cause. We understand that you cannot but join the Polish rebellion whatever form it may take; you give yourselves as atonement for the sins of the Russian Tsardom; moreover, to leave Poland to be beaten without any protest from the Russian militant party would have the fatal appearance of Russia taking a dumbly submissive, immoral part in the butchering for which Petersburg alone is responsible. Nevertheless, your position is hopeless and tragic. We see no chance of success. Even if Warsaw were free for one month, it would only mean that you had paid a debt by your share in the movement of *national independence*, but to raise the Russian socialist banner of "Land and Freedom" is not vouchsafed to Poland; while you are too few.

'This premature rebellion will obviously mean the ruin of Poland, while the Russian cause will be drowned for years to come in the flood of national hatred which goes hand in hand with devotion to the Tsar, and it will only rise again later, long years later, when your heroic deed will have become the same sort of tradition as that of the 14th of December and will stir the hearts of a generation not yet begotten. The moral of this is clear: put off the rebellion till a better time, when forces are united; put it off by your influence on the Polish Committee and by your influence on the Government itself, which may yet be alarmed into removing the unhappy decree; put it off by every means within your power.

'If your efforts are fruitless there is nothing else for you but to submit to your fate and accept your inevitable martyrdom, even though its consequence will be ten years' stagnation for Russia. Anyway, as far as possible be sparing of men and of strength, that elements may be left from this unhappy defeated struggle for victory in the distant future. But if you succeed and the rebellion is deferred, then you ought to adopt a firm line of conduct and not to depart from it.

'Then you ought to keep one object in view: to make the Russian cause a general one and not exclusively Polish, to create a complete unbroken chain of secret alliance between all the militant forces in the name of "Land and Freedom" and of the National Assembly, as you say in your letter to the Russian officers. For that, it is essential that the Russian Officers' Committee should be independent, and therefore its centre should be outside Poland. You ought to organise a centre outside yourselves to which you will owe allegiance, then you will be in a commanding position and at the head of a well-organised force which will take part in the rebellion, not in the name of Polish nationality exclusively, but in the name of "Land and Freedom," and will take part in it not in accordance with the needs of the moment, but at the time when all forces have been reckoned and success is assured.

'To us this plan seems so clear that you too cannot

but recognise what must be done. Accomplish it whatever labour it may cost.   N. OGARYOV.'

'FRIENDS AND BROTHERS,—The lines written by our friend Nikolay Platonovitch Ogaryov are full of true and boundless devotion to the great cause of our national and indeed Panslav emancipation. One cannot but agree with him that the premature and partial rising of Poland threatens to interrupt the general steady advance of the Slav, and especially of the Russian, progressive movement. It must be owned that in the present temper of Russia and of all Europe there is too little hope of success for such a rebellion, and that the defeat of the progressive party in Poland will inevitably be followed by the temporary triumph of the Tsarist despotism in Russia. But on the other hand, the position of the Poles is so insufferable that they can hardly be patient for long.

'The Government itself by its infamous measures of cruel and systematic oppression is provoking them, it seems, to a rebellion, the postponement of which would be for that very reason as good for Poland as it is essential for Russia. To defer it till a much later date would undoubtedly be the salvation of them as well as of us. You ought to devote all your efforts to bring this about, without, however, failing to respect their sacred rights and their national dignity. Persuade them so far as you can and so far as circumstances permit, but yet lose no time, be active in propaganda and organisation, that you may be ready for the decisive moment; and when, driven beyond the utmost limit of possible patience, our unhappy Polish brothers rise, do you rise too, not against them but for them; rise up in the name of Russian honour, in the name of Slav duty, in the name of the Russian people, with the battle-cry, "Land and Freedom"; and if you are doomed to perish, your death will serve the common cause . . . and God knows! Perhaps in opposition to every calculation of cold prudence your heroic deed may unexpectedly be crowned with success. . . .

'As for myself, whatever may await you, success or death, I hope that it may be my lot to share your fate.

'Good-bye—and perhaps till we meet again soon.

'M. Bakunin.'

APPENDIX

1

The Steamer 'Ward Jackson'

THIS is what happened two months before the Polish rebellion: a Pole, one Joseph Cwerczakiewicz, who had come for a brief visit from Paris to London, was on his return to Paris seized and arrested, together with C. and M., the latter of whom I have mentioned in connection with the interview with members of the Polish Committee.

There was a good deal that was strange about the whole arrest. C. had arrived between 9 and 10 in the evening; he knew no one in Paris and went straight to M.'s lodging. About 11 o'clock the police made their appearance and asked for his passport.

'Here it is,' and C. gave the police officer a passport with another name on it and a perfectly regular *visa*.

'To be sure, to be sure,' said the man, 'I knew you were travelling under that name. Now your portfolio,' he asked Cwerczakiewicz. It was lying on the table. The policeman took out the papers, looked through them, and handing his companion a brief letter addressed E. A., said: 'Here it is.'

All three were arrested, and their papers taken from them; afterwards they were released. C. was kept longer than the rest. For the sake of the prestige of the police they wanted him to tell his name. He would not give them this gratification. He, too, was released a week later. When, a year or more afterwards, the Prussian Government initiated the very absurd Posen Trial, the prosecutor presented among the incriminating documents papers sent him by the Russian police which had belonged to Cwerczakiewicz. When the question how these papers had found their way to

Russia was raised, the prosecutor calmly explained that when Cwerczakiewicz was under arrest, some of his papers had been handed over by the French police to the Russian Embassy.

The released Poles were ordered to leave France; they came to London. In London they themselves told me all the details of their arrest, and were very justly most surprised at the police officer's knowing that they had a letter addressed to E. A. Mazzini had given this letter with his own hands to Cwerczakiewicz, asking him to hand it to Étienne Arago.

'Did you tell any one about the letter?' I asked him.

'No one, absolutely no one,' answered Cwerczakiewicz.

'There is some sorcery about it; no suspicion can fall on you or on Mazzini. Think a little.'

Cwerczakiewicz mused. 'I know one thing,' he observed. 'I did go out for a short time, and I remember I left the portfolio in an unlocked drawer.'

'A clue! A clue! Now, allow me, where were you living?'

'In So-and-so Street in furnished apartments.'

'Was the landlord an Englishman?'

'No, a Pole.'

'Better still. And his name?'

'Tur; he is a specialist in agriculture.'

'And in many other things, since he lets furnished rooms. I know a little of that Tur. Did you ever hear a story about a fellow called Michalowski?'

'I have heard it alluded to.'

'Well, I will tell you the story. In the autumn of 1857 I received a letter from Petersburg *via* Brussels. An unknown person informed me with the fullest details that a shopman at Trübner's called Michalowski had offered his services to the Third Section for spying on us, asking for two hundred pounds for his trouble; that, in proof of his merit and capacity, he had presented a list of the persons who had been at our house of late, and promised to furnish specimens of manuscripts from the printing-press. Before I had properly considered what to do, I received a second letter to the same effect through Rothschild's.

'I had not the slightest doubt of the truth of the information. Michalowski, a cringing, repulsive, drunken, nimble Pole from Galicia, speaking four languages, had every qualification for the calling of a spy and was only waiting the opportunity *pour se faire valoir*.

'I made up my mind to go with Ogaryov to Trübner's to unmask Michalowski and make him commit himself, and in any case to get him dismissed from Trübner's. To add to the impressiveness of our visit, I invited Pianciani and two Poles to go with me. Michalowski was insolent, loathsome, and denied the charge; he declared that Napoleon Szestacowski, who lived in the same lodging with him, was a spy. I was quite prepared to believe that half of what he said was true, that is, that his friend was also a spy. I told Trübner that I asked for his immediate dismissal from the bookshop. The wretch contradicted himself and could not bring forward anything worth considering in his defence. "It is all envy," he said. "As soon as one of us has a good coat to wear, the others begin shouting 'Spy!'" "Why is it then," Zeno Swentoslawski asked him, "that though you have never had a good coat you have always been looked upon as a spy?" Every one laughed. "You don't seem to resent it," said Czenecki. "It is not the first time," answered the philosopher, "that I have had to do with crazy fellows like you." "You are used to it," observed Czenecki.

'The scoundrel walked away.

'All the decent Poles abandoned him, with the exception of gamblers who were complete drunkards and drunkards who were completely ruined at cards. Only one decent person has remained on friendly terms with this Michalowski, and that man is your landlord, Tur.'

'Yes, that is suspicious. I will go at once . . .'

'Why at once? You can't set things right now, but keep an eye on the man. What proofs have you?'

Soon after this, Cwerczakiewicz was appointed by the Polish Committee their diplomatic agent in London. He was allowed to visit Paris; it was just at that time that Napoleon felt that ardent sympathy with the fate of Poland which cost her one whole generation and may perhaps cost her the whole of the next one.

Bakunin was already in Sweden, making friends with every one, opening ways for 'Land and Freedom' across Finland, arranging for the despatch of the *Kolokol* and of books, and interviewing representatives of all the Polish parties. Received by the Ministers and the brother of the King, he assured every one of the approaching insurrection of the peasants and the state of intense mental ferment in Russia. He assured them the more readily as he himself *sincerely believed*, if not in the actual strength of these movements, at least in their growing power. No one dreamed at that time of Lapinski's expedition. Bakunin's intention was, after arranging everything in Sweden, to make his way into Poland and Lithuania.

Cwerczakiewicz came back from Paris with Demontowicz. In Paris he and his friends formed a design of fitting out an expedition to the shores of the Baltic. They wanted to find a steamer and wanted to find a capable leader; and with that end in view came to London. This is how they conducted secret negotiations.

One day I received a little note from Cwerczakiewicz: he asked me to go to see him for a minute, said it was a matter of urgent necessity and that he had caught a chill and was lying in bed with an acute migraine. I went. I did in fact find him ill and in bed. S. Tchorszewski was sitting in the next room, knowing that Cwerczakiewicz had written to me and that he had business with me. Tchorszewski would have gone out, but Cwerczakiewicz stopped him, and I am very glad that there is a living witness of our conversation.

Cwerczakiewicz asked me, laying aside all personal feelings and considerations, to tell him quite sincerely, and of course in dead secret, about a Polish exile in whom he had not complete confidence, though he had been introduced to him by Mazzini and Bakunin. 'You don't much care for him, I know, but now, where it is a matter of the utmost importance, I expect from you the truth, and the whole truth.'

'You are speaking of L. B.?' I asked.

'Yes.'

I hesitated. I felt that I might injure a man of whom, anyway, I knew nothing particularly bad; on the other hand, I knew what harm I might be doing to the common cause by arguing against Cwerczakiewicz's perfectly sound instinct of antipathy.

'Very well, I will speak openly and tell you everything. As regards Mazzini's and Bakunin's recommendation, I disregard that completely. You know how I love Mazzini; but he is so accustomed to carve his agents out of every sort of wood and mould them out of any sort of clay, and knows so well how to keep them in hand in the Italian party, that it is hard to rely on his opinion. Besides, though he makes use of everything he can get, Mazzini knows to what degree and with what business to trust each. Bakunin's recommendation is even worse: he is a great child—"a big Liza," as Martyanov used to call him—he likes every one. A fisher of men, he is so delighted when he comes upon a "Red," especially if he is a Slav, that he goes no further. You referred to my personal relations with L. B. I ought to speak of that too. Z. and L. B. tried to exploit me: it was not he but Z. who took the initiative. They did not succeed in that, they were very angry, and I should long ago have forgotten it; but they came between Worcell and me, and that I have not forgiven. I loved Worcell very much, but, being frail in health, he gave way to them and only realised his mistake (or acknowledged that he realised it) the day before his death. As he lay dying, he pressed my hand and whispered in my ear: "'Yes, you were right." (But there were none to hear, and it is easy to appeal to the witness of the dead.) But here is my opinion: taking everything into account, I cannot find a single action, or a single rumour even, which would compel one to suspect the political honesty of L. B., but I should not let him into any important secret. To my thinking, he is a spoilt *poseur*, filled with French phrases and immensely conceited; anxious to play a part at all costs, he would do everything to spoil the performance if it had not a part for him.'

Cwerczakiewicz got up; he was pale and troubled.

'Yes, you have taken a weight off my heart; I will do all I can, if it is not too late already.' Cwerczakiewicz began pacing about the room in perturbation. Soon after I went away with Tchorszewski.

'Did you hear the whole conversation?' I asked him as we were going.

'Yes, I did.'

'I am very glad of it; don't forget it; perhaps the day may come when I shall appeal to you . . . and do you know, it strikes me that he has told him everything already, and only thought to investigate the grounds of his antipathy afterwards. . . .'

'Not a doubt of it.'

And we almost burst out laughing, although we were anything but mirthful at heart.

Moral

A fortnight later Cwerczakiewicz entered into negotiations with Blackwood's Steam Company concerning the hiring of a steamer to make an expedition to the Baltic.

'Why,' we said, 'did you apply to the very company which for years past has carried out all the shipping commissions for the Petersburg Admiralty?'

'I don't like it myself, but the company knows the Baltic Sea so well. Besides, it is against its interests to betray us; and it is not in the English character either.'

'All very true, but what made you think of applying to them?'

'It was done by our agent.'

'That is?'

'Tur.'

'What, *that* Tur?'

'Oh, you can set your mind at rest about him. He was most highly recommended to us by L. B.'

For a minute all the blood rushed to my head. I was overwhelmed with the feeling of fury, indignation, resentment—yes, yes, personal resentment—while the delegate of Poland, observing nothing, went on: 'He has a splendid knowledge of English.'

'Both of the language and of the laws.'

'I have no doubt of it.'

'Tur has been in prison in London for some rather shady affair; and he was employed as an official interpreter in the law courts.'

'How was that?'

'You must ask L. B. or Michalowski; don't you know him?'

'No.'

Tur was indeed a fellow! He had been a specialist in agriculture, but here he was a specialist in marine affairs. But now all eyes were turned on the head of the expedition, Colonel Lapinski, who arrived upon the scene.

2

COLONEL LAPINSKI AND AIDE-DE-CAMP POLLES

At the beginning of 1863 I received a letter written in a tiny, extraordinarily fine handwriting, and headed with the text: *Licite Venire Parvulos*. In the most elaborately flattering and cringing expressions the *parvulus*, whose name was Polles, asked permission to call upon me. I did not like the letter at all. The man himself I liked even less. A cringing, subdued, furtive man, with a shaven chin and a pomaded head, he told me that he had been at a dramatic school in Petersburg and had received some sort of pension there. He almost overdid the patriotic Pole, and after sitting a quarter of an hour with me, confided that he came from France, that he had been miserable in Paris, and that the centre of everything there was Napoleon.

'Do you know, it has often struck me, and I am more and more convinced that I am right: the thing to do is to kill Napoleon.'

'What prevents you then?'

'What do you think about it?' Parvulus asked, somewhat embarrassed.

'I don't think about it at all. Why, it is you who are thinking about it.' And I immediately told him the story which I always make use of when people rave about bloody deeds and ask advice concerning them.

'No doubt you know that when Charles v. was in Rome a page took him over the Pantheon. On returning home, the boy told his father that the idea had occurred to him to push the emperor down from the top gallery. The father flew into a rage: "You" (here I vary the term of abuse to suit the character of the would-be Tsaricide[1]) "wretch, scoundrel, fool, and so on. How

[1] 'I have come to ask your advice,' a youthful Georgian, who

can such criminal ideas occur to you? If they can, they are sometimes acted upon, but never spoken of."'

When Polles had gone, I made up my mind not to be at home to him again. A week later he met me near my house; he told me that he had called twice and had not found me in, talked some sort of nonsense, and added: 'I called to see you partly to tell you of an invention I have made for sending anything secretly by post, to Russia for instance. You are probably often in need of communicating something in secret?'

'Quite the contrary, never. I never write to any one in secret. Good morning.'

'Good-bye. Remember, if ever you or Ogaryov would like a little music, my violoncello and I are at your service.'

'Very much obliged to you.'

And I lost sight of him in the full conviction that he was a spy—whether a Russian or a French one, I don't know; perhaps international, as the paper *Le Nord* is international.

He never turned up among the real Polish exiles, and not one of them knew him.

After a prolonged search, Demontowicz and his Parisian friends had pitched on Colonel Lapinski as the most capable military leader for the expedition. He had fought for a long time in the Caucasus on the side of the Circassians, and understood mountain warfare so thoroughly that there could be no doubt of his skill on the sea. It could not be called a bad choice. Lapinski was in the fullest sense of the word a condottiere. He had no settled political convictions. He could have fought on the side of the White or the Red, the

looked like a young tiger, said to me one day, 'I want to give Skaryatin a thrashing.'

'No doubt you know that when Charles v. was in Rome, et cetera. . . .' 'I know, I know; for God's sake don't tell me!'

And the tiger with milk in his veins departed.—(*Author's Note*.)

clean or the dirty; belonging by birth to the Galician gentry, by education to the Austrian army, he was strongly inclined towards Vienna. Russia and everything Russian he hated with a savage, irrational and incorrigible hatred. He probably knew his trade, he had spent years in active warfare and had written a remarkable book about the Caucasus.

'This is what happened to me once in the Caucasus,' Lapinski used to tell. 'A Russian major, living with a whole household not far from us, seized some of our people, I don't know how or why. I heard about it and said to my men, "Look here, it is a sin and a shame; are you stolen like women? Go to his place, take everything you find and bring it here." They are mountaineers, you know; you don't need to say much to them. A day or two afterwards they brought me the whole family—servants, wife and children—but they did not find the major himself at home. I sent word to him that if he released our people and paid a ransom, we would give him back our prisoners at once. Of course they sent our men, paid the fine, and we released our Moscow visitors. The next day a Circassian came to me: "Look here," he said, "what's happened; when we let the Russians go yesterday," he said, "a boy of four was forgotten; he was asleep, so he was forgotten; what is to be done?"

'"Ah, you dogs, you can't do anything properly; where's the child?"

'"With me. He screamed and screamed—well, I was sorry for him and took him home."

'"Allah has sent you luck, it seems; I won't hinder it. Let them know that they have forgotten the child and you have found him, and ask for a ransom." My Circassian's eyes fairly sparkled. Of course the father and mother were in a fluster, they gave anything he liked to ask. It was funny.'

PREPARATIONS FOR EXPEDITION

'Very.'

Here is another trait showing the character of the future hero of Polish independence.

Before he set off, Lapinski came to see me. He arrived not alone, and somewhat disconcerted by the expression on my face, made haste to say: 'Allow me to introduce my adjutant.'

'I have had the pleasure of meeting him already.'

It was Polles.

'Do you know him well?' Ogaryov asked Lapinski when they were alone.

'I met him in the boarding-house in which I am staying now. He seems a nice fellow and very obliging.'

'But do you trust him?'

'Of course. Besides, he plays the violoncello charmingly and will entertain us on the voyage.'

It was said that the colonel found him entertaining in other ways.

We told Demontowicz later on that to our thinking Polles was a very suspicious character. Demontowicz observed: 'Yes, I don't trust either of them much, but they won't play us any tricks'; and he took his revolver out of his pocket.

The preparations proceeded slowly; rumours of the expedition spread more and more widely. At first the company furnished a steamer which on being inspected by an experienced sailor, Count S., turned out to be good for nothing. All the cargo had to be shifted. When everything was ready and a good part of London knew all about it, the following incident occurred: Cwerczakiewicz and Demontowicz informed all who were taking part in the expedition that they were to assemble at ten o'clock on such and such a railway platform to go to Hull by a special train provided by the railway company. And so at ten o'clock the future warriors began to assemble. Among them were Italians and a few

Frenchmen; poor, reckless men, sick of a life spent in homeless wandering, and men who were true lovers of Poland. And ten o'clock came and eleven o'clock, but still no train appeared. Little by little, rumours of this long journey reached the homes from which our heroes had mysteriously vanished, and by twelve o'clock the future warriors were joined in the station waiting-rooms by a troop of women, inconsolable Didos deserted by their fierce adorers, and ferocious landladies who had not been paid, probably for fear they should spread the news abroad. In violent excitement they raised a furious uproar, and wanted to complain to the police; some of them had children; all the latter screamed and all the mothers screamed. The English stood round, staring in astonishment at the picture of 'The Exodus.' In vain some of the elders of the party inquired whether the special train would soon come in, and showed their tickets. The railway officials had never heard of any such train. The scene was becoming more and more uproarious . . . when suddenly a messenger from the leaders galloped up to tell the waiting warriors that they had all gone mad, that the train was at ten o'clock in the evening, not in the morning, and that they had thought this so evident that they had not even written it. The poor warriors returned with their bags and their wallets to their deserted Didos and softened landladies.

At ten o'clock in the evening they went off. The English gave them three cheers.

Next morning a marine officer whom I knew came to me from one of the Russian steamers.

The steamer had received an order the previous evening to set off full steam next morning and follow the *Ward Jackson*.

Meanwhile the *Ward Jackson* had stopped at Copenhagen for water, had spent some hours at Malmö waiting for Bakunin, who was intending to go with them to incite the peasants in Lithuania to rise, and had been seized by the orders of the Swedish Government.

The details of this affair and of Lapinski's second attempt have been described by himself in the papers. I will only add that even in Copenhagen the captain had said he would not take the steamer to the coast of Russia, as he did not want to expose it and himself to danger; that even before they reached Malmö things had come to such a pass that Demontowicz threatened not Lapinski but the captain with his revolver. He did, however, quarrel with Lapinski too, and sworn foes they went to Stockholm, leaving their luckless followers at Malmö.

'Do you know,' Cwerczakiewicz or some of his associates said to me, 'the person who is most suspected of being chiefly responsible for the vessel being stopped at Malmö is Tugenbold?'

'I don't know him at all. Who is he?'

'Oh yes, you do, you have seen him with us: a young fellow without a beard—Lapinski brought him to see you once.'

'Then you are speaking of Polles?'

'That is his pseudonym, his real name is Tugenbold.'

'What are you saying?' and I rushed to my writing-table. Among letters I had put aside as of special importance I found one sent me two months previously. This letter was from Petersburg; it warned me that a certain Dr. Tugenbold was in relations with the Third Section, that he had returned, but had left his younger brother as his agent, and that the younger brother was to come to London.

That Polles and he were one and the same person there could be no doubt. I let my hands fall in despair.

'Did you know before the expedition started that Polles was Tugenbold?'

'Yes I knew. It was said he had changed his name

because his brother was known in the country for a spy.'

'Why didn't you say a word to me?'

'Oh, it just didn't come up.'

And Tchitchikov's Selifan[1] knew that the chaise was broken and did not say a word.

We had to telegraph to Malmö after the arrest. Even then neither Demontowicz nor Bakunin[2] could do anything effective; they quarrelled. Polles was thrown into prison over some diamonds collected from Swedish ladies for the Polish cause and spent by him on riotous living.

At the same time that a crowd of armed Poles, a large quantity of expensive ammunition, and the *Ward Jackson* remained honourable prisoners on the coast of Sweden, another expedition was being got up by the Whites; it was to go by way of the Straits of Gibraltar. At the head of it was Count Sbyszewski, brother of the man who wrote the remarkable pamphlet, *La Pologne et la Cause de l'Ordre*. He was a first-rate naval officer in the Russian service, but he abandoned it when the insurrection broke out, and now took a steamer, which had been secretly equipped, to the Black Sea. He had been to Turin for a secret interview with the leaders of the opposition there, among others with Mordini.

'The day after my interview with Sbyszewski,' Mordini himself told me, 'the Minister of Internal Affairs drew me aside in the evening and said: "Do please be more careful; you were visited yesterday by a Polish emissary who wants to take a steamer through the Straits of Gibraltar; be that as it may, why do they chatter about it beforehand?"'

---

[1] Characters in Gogol's *Dead Souls*.—(*Translator's Note*.)

[2] Demontowicz, after prolonged arguments with Bakunin, said: 'I tell you what, gentlemen, hard as it may be for us with the Russian Government, anyway our position under it is better than what these Socialist fanatics are preparing for us.'—(*Author's Note*.)

The steamer, however, did not reach the shores of Italy: it was seized at Cadiz by the Spanish Government. When they no longer needed them, both the Governments allowed the Poles to sell their arms and let the steamers go.

Disappointed and incensed, Lapinski arrived in London. 'The only thing left to do,' he said, 'is to form a society of assassins and kill the greater number of all the rulers and their advisers, or to go back again to the East, to Turkey.'

Disappointed and incensed, Sbyszewski arrived.

'Well, are you going off to kill kings, like Lapinski?'

'No, I am going to America. . . . I am going to fight for the Republic. By the way,' he asked Tchorszewski, 'where can one enlist here? I have a few comrades with me, and all without bread to eat.'

'Simply, at the Consul's.'

'No, we want to go on to the South; they are short of men now, and they offer more favourable conditions.'

'Impossible; you could not go to the South!'

. . . Fortunately Tchorszewski guessed right; they did not go to the South.

May 3, 1869.

FRAGMENTS

(1867 TO 1868)

1

Swiss Views

TEN years ago, as I was going through the Haymarket late one cold damp winter evening, I came upon a negro, a lad of seventeen; he was barefooted and without a shirt, and in fact rather undressed for the tropics than dressed for London. Shivering all over, with his teeth chattering, he begged from me. Two days later I met him again, and then again and again. At last I got into conversation with him. He spoke a broken English-Spanish, but it was not hard to understand the meaning of his words.

'You are young and strong,' I said to him,' why don't you get work?'

'No one will give it me.'

'Why is that?'

'I know no one here who would give me a character.'

'Where do you come from?'

'From a ship.'

'What sort of ship?'

'A Spanish one; the captain beat me very much, so I went away.'

'What did you do on board ship?'

'Everything: brushed the clothes, washed up, did the cabins.'

'What do you mean to do?'

'I don't know.'

'But you will die of cold and hunger, you know, or anyway you will certainly get a bad cold.'

'What am I to do?' said the negro in despair, looking at me and shivering all over with cold.

'Well,' I thought, 'here goes. It is not the first silly thing I have done in my life.'

'Come with me. I'll give you clothes and a corner to sleep in; you shall scrub my rooms, light the fires and stay as long as you like, if you behave quietly and properly. *Si no—no*.'

The negro jumped with joy.

Within a week he was fatter, and gaily did the work of four. So he spent six months with us; then one evening he made his appearance at my door, stood a little while in silence, and then said to me:—

'I have come to say good-bye to you.'

'How's that?'

'For now it is enough, I am going.'

'Has anybody been nasty to you?'

'No, indeed, I am content with all.'

'Then where are you going now?'

'To some ship.'

'What for?'

'I am dreadfully sick of it, I can't stand It, I shall do a mischief if I stay. I want the sea. I will go away and come back again, but for now it is enough.'

I made an effort to keep him; he stayed on for three days, and then announced for the second time it was more than he could stand, that he must go away, that 'for now it is enough.'

That was in the spring.

In the autumn he turned up again, tropically divested, and again I clothed him; but he soon began playing various nasty tricks, and even threatened to kill me, and I was obliged to turn him away.

These last facts are irrelevant, but the point is that I completely share the negro's outlook. After staying a long time in the same place and sticking in the same rut, I feel that for a time *it is enough*, that I must refresh myself with other horizons and other faces . . . and at the same time must retire into myself, strange as that sounds. The superficial distractions of the journey do not prevent it.

There are people who prefer to get away *inwardly*, some with the help of a powerful imagination and faculty of abstracting themselves from their surroundings (a peculiar gift bordering on genius and insanity is necessary for this), some with the help of opium or alcohol. Russians, for instance, will have a drinking-bout for a week or two, and then go back to their duties. I prefer shifting my whole body to shifting my brain, and going round the world to letting my head go round.

Perhaps it is because I have a bad time after too much wine.

So I meditated on the 4th of October 1866 in a little room of a wretched hotel on the Lac de Neufchâtel where I felt as much at home as though I had lived in it all my life. The craving for solitude, and still more for tranquillity, develops strangely with years . . . It was rather a warm night; I opened my window. . . . Everything was plunged in deep sleep: the town and the lake and the boat which was moored to the bank and faintly heaving, as I could hear from a slight creaking and see from the swinging of the mast which shifted first to the right then to the left. . . .

To know that no one is expecting you, no one will come in to you, that you can do what you like, die perhaps, and no one will hinder you . . . no one will care . . . is at once dreadful and good. I am certainly beginning to be unsociable, and sometimes regret that I have not the strength to become a secular hermit.

Only in solitude can a man work to the utmost of his power. The free disposal of one's time and the absence of inevitable interruptions is a great thing. If a man begins to feel dull and tired, he can take his hat and go himself in search of his fellows and rest with them. He has but to go out into the street; the everlasting stream of faces floats by, unending, changing and unchanged, with its flashing rainbow hues and grey froth, its uproar and din. You look at this river of life as an artist, you look at it as at an exhibition, just because you have nothing to do with it.' It is all apart from you, and you need nothing from any one.

Next day I got up early, and by eleven o'clock was so hungry that I went for *déjeuner* to a big hotel which could not take me the evening before for lack of room. In the dining-room there was an Englishman with his wife, from whom he concealed himself with a sheet of *The Times*, and a Frenchman of about thirty, one of the new types which have come up of late: stout, flabby, white, fair-haired, and softly fat, he looked as though he were on the point of melting like jelly in a warm room, but his ample overcoat and trousers of springy material fortunately held him together. No doubt he was the son of some prince of the Bourse or aristocrat of the democratic empire. Listlessly, in a spirit of mistrust and investigation, he was proceeding through his lunch. One could see that he had been engaged upon it for a long time already and was tired of it.

This type, which scarcely existed in old days in France, began to appear in the time of Louis-Philippe and has reached its full blossoming during the last fifteen years. It is very repulsive, and that is perhaps a compliment to the French. The life of an epicure of the *cuisine* and of wines does not so distort an Englishman or a Russian as it does a Frenchman. The Foxes and the Sheridans drank and ate more than enough, but they remained Foxes and Sheridans. The Frenchman is with impunity devoted only to *literary* gastronomy, consisting in an elaborate *knowledge* of dainties and in the ordering of dishes. No other nation *talks* as much about dinner, about sauces and culinary refinements, as the Frenchman, but that is all a form of flourish and rhetoric. Real gluttony and drunkenness destroy a Frenchman, swallow him up . . . his nerves are not fit for that. A Frenchman remains sound and uninjured only when he spends his time flirting with every aspect of life; that is his national passion and favourite weakness—in it he is strong.

'Will you take dessert?' asked the waiter, who evidently had more respect for the Frenchman than for us. The young gentleman was at the moment engaged in digestion, and therefore, slowly lifting his weary and lustreless eyes to the waiter, he said: 'I don't know yet,' thought a little, and then added: '*Une poire!*'

The Englishman, who had all this time been eating in silence behind the screen of his paper, stirred and said: '*Et à moa aussi!*'

The waiter brought two pears on two plates and handed one to the Englishman; but the latter vigorously and emphatically protested: 'No, no! *aucune chose pour poire!*' He simply wanted something to drink. He got his drink and stood up; I only then observed that he was wearing a child's jacket, or spencer, of a light brown colour, and tight-fitting light trousers terribly creased above his boots. The lady too got up; she rose higher and higher still, and at last, terrifically tall, took the arm of her squat husband and went out.

I followed them out with an involuntary smile, completely free from malice; they seemed to me to have ten times as much human dignity as my neighbour, who was unbuttoning the third button of his waistcoat as the lady withdrew.

BASLE.

The Rhine is a natural frontier, not shutting off anything, but dividing Basle into two parts, which does not prevent both sides from being inexpressibly dull. Everything here is oppressed by a threefold dullness: German, commercial and Swiss. It is no wonder that the only artistic work that originated in Basle took the form of a dance of the dying with Death[1]; none but the dead rejoice here, though the German inhabitants are extremely fond of music—of a very grave and elevated character, however. The town is a place of transit; every one passes through it, but nobody stays here except commissioners and carriers of the higher order.

No one could live in Basle apart from a passion for money. Though, indeed, life is dull in Swiss towns as a rule, and not only in Swiss towns, but in all little towns. 'Florence is a wonderful town,' said Bakunin, 'like a delicious sweetmeat . . . you are delighted while you eat it, but in a week you are deadly sick of everything sweet.' That is perfectly true, and nothing need be said about Swiss towns after that. In old days it was quiet and pleasant on the shores of Lake Leman; but since villas have been built all the way from Vevey and whole families of the Russian nobility, impoverished by the calamities of the 19th of February 1861, have taken up their abode in them, it is no place for such as us.

LAUSANNE.

I am passing through Lausanne. Every one passes through Lausanne except the aborigines.

Outsiders do not live in Lausanne, in spite of the marvellous scenery round it and of the fact that the English three times discovered it: once after the death of Cromwell, once in the time of Gibbon, and now when they are building houses and villas in it. Tourists stay only in Geneva.

The thought of that town is in my mind inseparable from the thought of the coldest and driest of great men

---

[1] The 'Dance of Death' on the cloister walls of a convent in Basle, attributed to Holbein.—(*Translator's Note.*)

and the coldest and driest of winds—of Calvin and of the *bise*; I can't endure either of them. And certainly in every native of Geneva there is something left of the *bise* and of Calvin, both of which have blown upon him physically and spiritually from the day of his conception and even before, one from the mountains, the other from the prayer-book.

Those two chilling influences, checked and diversified by different currents from Savoy, from Valais, most of all from France, make up the fundamental character of the citizens of Geneva—an excellent character, but not a particularly agreeable one.

However, I am now writing my *impressions de voyage* while I am *living* in Geneva. Of that town I will write when I have retreated to an artistic distance. . . .

I reached Freiburg at ten o'clock in the evening and went straight to the Zöhringhof. The same landlord in a black velvet cap who met me in 1851, with the same regular features and condescendingly polite face of a Russian master of the ceremonies, or an English porter, came up to the omnibus and congratulated us on our arrival.

And the dining-room is the same, the same rectangular folding little sofas upholstered in red velvet. Fourteen years have passed over Freiburg like fourteen days! There is the same pride in the cathedral-organ, the same pride in their hanging bridge.

The breath of the new restless spirit, continually shifting and casting down barriers, that was raised by the equinoctial gales of 1848, scarcely touched towns which morally and physically stand apart, such as the Jesuitical Freiburg and the pietistic Neufchâtel. These towns, too, have advanced, though at the pace of a tortoise; they have improved, though they seem to us out of date in their old-fashioned stony garb. . . . And of course much in the life of old days was not bad; it was more comfortable, more durable; it was better fitted for the small number of the elect, and so it does not do for the vast number of the newly invited, who are far from being spoiled or difficult to please.

Of course, in the present state of technical development, with the discoveries that are being made every day, with the improvement of the resources at our disposal, it is possible to organise modern life on a free and ample scale. But the Western European, as soon as he has a place of his own, is satisfied with little. As a rule, he has been falsely charged, or rather he has charged himself, with the passion for comfort and that love of luxury of which people talk. All that, like everything else in him, is rhetoric and flourish. They have had free institutions without freedom, why not have a brilliant setting for a narrow and clumsy life? There are exceptions. One may find all sorts of things among English aristocrats and French Camélias and the Jewish princes of this world. . . . All that is personal and temporary; the lords and bankers have no future and the Camélias have no heirs. We are talking about the whole world, about the golden mean, about the chorus and the *corps de ballet*, which now is on the stage, leaving aside the father of Lord Stanley, who has twenty thousand francs a day, and the father of that child of twelve who flung himself into the Thames the other day to relieve his parents of the task of feeding him.

The old tradesman who has grown rich loves to talk of the comforts of life. For him it is a novelty that he is a gentleman *qu'il a ses aises*, 'that he has the means to do this, and that doing that will not ruin him.' He glories in money and knows its value and how quickly it flies, while his predecessors in fortune believed neither in its value nor that it could be exhausted, and so have been ruined. But they ruined themselves with good taste. The bourgeois has little notion of making full use of his accumulated riches. The habits of the old narrow, niggardly life he has inherited from his forbears remain. He may indeed spend a great deal of money, but he does not spend it on the right things.

A generation which has come from behind the counter has absorbed standards and ambitions of no wide horizon and cannot get away from them. Everything with them is done as though for sale, and they naturally aim at the greatest possible profit, gain and good bargain. The *propriétaire* instinctively diminishes the size of his rooms and increases their number, not knowing why he makes the windows small and the ceilings low; he takes advantage of every corner to snatch it from his lodger or from his own family. That corner is of no use to him, but in case he may need it, he will take it from somebody. With peculiar satisfaction he builds two uncomfortable kitchens instead of one good one, puts up a garret for his maid in which she can neither work nor move, but succeeds in making it damp. To compensate for this economy of light and space, he paints the front of the house, loads the drawing-room with furniture, and lays out before the house a flower-bed with a fountain in it, which is a source of tribulation to children, nurses, dogs and workmen. What is not spoilt by miserliness is ruined by lack of intelligence. Science, which cuts its way through the muddy pond of daily life without mingling with it, flings its wealth to right and left, but the boatmen do not know how to catch it. All the profit goes to the wholesale dealers and filters in scanty drops to others; the wholesale dealers are changing the face of the earth, while private life trails along beside their steam-engines in its old lumbering waggon with its broken-down nags. . . .

The fire which does not smoke is a dream. A landlord in Geneva said to me soothingly: 'This fire *only* smokes in the *bise*.' That is only just when one most wants a fire; and he says this as though the *bise* were something casual or newly invented, as though it had not been blowing since before the birth of Calvin and would not blow after the death of Fazy. In all Europe, not excepting Spain or Italy, one must make one's will at the approach of winter, as men used to do when they set off on a journey from Paris to Marseilles, and must have a thanksgiving service sung to the Iversky Madonna at mid-April.

Let these people tell me that they are not occupied with such vanities, that they have many other things to do, and I would forgive them their smoky chimneys, and the locks which at once open the door and bleed you, and the stench in the passage, and so on; but I ask, what other work have they, what are their higher interests? They have *none*. . . . They only make a display of them to cover the inconceivable emptiness and senselessness of their lives.

In the Middle Ages men lived in the very nastiest way and wasted their efforts on utterly useless edifices which did not add to their comfort. But the Middle Ages did not talk about their passion for comfort; on the contrary, the more comfortless their life, the more nearly it approached their ideal; their luxury took the form of the magnificence of the House of God and of their assembly-hall, and there they were not niggardly, they grudged nothing. The knight in those days built a fortress, not a palace, and did not select for a site the most convenient road, but an inaccessible precipice. Now there is no one to defend oneself against, and nobody believes in saving his soul by adorning the church; the peaceful and orderly citizen has dropped out of the forum and the *Rathhaus*, out of the opposition and the club; passions and fanaticisms, religions and heroisms, have all given way to material prosperity: *and that has not been successfully organised.*

For me there is something melancholy, tragic, in all this, as though the world were living anyhow, in expectation of the earth's giving way under its feet, and were seeking not reconstruction but forgetfulness. I see this not only in the careworn, wrinkled faces, but also in the fear of any serious thinking, in the turning away from any analysis of the position, in the nervous thirst to be busy, to fill up the time with external distractions. The old are ready to play with toys, 'if only to keep from thinking.' The fashionable mustard-plaster is an International Exhibition. The remedy and the disease form a sort of intermittent fever centred first in one part and then in another. All are moving, rushing, flying, spending money, striving, staring and growing weary, living even more uncomfortably in order to keep up with *progress*—in what? Why, just progress. As though in three or four years there can be much progress in anything, as though, when we have railways to travel by, there were any necessity to drag from place to place things like houses, machines, stables, cannon, even perhaps parks and kitchen-gardens.

And when they are sick of exhibitions they will take to war and find distraction in the sheaves of dead—anything to avoid seeing certain *black spots* on the horizon.

2

Chatter on the Road and Fellow-Countrymen in the Buffet

'Is there a seat free for Andermatt?'
'Most likely there will be.'
'In the *cabriolet*?'
'Perhaps; you must come at half-past ten. . . .'
I look at my watch, it is a quarter to three . . . and with a feeling of fury I sit down on a seat in front of the café. Noise, shouting, trunks dragged about, horses

led, horses needlessly stamping on the stones, waiters from the restaurants fighting over travellers, ladies rummaging among the portmanteaus. . . . Clack, clack, our diligence has galloped off; clack, clack, another has galloped after it. . . . The square grows empty, everything has gone away. . . . The heat is deadly, the sunlight is hideously bright, the stones grow whiter; a dog lies down in the middle of the square, but suddenly leaps up with indignation and runs into the shade. The fat landlord sits in his shirt-sleeves before the café, continually dropping asleep. A peasant-woman comes along with fish. 'How much are the fish?' the landlord asks with an expression of intense anger. The woman tells the price. '*Carrogna!*' shouts the landlord. '*Ladro!*' shouts the woman. 'Go along with you, old she-devil.' 'Will you take it, you robber?' 'Well, let me have it for *tre venti* the pound.' 'May you die unshriven!' The landlord takes the fish, the woman takes the money, and their parting is friendly. All their abusive epithets are just an accepted etiquette, like the forms of politeness employed by us.

The dog goes on sleeping, the landlord has taken in the fish and is dozing again, the sun is baking. I can't sit there any longer. I go into the café, take up a sheet of paper and begin writing, not knowing in the least what I am going to write: a description of the mountains and precipices, of the flowering meadows and bare granite rocks—all that is in the guide . . . better talk gossip. . . . Gossip is the repose of conversation, its dessert, its sauce; only idealists and theoretical people do not like gossip. . . . But about whom? Why, of course about the subject nearest to our patriotic heart, our charming fellow-countrymen. There are plenty of them everywhere, especially in good hotels.

It is still just as easy to recognise Russians as it always has been. The zoological features noted long ago have not been effaced, though the number of travellers has been so greatly increased. Russians speak in a loud voice where others speak in a low voice, and do not speak at all where others speak loud. They laugh aloud and tell funny stories in a whisper, they quickly make friends with the waiters and slowly with their neighbours. They eat with their knives. The military people look like Germans, but are distinguished from them by the peculiar insolence of the back of their heads and their original bristling hair; the ladies attract attention by their dress in railway trains and steamers, just as Englishwomen do at *table d'hôte*, and so on.

The lake of Thun has become a tank about which our tourists of the higher sort have settled. The *Fremden List* might have been copied out of a reference book; ministers and grandees, generals of every branch of the service, even of the secret police, are recorded in it. In the hotel-gardens the great *mit Weib und Kind* enjoy nature, and in the hotel dining-room her gifts.

'Did you come by Gemmi or Grimsel?' an Englishwoman will ask her fellow-countrywoman.

'Are you staying at the Jungfraublick or at the Victoria?' a Russian woman will ask her fellow-countrywoman.

'There is the Jungfrau!' says an Englishwoman.

'There is Reytern, the Minister of Finance!' says a Russian.

. . . . .

'Intcinq minutes d'arrêt. . . .'

'Intcinq minutes d'arrêt. . . .'

And every one in the railway carriages hurries into the restaurant and rushes to a table in haste to devour dinner in some twenty minutes, from which the railway authorities will inevitably steal five or six, besides scaring away the appetite with a terrifying bell and shout of '*En voiture!*'

A tall lady in black walked in, together with her husband in light-coloured clothes, and with them two children. . . . A poorly dressed girl with her arms full of bags and parcels walked in with a shy awkward air. She stood a little, then went into a corner and sat down almost beside me. The sharp eye of the waiter detected her; after flying past her with a plate on which lay a slice of roast beef he pounced like a hawk on the poor girl and asked her what she wished to order. 'Nothing,' she answered, and the waiter, summoned by an English clergyman, ran off to him. . . . but a minute later he flew down upon her again, and waving his napkin asked her: 'What was it you ordered?'

The girl muttered something, flushed crimson and stood up. It sent a pang to my heart. I longed to offer her something, but I did not dare.

Before I had made up my mind what to do, the lady in black turned her dark eyes about the room, and seeing the girl, beckoned to her with her finger. She went up, the lady pointed her to the soup that the children had not finished, and she, standing among rows of sitting and astonished travellers, confused and helpless, ate two spoonfuls and put down the plate.

'*Essieurs les voyageurs pour Ucinnungen onction, et tontuyx-en voiture!*'

All rushed with unnecessary haste to their carriages.

I could not refrain from saying to the waiter (not the hawk, another one): 'Did you see?'

'To be sure I did—they are Russians.'

3

Beyond the Alps

The architectural monumental character of the Italian towns together with their neglected condition palls on one at last. In them a modern man feels not at home, but as though in an uncomfortable box at the theatre, with magnificent scenery on the stage.

Life in them has not found its own level, is not simple, and is not convenient. The tone is elevated; in everything there is declamation, and Italian declamation (any one who has heard Dante read aloud knows what it is like). In everything there is the strained intensity which used to be the fashion among Moscow philosophers and German learned artists; everything is looked at from the highest standpoint, *vom höhern Standpunkt.* This artificial strain excludes all *abandon*, and is for ever prepared for controversy and exposition in set phrases. Chronic enthusiasm is exhausting and irritating.

Man does not want to be always admiring, always spiritually elevated; he does not want to have the *Tugenden* always in evidence; he does not want to be touched and carried mentally far back into the past; while Italy will never let him drop below a certain high pitch, but is incessantly reminding him that her street is not simply a street but also a monument, that he may not merely walk through her squares but ought to be studying them.

At the same time everything in Italy, particularly what is beautiful and grand (possibly it is the same everywhere), borders upon insanity and absurdity—or at least is suggestive of childishness . . . The Piazza Signoria is the nursery of the Florentine people; granddad Buonarroti and uncle Cellini presented it with marble and bronze playthings, and it has strewn them about at random in the square where blood has so often been shed and its fate has been decided—without the slightest connection with David or Perseus. . . . There is a town in the water so that pike and perch can wander through the streets . . . there is a town built of stone crevices such as would suit centipedes or lizards to creep and run through—between precipices made up of palaces . . . and then a primaeval wilderness of marble. What brain dared create the outlines of that stone forest called Milan Cathedral, that mountain of stalactites? What brain had the hardihood to carry out that mad architect's dream? . . . And who gave the money for it, the incredible immense sums of money?

People only make sacrifices for what is unnecessary. Their fantastic aims are always the most precious to them, more precious than daily bread, more precious than self-interest. To develop egoism a man must be trained, just as for humane culture. But imagination will carry him away without training, will fill him with enthusiasm without reflection. The ages of faith were the ages of miracles.

A town which is more modern but less historical and decorative is Turin.

'It simply overwhelms one with its prose.'

Yes, but it is easier to live in, just because it is simply a town, a town that exists not only for its own memories but for everyday life, for the present; its streets are not archaeological museums, and do not remind us at every step: *memento mori*; but glance at its working population, at their aspect, keen as the Alpine air, and you will see that they are a sturdier stamp of men than the Florentines or the Venetians, and have perhaps even more staying power than the Genoese.

The latter, however, I do not know. It is very difficult to get a view of them, they are always flitting before one's eyes, bustling and running to and fro in a hurry. There are swarms of people in the lanes leading to the sea, but those who are standing still are not Genoese; they are sailors of every land and ocean — skippers, captains. A bell rings here, a bell rings there: *Parienta!—Partenxa!*—and part of the ant-heap begins scurrying about, some loading, others unloading.

4

Zu Deutsch

It has been raining continuously for three days. I cannot go out and I am not inclined to work. . . . In the bookshop window there are two volumes of Heine's *Correspondence*; here is salvation. I take them and proceed to read them till the sky clears again.

Much water has flowed away since Heine was writing to Moser, Immermann, Varnhagen.

It is a strange thing: since 1848 we have all faltered and stepped back, we have thrown everything overboard and shrunk into ourselves, and yet something has been done and everything has gradually changed. We are nearer to the earth, we stand on a lower, that is a firmer, level, the plough cuts more deeply, our work is not so attractive, it is rougher—perhaps because it really is work. The Don Quixotes of the reaction have burst many of our balloons, the smoky gases have evaporated, the aeronauts have come down, and we no longer float like the spirit of God over the waters with chants and prophetic songs, but catch at the trees, the roofs, and damp Mother Earth.

Where are those days when 'Young Germany' in its spiritual heights theoretically set the Fatherland free, and in the spheres of Pure Reason and Art made an end of the world of tradition and superstition? Heine hated the highly enlightened frosty heights upon which Goethe majestically slumbered in his old age, dreaming the clever but not quite coherent phantasies of the second part of *Faust*. But even Heine never sank below the level of the bookshop, even with him it was still the academic precinct, the literary circle, the journalistic clique with its gossip and its babble, with its bookish

Shylocks in the form of Cotta,[1] Hoffmann,[2] and Campe,[3] with its Göttingen high priests of philology and its bishops of jurisprudence in Halle or Bonn. Neither Heine nor his circle knew the people, and the people did not know them. The sorrows and the joys of the lowly plains did not rise up to those heights; to understand the moan of humanity in the bogs of to-day they had to translate it into Latin and to arrive at their thoughts through the Gracchi and the proletariate of Rome.

The graduates of a *sublimated* world, they sometimes emerged into life, beginning like Faust with the beer-shop and always, like him, with a spirit of scholastic scepticism, which with its reflections hindered them as it did Faust from simply looking and seeing. That is why they immediately hastened back from living sources to the sources of history; there they felt more at home. Their pursuits, it is particularly worth noting, were not only not *work*, but were not *science* either, but, so to speak, erudition, and above all, literature.

Heine at times revolted against the scholastic atmosphere and the passion for analysis, he wanted something different, but his letters are typically German letters of that period, on the first page of which stands Bettina the child and on the last Rahel the Jewess. We breathe

---

[1] One of the members of the great German publishing firm of Cotta, which brought out the works of Schiller, Goethe, Herder, Fichte, Schelling, the Humboldts, etc., is meant. One of them was responsible for the. *Allgemeine Zeitung*, which first appeared in 1798, and he was also the first Würtemberg landowner to abolish serfdom on his estates.

[2] Hoffmann, A. H. (commonly called Hoffmann von Fallersleben), the poet and author of many philological and antiquarian works, is no doubt referred to here, not the better-known musical composer and story-writer of that name.

[3] Campe, J. H., was the author of works on education, a German dictionary, and numerous stories for children, of which *Robinson der Jüngere* was the most popular.—(*Translator's Notes.*)

more freely when we meet in his letters passionate outbursts of Judaism, then Heine is genuinely carried away; but he quickly lost his warmth and turned cold to Judaism, and was angry with it for his own by no means disinterested faithlessness.

The revolution of 1830 and Heine's moving afterwards to Paris did much for his progress. *Der Pan ist gestorben!* he says with enthusiasm, and hastens to the city to which I once hastened with the same feverish eagerness—to Paris; he wanted to see the 'great people' and 'grey-headed Lafayette' riding about on his grey horse. But literature soon gets the upper hand again; his letters are filled in and out with literary gossip, personalities, interspersed with complaints of destiny, of health, of nerves, of depressed spirits, through which an immense revolting vanity is apparent. And then Heine takes a false note. His coldly inflated rhetorical Buonapartism grows as detestable as the squeamish horror of the well-washed Hamburg Jew at the tribunes of the people when he meets them not in books but in real life. He could not stomach the fact that the workmen's meetings were not staged in the frigidly decorous setting of the study and salon of Varnhagen, 'the fine-china' Varnhagen von Ense, as he himself calls him.

His feeling of personal dignity, however, did not go beyond having clean hands and being free from the smell of tobacco. It is hard to blame him for that. That feeling is not a German nor a Jewish one, and unhappily not a Russian one either.

Heine coquettes with the Prussian Government, seeks its favour through the ambassador and through Varnhagen, and then abuses it.[1] He coquetted with the

[1] Did not the *kept* genius of the Prussian King do the same? His double personality drew down a biting sarcasm. After 1848 the Hanoverian King, an ultra-conservative and feudalist, arrived in

King of Bavaria and pelted him with sarcasms; he more than coquetted with the German Diet, and tried to atone for his abject behaviour with biting taunts.

Does not all this explain why the scholastically revolutionary flare-up in Germany so quickly came to grief in 1848? It too was merely a literary effort, and it vanished like a rocket: its leaders were professors and its generals came from the Faculty of Philology; its rank and file in high boots and *bérets* were students who deserted the revolutionary cause as soon as it passed from metaphysical audacity and literary recklessness into the market-place. Apart from a few stray workmen, the people did not follow these pale *Führer*, they simply held aloof from them.

'How can you put up with all Bismarck's insults?' I asked a year before the war of a deputy of the Left from Berlin at the time when the former was practising violent methods, and more successfully than Grabow and Company.

'We have done everything we could, *innerhalb* the constitution.'

'Well, then, you should follow the example of the Government and try *ausserhalb*.'

'How do you mean? Make an appeal to the people, stop paying taxes? . . . That's a dream. . . . Not a single man would follow us or would make a move to support us. . . . And we should only provide a fresh triumph for Bismarck by ourselves proving our weakness.'

'Well, then, I can only say like your President at every fresh blow: "Shout three times *Es lebe der König* and go home peaceably!"'

Potsdam. On the palace staircase he met various courtiers, and among them Humboldt in a livery dress-coat. The malicious king stopped and said to him, smiling: '*Immer derselbe, immer Republikaner und immer im Vorzimmer des'Palastes.*'—(*Author's Note*.)

5

This World and the Other

I

THE OTHER WORLD

. . . Villa Adolphina . . . Adolphina? . . . Villa Adolphina, *grands et petits appartements*, *jardin*, *vue sur la mer*. . . .

I go in. Everything is clean and nice; there are trees and flowers in the garden, and English children, fat, soft and rosy, who make you hope from the bottom of your heart that they will never meet with cannibals. An old woman comes out, and after asking what I have come for, begins a conversation by telling me that she is not a servant, but 'more like a friend,' that Madame Adolphine has gone to a hospital, or almshouse, of which she is a patroness. Then she takes me to see 'an exceptionally convenient apartment' which this season for the first time is unoccupied, and which two Americans and a Russian princess had been only that morning to look at—for which reason the old woman who was 'more a friend than a servant' sincerely advised me not to lose time. Thanking her for this sudden sympathy and solicitude on my behalf, I asked her the question: '*Sie sind eine Deutsche?*'

'*Zu Diensten, und der gnädige Herr?*'

'*Ein Russe.*'

'*Das freut mich zu sehr. Ich wohnte so lange, so lange* in Petersburg. I must say I believe there is no other town like it and never will be.'

'It is very pleasant to hear that. Is it long since you left Petersburg?'

'Yes, it is not yesterday; why, we have been living here twenty years. I have been a friend of Madame

Adolphine from my childhood, and so I never wanted to leave her. She does not care much for housekeeping; everything is at sixes and sevens in her house with no one to look after it. When *meine Gönnerin* bought this little *Paradise* she sent for me at once from *Braunschweig*.'

'And where did you live in Petersburg?' I asked.

'Oh, we lived in the very best part of the town, where the *Laute Herrschaften und Generäle* live. How many times I have seen the late Tsar driving by in a carriage or a one-horse sledge *so ernst*. . . . He was a real potentate, one may say.'

'Did you live on the Nevsky or in Morsky Street?'

'Yes; that is, not quite on the Nevsky, but close by, at the *Polizei-brücke*.'

'Enough . . . enough, I might have known,' I thought, and I asked the old woman to say that I would come to discuss terms with Madame Adolphine herself. I could never without a peculiar tenderness meet the relics of old days, the half-ruined monuments from the temple of Vesta or some other god, it does not matter. . . . The old woman who was 'more like a friend' escorted me across the garden to the gate.

'Here is our neighbour, he too lived for years in Petersburg. . . .' She pointed to a big, smartly decorated house, inscribed this time in English: 'Large and small Apartments, Furnished or Unfurnished. . . .' 'No doubt you remember Floriani? He was the *coiffeur de la cour* near Millionnaya Street; he was mixed up in a very unpleasant affair . . . he was prosecuted and almost sent to Siberia . . . you know, for being too indulgent, there were such severe measures.'

'Well,' I thought, 'she will certainly exalt Floriani into being my "comrade in misfortune"!'

'Yes, yes, now I vaguely remember the story; the Procurator of the Holy Synod and other divines and officers in the Guards had a hand in it. . . .'

'Here he comes.'

A little dried-up, toothless old man in a small straw hat like a sailor's or a child's, with a blue ribbon round the crown, a short, light pea-green overcoat and striped breeches, came out to the gate. He raised his dull, lifeless eyes, and munching with his thin lips, nodded to the old lady.

'Would you like me to call him?'

'No, thank you very much. . . . I am not in that line—you see, I don't shave my beard. . . . Good-bye. And tell me, please, am I mistaken or not, has M. Floriani a red ribbon?'

'Yes, yes, he has subscribed largely to charities!'

'A very good heart, no doubt.'

In classical times writers were fond of bringing back into this world the shades of the dead, that they might have a chat about this and that. In our realistic age everything is on the earth, and even part of the other world is in *this* world. The Champs-Élysées extend to the shores and strands of Elysium, and are scattered here and there by warm or sulphurous springs at the foot of mountains or the borders of lakes; they are sold in acres or laid out into vineyards. . . . Part of a man who has died to the life of excitement and agitation is here passing through the first course of the transmigration of souls and the preparatory class of Purgatory.

Every man who has lived for fifty years has buried a whole world or even two; he has grown used to its disappearance and accustomed to the new scenery of another act: but suddenly the names and faces of times long dead appear more frequently on his way, calling up series of shadows and pictures kept somewhere in readiness in the endless catacombs of the memory, making him smile or sigh, and sometimes almost weep. . . .

Those who like Faust want to see 'the mothers,' and even 'the fathers,' need no Mephistopheles; it is enough to take a railway ticket and travel to the South. By the time Cannes and Grasse are reached, shades of days long fled stray about, warming themselves in the sun; quietly huddled up, close to the sea, they wait for Charon and their turn.

On the way to this *Città*, which is not so very *dolente*, the tall, bent and majestic figure of Lord Brougham stands as keeper of the gate. After a long and honourable life spent in useless toil, he seems, with one grey eyebrow lower than the other, like the living embodiment of part of Dante's inscription: '*Voi che'ntrate*,' with the idea of correcting old-standing historical evils by amateurish means, '*lasciate ogni speranza.*' Old Brougham, the best of the ancients, the defender of the luckless Queen Caroline, the friend of Robert Owen, the contemporary of Canning and Byron, the last unwritten volume of Macaulay, built his villa between Grasse and Cannes, and he did well to do so. Who, if not he, should be put as a conciliatory signboard at the portal of the temporary purgatory to avoid scaring away the living?

Here we are *en plein* in the world of the tenors, now silent, that set our bosoms quivering at eighteen—thirty years ago; of the feet which set our hearts and the hearts of the whole parterre melting and thrilling, feet now ending their career in down-trodden, home-knitted slippers, that go flopping after the servant-girl from aimless jealousy or from very justifiable niggardliness.

And all this, with a few intervals, goes on right up to the Adriatic, to the shores of Lake Como, and even to some German watering-places. Here is the Villa Taglioni, there is the Palazzo Rubini, there the Campagne Fanny Elsner and others. . . . *du prétérit-défini et du plus-que-parfait*.

Beside the actors retired from the small stage of the theatre, the actors of the greatest stages of the world, whose names have long ago been cut out of the playbills and forgotten, live out their days in peace as followers of Cincinnatus and philosophers against their will. Side by side with artists who have once magnificently played the parts of kings are met kings who have played their parts very poorly. Like the dead in India who take their wives to the other world with them, these kings have carried off two or three devoted ministers who zealously helped to bring about their downfall and have themselves come to grief with them. Among them are crowned heads who were hissed at their début and are still expecting that the public will return to a juster sense of values and call them on again. There are others whom the impresarios of the theatre of history have not permitted even to make their début—the stillborn who have a yesterday but no to-day; their biography ended on their appearance in the world; the Aztecs of a long-abolished law of royal inheritance, they remain the moving monuments of extinguished dynasties.

Then come the generals, famous for the victories they have lost; subtle diplomats, who have wrecked their countries; gamblers who have wrecked their fortunes; and grey-headed, wrinkled old women who in their day wrecked the hearts of these diplomats and gamblers. Political fossils, still taking their pinch of snuff, as once they took it at Pozzo di Borgo's,[1] Lord Aberdeen's, and Princess Esterhazy's, discuss with extinct beauties of the days of Madame Récamier reminiscences of the salon of Princess Lieven, the youth of Lablache, the débuts of Malibran, and wonder that Patti dare sing after them . . . and at the same time gentlemen of the green cloth, hobbling and limping, half-crippled with paralysis, half-drowned in dropsy, talk with other old ladies of

[1] Pozzo di Borgo, C. A. (1764-1842), a Corsican, was a diplomat in the Russian service and a privy councillor of Alexander 1.—(*Translator's Note*.)

other salons and other celebrities, of reckless stakes, of Countess Kisselyov, of roulette at Homburg and at Baden, of the late Suhozanet's[1] play, of the patriarchal days when the hereditary princes of the German Spas were partners with the keepers of the gambling-halls and exchanged the risky mediaeval plundering of travellers for the peaceful practice of the bank and *rouge et noir*.

And all this world is still breathing, still moving; some lie crippled in a bath-chair or a carriage under a fur rug, others lean on a servant by way of a crutch, or sometimes on a crutch for lack of a servant. The visitors 'lists are like old-fashioned directories or bits of torn newspapers' of the days of Navarino and the Conquest of Algiers.'

Besides the smouldering stars of the three first magnitudes there are other comets and luminaries with which thirty years ago idle and greedy curiosity was very busy, thanks to the peculiar bloodthirsty lust which prompts men to watch the trials that lead from the murdered victim to the guillotine, and from heaps of gold to hard labour. Among them there are all manner of criminals acquitted for lack of proof, poisoners, coiners, as well as men who have completed their course of moral regeneration in some central prison or penal colony, '*contumaces*' and so on.

The shades least often met with in these warm purgatories are those of survivors from the revolutionary storms and unsuccessful rebellions. The gloomy and embittered Montagnards of the Jacobin heights prefer the austere *bise*, or like stern Spartans hide in the fogs of London....

---

[1] Suhozanet, a Russian general under Alexander 1. and Nicholas. He took a prominent part in the suppression of the Fourteenth of December 1825.—(*Translator's Note*.)

II

THIS WORLD

A. *Living Flowers—The Last of the Mohicans*

'Let us go to the *Bal de l'Opéra*; now is just the right time, half-past one,' I said, getting up from the table in a little room of the Café Anglais, to a Russian artist who was always coughing and never quite sober. I had a longing for the open air and bustle. And besides, I dreaded a long *tête-à-tête* with my Claude Lorraine from the Neva.

'Let us go,' he said, and poured out another glass of brandy.

This was at the beginning of 1849, at that moment of delusive convalescence between two bouts of sickness when one still sometimes thought that one wanted to play the fool and be merry.

Strolling about the opera-hall, we stopped before a particularly pretty quadrille of powdered *débardeurs* and pierrots with chalked faces. All the four girls were very young, eighteen or nineteen, charming and graceful, dancing and enjoying themselves with all their hearts, and unconsciously passing from the quadrille to the *cancan*. We had hardly admired it enough when suddenly the quadrille was disturbed 'owing to circumstances in no way connected with the dancers,' as our journalists used to express it in the happy days of the censorship. One of the dancing girls, and alas! the handsomest, so skilfully, or so unskilfully, dropped her shoulder that her shift slipped down, displaying half her bosom and part of her back—a little more than is done by elderly Englishwomen (who have nothing with which they can attract except their shoulders) at the most decorous receptions and in the most conspicuous

LIVING FLOWERS

boxes at Covent Garden. (So that it is absolutely impossible in the second tier to listen to *Casta Diva* or *Sul Salice* with befitting modesty.) I had scarcely had time to say to the chilled artist: 'If only Michael Angelo or Titian were here! Seize your brush or she will pull it up again,' when an immense black hand, not that of Michael Angelo nor Titian, but of a *gardien de Paris*, seized her by the collar, tore her away from the quadrille, and dragged her off. The girl would not go, and struggled as children do when they are to be washed in cold water, but order and human justice gained the upper hand and were satisfied. The other girls and their pierrots exchanged glances, found a fresh *débardeur*, and began again kicking above their heads and darting apart from each other in order to rush together with the more fury, taking scarcely any notice of the rape of Proserpine. 'Let us go and see what the policeman does to her,' I said to my companion. I noticed the door through which he had led her.

We went down by a side-staircase. Any one who has seen and remembers a certain dog in bronze looking attentively and with some excitement at a tortoise can easily picture the scene which we came upon. The luckless girl in her light attire was sitting on a stone step in the piercing wind in floods of tears; facing her stood a dry, tall *municipal* in full uniform with a predatory and earnestly stupid expression, with a comma of hair on his chin and half-grey moustaches.

He was standing in a dignified attitude with folded arms, looking intently for the end of these tears and urging: '*Allons, allons.*'

To complete the effect, the girl, whimpering, was saying through her tears: '. . . *Et . . . et on dit . . . on dit que . . . que . . . nous sommes en République . . . et . . . on ne peut dans er com me l'on veut! . . .*'

All this was so absurd, and in reality so pathetic, that

I resolved to go to the rescue of the captive and to the restoration in her eyes of the republican form of government.

'*Mon brave*,' I said with calculated and insinuating courtesy to the policeman, 'what will you do with mademoiselle?'

'I shall put her *au violon* till to-morrow,' he answered grimly. The wails were redoubled. 'To teach her to take off her shift,' added the guardian of order and of public morality.

'It was an accident, *brigadier*, you should pardon her.'

'I can't. *La consigne* . . .'

'After all, at a fête . . .'

'But what is it to do with you? *Êtes-vous son réciproque?*'

'It is the first time I have seen her in my life, *parole d'honneur*. I don't know her name, ask her yourself. We are foreigners, and are surprised to see you in Paris so stern with a weak girl, *avec un être frêle*. We always thought the police here were so kind. . . . How is it that they are allowed to dance the *cancan*, for if they are allowed, *monsieur le brigadier*, sometimes without meaning it a foot will be kicked too high or a blouse will slip too low.'

'That may be so,' the *municipal* observed, impressed by my eloquence, and still more stung by my observation that foreigners have such a flattering opinion of the Parisian police.

'Besides,' I said, 'look what you are doing. You are giving her a cold—how can you bring the child, half-naked, out of the heated room and sit her down in the biting wind?'

'It is her own fault, she won't come. But there, I'll tell you what: if you will give me your word of honour that she shan't go back into the dancing-room to-night, I'll let her off.'

'Bravo! Though, indeed, I expected no less of you, *monsieur le brigadier*, I thank you with all my heart.'

I had now to enter into negotiations with the rescued victim. 'Excuse me for interfering on your behalf without having the pleasure of being personally acquainted with you.' She held out a warm, moist little hand to me and looked at me with still moister and warmer eyes. 'You heard what was said? I can't answer for you if you won't give me your word, or better still if you won't come away at once. It is not a great sacrifice really; I expect it is half-past three by now.'

'I am ready. I'll go and get my cloak.'

'No,' said the implacable guardian of order, 'not a step from here.'

'Where is your cloak and hat?' 'In *loge* so-and-so, row so-and-so.' The artist was rushing off, but he stopped to ask: 'But will they give them to me?'

'Only tell them what has happened and that you come from "Little Leontine." . . . Here's a ball!' she added with the expression with which people say in a graveyard: 'Sleep in peace.'

'Would you like me to take a *fiacre?*'

'I am not alone.'

'With whom then?'

'With a friend.'

The artist returned, his cold worse than ever, with a hat and cloak, and a young shopman or *commis-voyageur*.

'Very much obliged,' he said to me, touching his hat, then to her: 'Always making scandals!' He seized her by the arm almost as roughly as the policeman had by the collar, and vanished into the big vestibule of the Opéra. . . . Poor girl . . . she will catch it . . . and what taste . . . she . . . and he!

I felt positively vexed. I suggested to the artist a drink. He did not refuse.

A month passed. Six of us, the Vienna agitator Tauzenau, General Haug, Müller, S., and another, agreed to go once more to a ball. Neither Haug nor Müller had ever been to one. We stood together in a group. All at once a masked figure pressed forward through the crowd straight up to me, almost threw herself on my neck, and said to me: 'I had not time to thank you then.'

'Ah, Mademoiselle Leontine . . . delighted to meet you. I can see before me now your tear-stained face, your pouting lips—you were awfully charming—that does not mean that you are not charming now.' The sly little rogue looked at me, smiling, knowing quite well that that was true.

'Didn't you catch cold then?'

'Not a bit.'

'In memory of your captivity, you ought, if you would be very, very kind . . .'

'Well what? *Soyez bref.*'

'You might have supper with us.'

'With pleasure, *ma parole*, only not now.'

'Where shall I find you then?'

'Don't trouble. I'll come and find you myself at four o'clock; but I say, I am not alone here. . . .'

'With your friend again . . .?' and a shiver ran down my back.

She burst out laughing. 'Not a very dangerous one,' and she led up to me a fair-haired, blue-eyed girl of seventeen. 'This is my friend.'

I invited her too.

At four o'clock Leontine ran up, gave me her hand, and we set off to the Café Riche. Though that is not far from the Opera House, yet Haug had time on the way to fell in love with the Madonna of Andrea del Sarto, that is, the fair girl. And at the first course, after long and curious sentences concerning the Tintoretto charm of her hair and eyes, Haug began discoursing on the aesthetic sin of dancing the *cancan* with the face of a madonna and the expression of an angel of purity. '*Armes, holdes Kind!*' he added, addressing us all.

'Why is it your friend talks such boring *fatras?*' Leontine whispered in my ear, 'and why does he go to fancy-dress balls at all—he'd better go to the Madeleine?'

'He is a German, they all suffer from that complaint,' I whispered to her.

'*Mais c'est qu'il est ennuyeux, votre ami avec son mal de sermon. Mon petit saint, finiras-tu donc bientôt?*'

And while waiting for the sermon to end, Leontine, tired out, flung herself on the sofa. Facing her was a big looking-glass; she kept looking in it, and at last could not refrain from pointing to herself and saying to me: 'Why, with my hair so untidy and in this crumpled dress and this position, I really don't look bad.'

When she had said it, she suddenly dropped her eyes and blushed—blushed openly up to her ears. To cover her confusion she began humming the well-known song which Heine has distorted in his translation, and which is terrible in its artless simplicity:—

> '*Et je mourrai dans mon hôtel,*
> *Ou à l'Hôtel-Dieu.*'

A strange creature, elusive, full of life; the 'Lacerta' of Goethe's Elegies, a child in a sort of unconscious delirium. Like a lizard, she could not sit still for a single instant, and she could not keep silent either. When she had nothing to say, she was singing, making grimaces before the looking-glass, and all with the unconstraint of a child and the grace of a woman. Her *frivolité* was naïve. Carded away by chance, she was still whirling round, still floating. . . . The shock which would have stopped her on the edge or finally thrust her over the precipice had not yet come. She had gone a good bit of the road but could still turn back. Her clear intelligence and innate grace were still strong enough to save her.

Her type, her circle, her surroundings, exist no longer. She was '*la petite femme*' of the student of old days, the *grisette* who passed from the Latin Quartier to this side of the Seine without sinking to the level of the streetwalker nor rising to the secure social position of the Camélia. That type has passed away, just as conversations by the fireside, reading aloud at a round table, chatting over tea have gone. There are other forms, other notes, other people, other words. . . . This too has its own scale, its own *crescendo*. The mischievous, rather abandoned element of the'thirties—*du lest, de l'espièglerie*—passed into *chic*; there was cayenne pepper in it, but it still retained a careless exuberant grace, it still retained wit and cleverness. As things began to be done on a larger scale, commerce cast off everything superfluous, and sacrificed everything spiritual to the shop-front, the *étalage*. The type of Leontine, the lively Parisian *gamine*, mobile, clever, spoilt, sparkling, free, and on occasion proud, is not wanted, and *chic* has passed into *chienne*. What the Lovelace of the boulevards wants is the woman-*chienne*, and above all, one who has her master. It is more economical and disinterested: with another man running the show, he can get his sport by simply paying the extras. '*Parbleu*,' an old man whose best years had been at the beginning of Louis-Philippe's reign said to me, '*je ne me retrouve plus—où est le fion*,[1] *le chic, où est l'esprit? . . . Tout cela est beau*, well-bred, *mats . . . c'est de la charcuterie . . . c'est du Rubens.*'

That reminds me how in the'fifties dear good Talan-

[1] 'Fion' is a colloquial word about equivalent to 'esprit.'— (*Translator's Note.*)

dier, with the vexation of a man in love with his France, explained to me with a musical illustration its downfall. 'When,' he said to me, 'we were great, in the early days after the revolution of February, nothing was heard but the Marseillaise—in the cafés, in the street-processions, always the Marseillaise. Every theatre had its Marseillaise, here with cannon, there with Rachel. When things grew duller and quieter, the monotonous sounds of *Mourir pour la Patrie* took its place. That was no harm yet, but we sank lower. . . . *Un sous-lieutenant accablé de besogne* . . . *drin, drin, din, din, din* . . . the whole city, the capital of the world, the whole of France was singing that silly thing. That is not the end; after that, we began playing and singing *Partant pour la Syrie* at the top and *Qu'aime done Margot* . . . *Margot* at the bottom: that is, senselessness and indecency. One can sink no lower.'

One can! Talandier did not foresee either *Je suis la femme a barbe* or *The Sapper*; he stopped short at *chic* and never reached the *chienne* stage. Hurried carnal corruption superseded all embellishments. The body conquered the spirit, and, as I said ten years ago, *Margot, la fille de marbre*, crowded out Béranger's Lisette and all Leon the Leontines in the world. The latter had their humanity, their poetry, their ideas of honour. They loved uproar and spectacles better than wine and supper, and they loved their supper more for the sake of the surroundings, the candles, the sweets, the flowers. They could not exist without dancing and balls, without laughter and chatter. In the most luxurious harem they would have been stifled, would have pined away in a year. Their finest representative was Déjazet— both on the great stage of the world and the little one of the *Théâtre des Variétés*. She was the living embodiment of a song of Béranger, a saying of Voltaire, and was young at forty—Déjazet, who changed her adorers like a guard of honour, capriciously flung away gold by the handful, and gave herself to the first-comer to get a friend out of trouble.

Nowadays it is all simplified, curtailed. One gets there sooner, as old-fashioned country gentlemen used to say who preferred vodka to wine. The woman of *fion* intrigued and interested, the woman of *chic* stung and amused, and both, apart from money, took up time. The *chienne* pounces straight away upon her victim, bites with her beauty, and pulls him by the coat *sans phrase*; in this there is no preface, in this the epilogue comes at the beginning. Thanks to a paternal Government and the medical faculty, even the two dangers of the past are gone; police and medicine have made great advances of late years.

And what will come after the *chienne?* Hugo's pieuvre has completely failed, perhaps because it is too much like a *pleutre*. And yet we cannot stop at the *chienne*.

However, let us leave prophesying. The designs of providence are unfathomable.

What interests me is something else.

Which of the two prophecies of Cassandra will come true for Leontine? Is her once graceful little head resting on a lace-trimmed pillow in *her own hotel*, or has it been laid on the rough hospital-bolster to fall asleep for ever, or awaken to poverty and sorrow? Though maybe neither the one fate nor the other is hers, and she is busy getting her daughter married or saving money to buy a recruit to replace her son in the army. She is no longer young now, and must be long past the'thirties.

B. *Garden Flowers*

In *our Russian Europe* everything done in *European Europe* has been repeated on a smaller scale as to quantity and on a greater or distorted scale as to quality.

We have had our Orthodox ultra-catholics, our titled liberal-bourgeois, our imperial Royalists, our democrat-officials, our Preobrazhensky Buonapartist horseguards and lifeguards. It is no wonder that among the ladies too we have not escaped our *chic* and *chienne* types: with this difference, that our *demi-monde* was a whole world and a little over.

Our Traviatas and Camélias, for the most part titular, that is honorary ones, grow on quite a different soil and flourish in different spheres from their Parisian prototypes. They must be sought, not in the valley but on the heights; they do not rise up like mist, but drop like dew from above. The Princess Camélia or the Traviata with an estate in the province of Tambov or Voronezh is a purely Russian phenomenon, and I think there is a good deal to be said for it.

As for our non-European Russia, its morals have been to a great extent saved by serfdom, which is now so much maligned. Love was a melancholy thing in the village; it called its sweetheart 'my heart's yearning,' as though feeling that it was stolen from the master, who might at any time miss his property and take it back. The village furnished the master's house with wood, hay, sheep, and its daughters, as part of its duties. It was a consecrated duty, the Crown service which could not be refused without a crime against morality and religion, which would provoke the landowner's rod and the knout of the whole empire. Here it was no question of *chic*, but sometimes of the axe, more often of the river, in which a Palashka or Lushka perished unnoticed.

What has happened since the Emancipation we hardly know, and therefore we cling the more to our ladies. They certainly do in masterly style and with extraordinary rapidity and adroitness assimilate abroad all the ways, all the *habitus* of the *lorettes*. It is only on careful scrutiny that it can be discerned that something is lacking. And what is lacking is the very simplest thing—being a *lorette*. It is just like Peter the Great working with hammer and mallet at Saardam, fancying he was doing real work. From cleverness and idleness, from superfluity and boredom, our ladies *play* at the trade, as their husbands play with a carpenter's lathe.

This absence of necessity, this character of artificiality, changes the whole thing. On the Russian side there is the feeling of a superb *mise-en-scène*; on the French, of reality and inevitability. Hence the vast differences. One is often genuinely sorry for the Traviata *tout de bon*, for the *dame aux perles* hardly ever; over the first one sometimes wants to weep, at the other always to laugh. A woman who has inherited two or three thousand souls of peasants, at first perpetually but now only temporarily ruined, can do a great deal—intrigue at the gambling Spas, dress eccentrically, loll in a carriage, whistle and make a row, get up scenes in restaurants, make men blush, change her lovers, go with them to *parties fines* and to all sorts of 'calisthenic exercises and conversations,' drink champagne, smoke Havana cigars, and stake pots of gold on the *rouge et noir*. . . . She can be a Messalina and a Catherine—but, as we have said already, she cannot be a *lorette*, although *lorettes* are not, like poets, born, but made. Every *lorette* has her story, her initiation induced by circumstances. As a rule, the poor girl drifts, not knowing whither, and is brought low by coarse deception, coarse ill-treatment. From outraged love, from outraged shame, she develops *dépit*, resentment, a sort of thirst of vengeance and at the same time a craving for excitement, for gaiety, for dress—with poverty all about her and money only to be gained in *one* way, and so *vogue la galére*. The deceived child with no training steps into the fray; her triumphs spoil her, spur her on (of those who have had no triumphs we know nothing, they are lost and never heard of); she remembers her Marengo and her Arcole; the habit of domination and of luxury is absorbed into her blood; she owes everything to herself alone. Beginning with nothing but her body, she too acquires 'souls,' and she too ruins the rich men who are temporarily devoted to her, as our great ladies ruin their poor peasants.

But in that also lies the whole impassable gulf between the *lorette* by profession and the amateur Camélia. That gulf and that opposition are vividly expressed in the fact that the *lorette*, supping in some stuffy room of the Maison d'Or, dreams of her future drawing-room, while the Russian lady, sitting in her sumptuous drawing-room, dreams of the restaurant.

The serious side of the question is to determine what has given rise in our ladies to this craving for dissipation and debauchery, this need to brag of their emancipation, to trample insolently, capriciously, on public opinion, and to fling off every veil and mask, while the chaste and patriarchal mothers and grandmothers of our lionesses blushed till they were forty at an indiscreet word, and with stealthy modesty contented themselves with a lover like the one in Turgenev's *The Bread of Others*, or, lacking him, a coachman or a butler.

Note that our aristocratic Camélias go no further back than the beginning of the'forties.

And all the modern movement, all the stirring of thought, the groping, the dissatisfaction, the discontent, date from the same period.

Therein lies revealed the human, the historical aspect of our aristocratic ladies' debauchery. It is a half-conscious protest of a sort against the old-fashioned family that weighed upon them like lead, against the brutal debauchery of the men. The oppressed woman, the woman deserted at home, had leisure for reading, and as soon as she felt that the family maxims were incongruous with George Sand, and had heard too many enthusiastic descriptions of Blanches and Célestines, her patience broke down, and she took the bit between her teeth. Her protest was savage, but her position too was savage.

Her opposition was not clearly formulated, but was vague and instinctive; she felt outraged, she was conscious of being humiliated, of being oppressed, but had no conception of independent freedom apart from debauchery and dissipation. She protested by her behaviour: her revolt was full of self-indulgence and bad manners, of caprice, of sloppiness, of coquetry, sometimes of injustice; she was unbridled without becoming free. She retained a secret fear and diffidence, but longed to show her resentment and to try *that other* life. Against the narrow self-will of the oppressors she set the narrow self-will of patience strained till it snapped, with no firm guiding idea but the conceited bravado of youth. Like a rocket she flared up, went off into sparks and fell with a splash, but not very deep. There you have the history of our titled Camélias, our Traviatas in pearls.

Of course, in this case too we may recall the bilious Rastoptchin, who on his death-bed said of the tragedy of the Fourteenth of December: 'Everything is inside out with us: in France *la roture* tried to climb into the nobility—well, that one can understand; our nobility tried to become *canaille*, and that's silly!'

But it is just that side of it which to us does not seem silly at all. It follows very consistently from two primary facts: the alien character of the culture which is for us not inevitable, and the fundamental note of another social order to which consciously or unconsciously we are striving.

However, that forms part of our catechism, and I am afraid of being drawn into repetition.

In the history of our development our Traviatas will not disappear without a trace; they have their value and significance, and form the bold and reckless legion of the advance guard, the volunteers and singers, who, whistling and striking their tambourines, dancing and showing off, go first to face the fire, screening the more serious phalanx who have no lack of thought nor daring nor of sharpened weapons.

III

THE FLOWERS OF MINERVA

This phalanx is the revolution in person, austere at seventeen . . . the fire of her eyes subdued by spectacles that the light of the mind may shine more brightly; *sans-crinolines* advancing to replace *sans-culottes*.

The girl-student and the young-lady-*bursche* have nothing in common with the Traviata ladies. The Bacchantes have grown grey or bald, have grown old and retired, while the students have taken their place before they are out of their teens. The Camélias and the Traviatas of the salons belonged to the Nicholas period. They were like the parade-generals of the same period, the dandy martinets whose victories were won over their own soldiers, who knew every detail of military *toilette*, all the glitter of the parade, and never soiled their uniforms with the blood of an enemy. The courtesan-generals, jauntily 'street-walking' on the Nevsky, were crushed at once by the Crimean War; while 'the intoxicating glamour of the ball,' the love-making of the boudoir, and the noisy orgies of the generals' ladies, were abruptly replaced by the academic hall and the dissecting-room, where the cropped student in spectacles studied the mysteries of nature. Then all the camélias and magnolias had to be forgotten, it had to be forgotten that there were two sexes. Before the truths of science, *im Reiche der Wahrheit*, distinctions of sex are effaced.

Our Camélias stood for the Gironde, that is why there is such a flavour of Faublas about them.

Our student-girls are the Jacobins, Saint-Just in a riding-habit—everything sharp-cut, pure, ruthless. Our Camélia wore a *masque*, a *loup* from warm Venice.

Our students wear a mask too, but it is a mask of Neva ice. The first may stick on, but the second will certainly melt away; that, however, is in the future.

This is a real, conscious protest, a protest and dividing line. *Ce n'est pas une émeute, c'est une révolution*. Dissipation, luxury, persiflage and dress are shoved aside. Love, passion, are in the far background. Aphrodite with her naked archer sulks and withdraws, Pallas Athene takes her place with her spear and her owl. The Camélias were impelled by vague emotion, indignation, unsatisfied voluptuous desire. . . and they went on till they reached satiety. In this case they are impelled by an idea in which they believe, by the declaration of 'the rights of woman,' and they are fulfilling a duty laid upon them by their faith. Some abandon themselves on principle, others are unfaithful from a sense of duty. Sometimes these students go too far, but they always remain children—disobedient, conceited, but children. The gravity of their radicalism shows that it is a matter of the head, not of the heart. They are passionate in relation to what is universal, and show no more 'pathos' (as they used to call it in old days) in individual encounters than any Leontine. Perhaps less. The Leontines played, they played with fire, and very often, ablaze from head to foot, saved themselves in the Seine; seduced by life before they had developed any prudence, it was sometimes hard for them to conquer their hearts. Our students begin with criticism, with analysis; a great deal may happen to them too, but there will be no surprises, no downfalls; they fall with a parachute of theory in their hands. They fling themselves into the stream with a handbook on swimming, and intentionally swim against the current. Whether they will swim long *à livre ouvert* I do not know, but they will certainly take their place in history, and will deserve to do so.

The most short-sighted people in the world have guessed as much.

Our old gentlemen, senators and ministers, the fathers and grandfathers of their country, looked with a smile of indulgence and even encouragement at the aristocratic Camélias (so long as they were not their sons 'wives). . . . But they did not like the students . . . so utterly different from the' charming rogues' with whom they had at one time liked to warm in words their old hearts.

For a long time the old gentlemen were angry with the austere Nihilist girls and sought an opportunity of dealing with them as they deserved.

And then, as though of design, Karakozov fired his pistol-shot. . . . 'There it is, your Majesty,' they began to whisper, 'that is what dressing not according to set rule . . . these spectacles and shock-heads, come to.' 'What? not according to set rule?' says the Tsar. 'We must take sterner measures.' 'Slackness, slackness, your Majesty! We have only been waiting for your gracious permission to save the sacred person of your Majesty.'

It was no jesting matter; all set to work in earnest. The Privy Council, the Senate, the Synod, the ministers, the bishops, the military commanders, the police-captains and gendarmes of all sorts, took counsel together, talked and deliberated, and decided in the first place to turn students of the female sex out of the universities altogether. Meanwhile, one of the bishops, fearing deception, recalled how in the time of the false Catholic Church a Pope Anna had been elected to the papacy, and offered his monks as inspectors . . . since there is no bodily shame before the eyes of the dead. The living did not accept his suggestion: the generals for their part supposed that such expert's duties could only be entrusted to an official of the highest rank placed beyond temptation by his rank and his monarch's confidence; the military department wanted to offer the post to Adlerberg the Elder; while the civilians preferred Butkov. But this did not take place—it is said because the Grand Dukes were anxious to secure the job.

Then the Privy Council, the Synod and the Senate ordered that within twenty-four hours the girls were to grow their cropped hair, to remove their spectacles, and to be forced to have good sight and to wear crinolines. And in spite of the fact that in the Book of Heavenly Wisdom there is nothing said about 'distension of skirts' or widening of petticoats, while the plaiting of hair is positively forbidden in it, the clergy assented. For the first time the Tsar's life seemed secure till he reached the Elysian Fields. It was not their fault that in Paris also there were Champs-Élysées, and with an accent on them too.

These extreme measures were of enormous benefit, and this I say without the slightest irony, but to whom? To our Nihilist girls.

The one thing that they lacked was to fling off their uniform, their formalism, and to develop in that broad freedom to which they have the fullest claim. It is terribly hard for one used to a uniform to cast it off of himself. The garment grows to the wearer. A high priest in a dress-coat would give over blessing and intoning.

Our girl-students and *Burschen* would have been a

long time getting rid of their spectacles and emblems. They were stripped of them at the expense of the Government, which added to them the aureole of a *toilette* martyrdom.

After that, all they have to do is to swim *au large*.

P.S.—Some are already coming back with the brilliant diploma of Doctor of Medicine, and all glory to them!

Nice, *Summer* 1867.

VENEZIA LA BELLA

(February 1867)

THERE is no more magnificent absurdity than Venice. To build a city where it is impossible to build a city is madness in itself; but to build there one of the most elegant and grandest of cities is the madness of genius. The water, the sea, their sparkle and glimmer, call for a peculiar sumptuousness. Moluscs adorn their shells with mother-of-pearl and pearls.

A single superficial glance at Venice will show one that it is a city of strong character, of vigorous mind, republican, trading, oligarchical; that it is the knot tying something together over the waters—a warehouse for merchandise under a military flag, a city of noisy popular assemblies and a silent city of secret councils and measures; in its squares the whole population is jostling from morning till night, while the rivers of its streets flow silently to the sea. While the crowd surges and clamours in Saint Mark's Square, the boat glides by and vanishes unobserved. Who knows what is under its black awning? The very place to drown people, within hail of lovers' trysts.

The men who felt at home in the Palazzo Ducale must have been of a special caste of their own. They did not stick at anything. There is no earth, there are no trees, what does it matter? Give us more carved stones, more ornaments, gold, mosaics, sculptures, pictures, frescoes. Here there is an empty corner left; put a thin, wet sea-god with a beard in the corner! Here is a porch; get in another lion with wings, and a gospel of Saint Mark! There it is bare and empty; put a carpet of marble and mosaic! and here, lacework of porphyry! Is there a victory over the Turks or over Genoa? does the Pope seek the friendship of the city?

then more marble. A whole wall is covered with a curtain of carving, and above all, more pictures. Paul Veronese, Tintoretto, Titian must mount the scaffold with their brushes: every step of the triumphal progress of the Beauty of the Sea must be depicted for posterity in paint or sculpture. And so full of life was the spirit that dwelt in these stones that new routes and new seaports, Columbus and Vasco da Gama, were not enough to crush it. For its destruction the 'One and Indivisible' republic had to rise up on the ruins of the French throne, and on the ruins of that republic the soldier who in Corsican fashion stabbed the lion with a stiletto poisoned by Austria. But Venice survived the poison and is alive again after half a century.

But is she alive? It is hard to say what has survived except the grand shell, and whether there is another future for Venice. . . . And, indeed, what future can there be for Italy at all? For Venice, perhaps, it lies in Constantinople, in the free federation of the rising Slav-Hellenic nationalities, which begins to stand out in vague outlines from the mists of the East.

And Italy? . . . Of that later. Just now there is the carnival in Venice, the first carnival in freedom after seventy years' captivity. The Square has been transformed into the hall of the Parisian Opera. Old Saint Mark gladly takes his part in the fête with his pictures of saints and his gilt, with his patriotic flags and his pagan horses. Only the doves who come at two o'clock every day to the Square to be fed are shy and flutter from cornice to cornice to convince themselves that this really is their dining-room in such disorder.

The crowd keeps growing, *le peuple s'amuse*, plays the fool heartily with all its might, with great comic talent in declamation and language, in action and gesticulation, without the spiciness of the Parisian pierrots, without the vulgar jokes of the German, without our native filth. The absence of everything indecent surprises one, though the significance of it is clear. This is the recreation, the diversion, the playfulness of a whole people, and not the dress-parade of the brothels, of their *succursales*, whose inmates, while they strip off so much else, put on a mask, like Bismarck's needle on a gun, to intensify and make sure their aim. Here they would be out of place; here the people are amusing themselves; here their sister, wife and daughter are diverting themselves, and woe to him who insults a mask. For the time of carnival the mask is for the woman what the Stanislav ribbon in his buttonhole used to be for a Stationmaster.[1]

At first the carnival left me in peace, but it kept growing, and with its elemental force was bound to draw every one in.

Nothing is too nonsensical to happen when Saint Vitus' Dance takes hold of a whole population in fancy dress. Hundreds, perhaps more, of mauve dominoes were sitting in the big hall of a restaurant; they had sailed across the Square in a gilt ship drawn by bulls (everything that walks on dry land and with four legs is a luxury and rarity in Venice), now they were eating and drinking. One of the guests suggested a curiosity to entertain them, and undertook to obtain it; that curiosity was myself.

The gentleman, who scarcely knew me, ran to me at the Albergo Danieli, and begged and besought me to go with him for a minute to the masqueraders. It was

[1] A year ago I saw the carnival in Nice. There is a fearful difference; to say nothing of the soldiers fully armed and the gendarmes and the commissaires of police with their scarves . . . the conduct of the people themselves, not of the tourists, amazed me. Drunken masqueraders were swearing and fighting with people standing at their gates, white pierrots were violently knocked down into the mud.—(*Author's Note.*)

silly to go, it was silly to make a fuss. I went, I was greeted with '*Evviva!*' and full glasses. I bowed in all directions and talked nonsense, the '*Evvivas*' were more hearty than ever; some shouted: '*Evviva el amico de Garibaldi,*' others drank to the *poet a Russo*! Afraid that the mauve masks would drink to me as the *pittore Slavo scultore i maestro*, I beat a retreat to the Piazza San Marco.

In the Square there was a thick wall of people. I leaned against a pilaster, proud of the title of poet; beside me stood my conductor who had carried out the dominoes' *mandat d'amener*. 'My God, how lovely she is!' broke from my lips as a very young lady made her way through the crowd. My guide without a word seized me and at once set me before her. 'This is that Russian,' my Polish count began. 'Will you give me your hand after that word?' I interrupted. Smiling, she held out her hand and said in Russian that she had long wanted to see me, and glanced at me so sympathetically that I pressed her hand once more and followed her with my eyes so long as she was in sight.

'A blossom, torn by the hurricane, carried by the tide of blood from her Lithuanian fields!' I thought, looking after her. 'Your beauty shines for strangers now.'

I left the Square and went to meet Garibaldi. On the water everything was still. . . the noise of the carnival came in discordant snatches. The stern, frowning blocks of the houses pressed closer and closer upon the boat, peeped at it with their lanterns; at an entry the rudder splashes, the steel hook gleams, the gondolier shouts: '*Apri—sia statt*'. . . and'. . . again the water flows quietly in a side-street, and all at once the houses move apart, we are in the Grand Canal. . . . '*Ferrovia Signore,*' says the gondolier, lisping, as all the town does. Garibaldi had not arrived, he was still at

Bologna. The engine that was going to Florence moaned, awaiting the whistle. 'I had better go too,' I thought; 'to-morrow I shall be tired of the masks. To-morrow I shall not see my Slav beauty.'

The city gave Garibaldi a brilliant reception. The Grand Canal was almost transformed into a single bridge; to get into our boat we had to step across dozens of others. The Government and its retainers did everything possible to show that they were sulky with Garibaldi. If Prince Amadeus had been commanded by his father to show all those petty indelicacies, all that vulgar resentment, how was it the Italian boy's heart did not speak, how was it that he did not for the moment reconcile the city with the king and the king's son with his conscience? Why, Garibaldi had bestowed the crowns of the two Sicilies upon them.

I found Garibaldi neither ill nor any older since our meeting in London in 1864. But he was depressed, worried, and not ready to talk with the Venetians who were presented to him next day. The masses of the common people were his real followers; he grew more lively in Chioggia, where boatmen and fishermen were waiting for him. Mingling with the crowd, he said to those poor and simple people: 'How happy and at home I am with you, how deeply I feel that I was born a working man and have been a working man; the misfortunes of our country tore me away from peaceful work. I too grew up on the sea-coast and know all about your work. . . .' A murmur of delight drowned the former boatman's words, the people surged about him. 'Give a name to my new-born child,' cried a woman. 'Bless mine.' 'And mine,' shouted the others. You valiant general, La Marmora,[1] and you

[1] La Marmora, Alfonso Ferrero, Marquis of, was Italian Minister of War in 1849, Commander-in-Chief of the Army in 1861, and Prime Minister in 1864.—(*Translator's Note*.)

THE FUTURE OF ITALY

inconsolable widower, Ricasoli,[1] with all your Cialdinis[2] and Depretises,[3] you may as well give up your efforts to destroy that bond; it is tied by peasant working hands, and with a cord which you can never break with the help of all the Tuscan and Sardinian hirelings, of all your halfpenny Machiavellis.

Let us return to the question: what then lies before Italy, what future awaits her now that she is renewed, united, independent? Is it the future preached by Mazzini, or that to which Garibaldi is leading her, or perhaps that which Cavour has created?

This question at once leads us far away, into all the difficulties of the most painful and most disputed subjects. It touches directly upon those inner convictions which lie at the foundations of our life, and upon that conflict which so often divides us from our friends and sometimes sets us on the same side as our opponents.

I doubt of the *future of the Latin peoples*. I doubt their fertility in the future; they like the process of revolutions, but are bored by progress when they have attained it. They love to move headlong towards it without reaching it.

---

[1] Ricasoli, Baron Bettino, an Italian authority on agriculture, wrote on the cultivation of the olive, the vine and the mulberry, and took a leading part in the work of draining the Tuscan Maremma. In 1859 he was dictator of Tuscany. He worked for the unity of Italy, and on the accession of Victor Emmanuel was appointed governor-general of Tuscany.

[2] Cialdini, Enrico, took part in the insurrection of 1831, and escaped to France; fought in Spain, first against the Miguelists and then against the Carlists; fought in Italy in 1848, and fell wounded into the hands of the Austrians. In the Crimean War he commanded a Sardinian division. In the war of 1859 he gained the victory of Palestro. He was for a few months governor of Naples, and it was there in 1862 that he acted against Garibaldi in the second Sicilian expedition.

[3] Depretis, Agostino (1813-1887), an Italian politician, took a leading part in promoting the adhesion of Italy to the Triple Alliance. —(*Translator's Notts.*)

The ideal of Italian emancipation is poor. On the one hand, it lacks the essential element that makes for life, and unhappily, on the other hand, retains the old dying and dead element that makes for decay. The Italian revolution has been hitherto the struggle for independence.

Of course, if the terrestrial globe does not crack, if a comet does not come too close and overheat our atmosphere, Italy in the future too will be Italy, the land of the blue sky and the blue sea, of graceful outlines, of a lovely, attractive race of people, musical and artistic by nature. Of course, the changes in military and civilian government, and victory and defeat, and fallen frontiers, and rising assemblies will all be reflected in her life; she will change (and is changing) from clerical despotism to bourgeois parliamentarianism, from a cheap mode of living to an expensive one, from discomfort to comfort, and so on, and so on. But that is not much, and it does not take one far. There is another fine country whose shores are washed by the same blue sea, a fine race, valiant and stern, living beyond the Pyrenees; it has no internal enemy, it has an assembly, it has external unity . . . but with all that, what is Spain?

Nations are of strong vitality; they can lie fallow for ages, and again under favourable circumstances show themselves full of sap and vigour. But do they rise up the same as they were?

How many centuries, I had almost said thousands of years, was the Greek people wiped off the face of the earth as a nation, and still it remained alive, and at the moment when the whole of Europe was stifling in the fumes of Reaction, Greece awoke and stirred the whole world. But were the Greeks of Capo d'Istrias[1] like the

[1] Capo d'Istrias, Ioannos Antonios, Count of, was president of the Greek Republic from 1828 to 1831, when he was assassinated. —(*Translator's Note.*)

THE EXAMPLE OF GREECE

Greeks of Pericles or the Greeks of Byzantium? All that was left of them was the name and a remote memory. Italy too may be renewed, but then she will have to begin a new history. Her emancipation is no more than her right to existence.

The example of Greece is very apt; it is so far away from us that it awakens less passion. The Greece of Athens, of Macedon, deprived of independence by Rome, appears again politically independent in the Byzantine period. What does she create in it? Nothing, or worse than nothing: theological controversy, seraglio revolutions *par anticipation*. The Turks come to the help of backward nature and give the glow of conflagration to her death by violence. Ancient Greece *had lived out her life* when the Roman empire covered and preserved her as the lava and ashes of the volcano preserved Pompeii and Herculaneum. The Byzantine period only lifted the coffin-lid, and the dead remained dead, controlled by popes and monks as every tomb is, ordered about by eunuchs who were quite in place as types of barrenness. Who does not know the tales of crusaders in Byzantium? Incomparably inferior in culture, in refinement of manners, these savage warriors, these rude swashbucklers, were yet full of strength, daring, force; they were advancing, the *god of history* was with them. To him, men are precious, not for their good qualities but for their sturdy vigour and for their coming upon the stage *à propos*. That is why as we read the tedious chronicles we rejoice when the Varangians sweep down from their northern snows, or the Slavs float down in cockle-shells and brand with their shields the proud walls of Byzantium. As a schoolboy, I was overjoyed at the savage in his shirt[1] paddling his canoe and going with a gold earring in his ear to an interview

---

[1] Svyatoslav, prince of Kiev, is meant.—(*Translator's Note.*)

with the effeminate, luxurious, scholastic Emperor,[1] John Zimisces.

Think a little about Byzantium. Until our Slavophils have brought out another new chronicle adorned with old ikon paintings, and until it has received the sanction of Government, Byzantium will explain a great deal of what it is hard to put into words.

Byzantium could *live*, but there was nothing for her to *do*; and nations in general only take a place in history while they are on the stage, that is while they are doing something.

I remember I have mentioned already the answer Thomas Carlyle gave to me when I spoke to him of the seventies of the Parisian censorship. 'But why are you so angry with it?' he said. 'In compelling the French to keep quiet, Napoleon has done them the greatest service. They have nothing to say, but they want to talk. . . . Napoleon has given them a justification in their own eyes. . . .' I do not say how far I agree with Carlyle, but I do ask myself: Will the Italians have anything to say and do on the day after the taking of Rome?

And sometimes, without finding an answer, I begin to hope that Rome may remain a long time their living desideratum.

Till Rome is taken, everything will go fairly well; there will be energy and strength enough, if only there is money enough. . . . Till then, Italy will put up with a great deal: taxes and the yoke of Piedmont and the pillaging administration and the quarrelsome and vexatious bureaucracy; while waiting for Rome, everything seems unimportant. To gain it, her people may be cramped, they must stand together. Rome is the boundary-line, the flag; it is always before their eyes, it

---

[1] John Zimisces became Emperor in 969 by marriage with Thcophania, widow of Romanus 11., and reigned till 976. He was, as a fact, victorious over the Russians.—(*Translator's Note.*)

prevents their sleeping, it prevents their attending to business, it keeps up the fever. In Rome all will be changed, everything will snap. . . . There, they fancy, is the end, the crown; not at all . . . there is the beginning.

Nations that are redeeming their independence never know (and it is a very good thing too) that independence of itself gives them nothing except the rights of mature age, except a place among their peers, except the recognition of their rights as citizens to act for themselves, and that is all.

What acts will be announced to us from the heights of the Capitol and the Quirinal? What will be proclaimed to the world from the forum or from the balcony, where for ages the Pope has blessed the 'Universe and the City'?

To proclaim 'independence' *sans phrase* is not enough. But there is nothing else. . . . And at times it seems to me that on the day when Garibaldi flings aside his sword, no longer needed, and puts the *toga virilis* on the shoulders of Italy, there will be nothing left for him to do but publicly to embrace his *maestro* Mazzini on the banks of the Tiber and to repeat with him: 'Lord, now lettest thou thy servant depart in peace!'

I say this for them and not against them.

Their future is secured, their two names will stand high and radiant throughout all Italy, from Fiume to Messina, and will be more and more exalted throughout all gloomy Europe as her people grow pettier and the general level sinks.

But I doubt whether Italy will follow the programme of the great *carbonaro* and the great warrior. Their religion has worked miracles; it has awakened thought, it has lifted the Sword, it has been the trumpet awakening the sleepers, the standard under which Italy has conquered herself. . . . Half of Mazzini's ideal has been accompushed, precisely because the other half lay far beyond the possible. That Mazzini now has grown weaker shows his success and greatness; he is the poorer for that part of his ideal which has passed into reality, it is the weakness after giving birth. In sight of the shore Columbus had but to float, and had no need to use all the might of his invincible spirit. We have had experiences something like it in our circle. . . . Where now is the force given to our words in the past by our struggle against serfdom, against the lack of all justice, of all freedom of speech?

Rome is Mazzini's America . . . there are no more elements strong enough to survive in his programme, it has been based on the struggle for unity and for Rome.

'And the democratic republic?'

That is the great reward beyond the grave, with the hope of which men have advanced into action and achievement, and in which the prophets and martyrs have fervently and earnestly believed.

Even now it is the goal of a handful of resolute old men, the veteran followers of Mazzini, the undaunted, unyielding, incorruptible, untiring masons who have laid the foundations of the new Italy and when they had not cement enough gave their blood for it. But are there many of them? And who will follow them?

While the threefold yoke of the German, the Bourbon and the Pope weighed on the neck of Italy, these vigorous soldier-monks of the Order of Saint Mazzini found sympathy everywhere. *Principessi* and students, jewellers and doctors, actors and priests, artists and lawyers, the more educated of the petty bourgeois, the more awakened of the workmen, officers and soldiers— all, secretly or openly, were with them and working for them. A republic was the aim of few, independence and unity the aim of all; independence they have gained, unity after the French fashion is detestable to them, they do not want a republic. The present *régime* is in many ways just what fits the Italians; they have a longing to present 'a strong and majestic figure' in the councils of European states, and finding this *bella e grande figura* in Victor Emmanuel they cling to him.[1]

The representative system in its continental development really answers best of all when there is nothing clear in the mind and nothing possible in action. It is a great stop-gap, which rubs corners and extremes off both sides and gains time. Part of Europe has passed through this mill, the other parts will pass through it, and we sinners among them. What about Egypt? Why, that too has ridden on camels into the representative mill, urged on by the whip.

I do not blame the majority, ill-prepared, weary and cowardly, still less the masses, so long left to the teaching of priests; I do not blame the Government even—and indeed, how can it be blamed for its stupidity, its ignorance, its lack of impulse, of poetry, of tact? It was born in the Carignano Palace[2] among rusty Gothic swords, old-fashioned powdered wigs, and the starched etiquette of little courts with vast pretensions.

---

[1] A very charming Hungarian, Count Sandor Tétéki, who afterwards served as a colonel of cavalry in Italy, said to me once, laughing at the tawdry luxury of the Florentine dandies: 'Do you remember a race or a festival in Moscow?. . . It is silly, but it has character. The coachman is primed with liquor, his cap is on one side, the horses are worth some thousands of roubles, and the master lolls in bliss and in sables. Here our gaunt Count So-and-so hires lean nags with rheumatic legs and nodding heads, and the same thin, clumsy-looking Giacopo who is his cook and gardener sits on the box, dressed in a livery not made for him, and tugs at the reins, while the Count entreats him: "Giacopo, Giacopo, *fate una grande e bella figura*."' I asked leave of Count Téléki to borrow this expression.—(*Author's Note*.)

[2] The Dukes of Savoy were also Princes of Carignano, a little town of Piedmont. Charles Albert of Savoy came to the throne of Piedmont in 1831, and his son, Victor Emmanuel 11., became in 1860 the first king of united Italy.—(*Translator's Note*.)

It has not inspired love—quite the contrary; but it is none the weaker for that. I was surprised in 1863 to see the general dislike of the Government in Naples. In 1867, in Venice, I saw without the slightest surprise that three months after their deliverance the people could not endure the Government, but at the same time I saw even more clearly that it had nothing to be afraid of unless it committed a series of colossal blunders, though it gets over these, too, with extraordinary ease. There is an example before my eyes. I will describe it in a few lines.

To the various jests with which Governments sometimes deign to throw dust in their people's eyes, such as the '*Prisonniers de la paix*' of Louis-Philippe, and 'Empire is Peace' of Louis Napoleon, Ricasoli added one of his own, calling the law which secured the greater part of the property of the clergy the law of 'the freedom of the Church in a Free State.' All the immature followers of liberalism, all the people who read no further than a title, rejoiced. The Ministry, concealing a smile, triumphed in their victory; the trick was obviously profitable to the clergy. The Belgian publican and sinner[1] behind whom the Jesuit fathers hid themselves turned up. He brought with him piles of gold, the colour of which had not been seen for a long time in Italy, and offered the Government a large sum to secure for the clergy the lawful possession of the estates wrung out in the confessional, gained from dying sinners and from the poor in spirit generally.

The Government saw only one thing—the money; the fools saw something else—*American* freedom of the Church in a Free state. It is the fashion nowadays to measure European institutions by the American standard. The Due de Persigny finds a striking similarity between the Second Empire and the First Republic of our day.

[1] Leopold 11., uncle of the present King of the Belgians, is meant. —(*Translator's Note*.)

RICASOLI'S BLUNDER

However artful Ricasoli and Cialdini were, the Chamber of Deputies, though very mixed and mediocre in its composition, began to grasp that the dice were loaded, and loaded without their assistance. The banker played the *impresario* and tried to buy Italian voices, but it was February and the Chamber was hoarse. In Naples there were murmurs, in Venice a meeting was called in the Mali bran Theatre to protest. Ricasoli ordered the theatre to be closed and put sentries to guard it. There is no doubt that of all possible blunders nothing more foolish could have been thought of. Venice, which had only just been set free, wanted to enjoy its right of opposition and was handicapped by the police. To assemble in order to fête the King and offer bouquets *al gran comandatore La Marmora* means nothing. If the Venetians had wanted to assemble in honour of the Austrian archdukes, they would, of course, have been permitted. There was absolutely no danger in a meeting in the Malibran Theatre.

The Chamber woke up and asked for an explanation. Ricasoli gave a haughty and arrogant answer, as was befitting to the last representative of Raoul Barbe-Bleue, a mediaeval Count and feudal Lord. The Chamber, convinced that the Ministry did not desire to limit the 'right of public meeting,' would have passed on to the order of the day. Barbe-Bleue, already enraged that his law of the freedom of the Church, of which he had been certain, was beginning to be curtailed in committees, announced that he could not accept the *ordre du jour motivé*. The offended Chamber voted against him. For such insolence he suspended the Chamber on the next day, on the third dissolved it, and on the fourth was thinking of still harsher measures, but, I was told, Cialdini informed the King that he could not rely upon the troops.

There have been instances of blundering Governments

seeking a sensible pretext for doing something nasty or for covering it, but these worthies sought the most absurd pretext to prove their own defeat. If the Government goes further and more conspicuously along this road, it may break its neck. One can foresee and reckon upon only what is to some extent subject to reason. There is no limit to what senselessness may do, though there is almost always some Cialdini at hand to pour cold water on the heated head.

And if Italy puts up with this *régime* and grows inured to it, she will not endure it with impunity. It is hard for a people *less experienced* than the French to digest such a fantastic world of lies and empty words, of phrases without meaning. In France nothing exists in reality, but everything is for appearance and show; like an old man sunk into second childhood, she is taken up with playthings; at times she guesses that her horses are only wooden ones, but she wants to deceive herself.

Italy will not be able to deal with these shadows of a Chinese lantern: with this moonlight independence that is illuminated on three of its four sides by the sun of the Tuileries; with a despised and hated Church, waited upon like an aged grandmother in expectation of her speedy demise. The potato-yeast of parliamentarianism and the rhetoric of the Chambers will not provide wholesome food for an Italian. He will be stunned and driven out of his mind by this pretence of nourishment and unreal struggle. And there is nothing else being prepared for him. What is to be done? Where is the solution? I do not know. Perhaps, after proclaiming the unity of Italy in Rome, her dissolution into independent self-governing parts, loosely connected together, may be proclaimed, and that may be the solution. More development might be possible (if there is anything to develop) in a dozen living units, and the solution would be quite in the spirit of Italy.

QUINET

In the midst of these reflections I happened to come across Quinet's pamphlet, *France and Germany*. I was immensely pleased with it—not that I specially rely upon the judgments of the celebrated historical thinker, though I have a great respect for him personally, but I rejoiced not on my own account.

In old days in Petersburg a friend noted for his humour, finding on my table a book of the Berlin Michelet, *On the Immortality of the Soul*, left me a note as follows: 'Dear friend, when you have read the book, do be so good as to tell me briefly whether the soul is immortal or not. It does not matter for me, but I should like to know for the comfort of relations.'

Well, it is for the sake of relations that I am glad I have come upon Quinet. In spite of the conceited attitude many of them have taken up in regard to European authorities, our friends still pay more attention to them than to any of their own kin. That is why I try when I can to put my own thought in the charge of a European nurse. Clinging to Proudhon, I said that not Catiline but death was at the doors of France; hanging on to the skirts of Stuart Mill, I repeated what he said about the Chinese character of the English; and I am very glad that I can take Quinet by the hand and say: 'Here my honoured friend Quinet says in 1867 about Latin Europe what I said about it in 1847 and all the following years.'

Quinet sees with horror and sadness the degradation of France, the softening of her brain, her growing pettiness. He does not understand the cause; he seeks it in her estrangement from the principles of 1789 and in the loss of political liberty, and so through his grief there is a gleam in his words of the hidden hope of recovery by a return to a genuine parliamentary *régime*, to the great principles of the Revolution.

Quinet does not observe that the great principles of

which he speaks, and the political ideas of the Latin world generally, have lost their virtue, their spring has been overstrained and has almost snapped. *Les principes du 1789* were not mere words, but now they have become mere words, like the liturgy and the prayers. Their service has been immense: by them, through them, France has accomplished her revolution, she has drawn up the curtain of the future and has sprung back in horror.

A dilemma has arisen.

Either free institutions will again touch the sacred curtain, or there will be government control, external order and internal slavery.

If in the life of the peoples of Europe there had been a single aim, a single tendency, one solution or the other would have gained the upper hand long ago. But as the history of Western Europe is constituted, it leads to everlasting struggle. The underlying fundamental fact that its culture is of twofold nature forms the organic obstacle to consistent development. To live in two civilisations, on two levels, in two worlds, at two stages of development, to live not with a whole organism but with one part of it, while employing the other for the hewing of wood and the drawing of water, and to keep talking about liberty and equality, is becoming more and more difficult.

Attempts to reach a more harmonious, better-balanced system have not been successful. But if they have failed in any given place, that rather proves the unsuitability of the place than the faultiness of the principle.

The whole gist of the matter lies in that.

The States of North America with their unity of civilisation will easily outstrip Europe; their position is simpler. The standard of their civilisation is lower than that of Western Europe, but they have *one* standard and all reach it: that is their tremendous strength.

Twenty years ago France burst like a Titan into

another life, struggling in the dark without plan or understanding and with no knowledge except of her insufferable agony. She has been beaten 'by order and civilisation,' but it was the victor who retreated. The bourgeoisie have had to pay for their melancholy victory with all they had gained by ages of effort, of sacrifice, of wars and revolutions, with the best fruits of their culture.

The centres of force, the paths of development—all have changed; the hidden activity and suppressed work of social reconstruction have passed to other lands beyond the borders of France.

As soon as the Germans were convinced that the French tide had ebbed, that its terrible revolutionary ideas were old and feeble, that there was no need to fear her, the Prussian helmet appeared behind the walls of the fortresses on the Rhine.

France still drew back, the helmets became more and more conspicuous. Bismarck has never thought much of his own people, he has kept his ears cocked towards France, he has sniffed the air coming that way, and, convinced of the permanent degradation of that country, he saw that Prussia's day was at hand. He ordered Moltke to make a plan, he ordered the munition factories to make needles for the guns, and systematically, with German unceremonious coarseness, gathered the ripe German pears and threw them into the apron of the ridiculous Friedrich Wilhelm, assuring him that he was a hero by the especial grace of the Lutheran god.

I do not believe that the destinies of the world will remain for long in the hands of the Germans and the Hohenzollerns. It is impossible, it is contrary to the good sense of humanity, contrary to the aesthetics of history. I say, as Kent to Lear, only the other way about: 'In you, oh Prussia, there is nothing of that I could call a king.' But all the same, Prussia has thrust

France into the background and herself taken the front seat. But all the same, painting the parti-coloured rags of the German fatherland all one colour, she will lay down the law to Europe so long as her laws are laid down by the bayonet and carried out by grapeshot, for the very simple reason that she has more bayonets and more grapeshot.

Behind the Prussian wave there will arise another that will not trouble itself much whether the old men with their classical principles like it or not. England craftily preserves the appearance of strength, standing on one side, as though proud of her apparent aloofness. . . . She has felt deep within her the same social sore that she healed so easily in 1848 with policemen's staves, but the pains of birth are growing stronger . . . and she is drawing in her far-reaching tentacles to meet the conflict at home.

France, amazed, embarrassed by the change of her position, threatens to fight not Prussia but Italy, if the latter touches the temporal possessions of the eternal father, and she collects money for a monument to Voltaire.

Will the ear-splitting Prussian trumpet of the *last* judgment by battle rouse Latin Europe? Will the approach of the learned barbarians awaken her?

Chi lo sa.

I reached Genoa with some Americans who had only just crossed the ocean. They were impressed by Genoa. Everything they had read about the Old World in books they saw now face to face, and they were never tired of gazing at the precipitous, narrow, black, mediaeval streets, the extraordinary height of the houses, the half-broken arches, the fortresses, and so on.

We went into the hall of a palace. A cry of delight broke from one of the 'How these people did live! How they did live! What proportions, what elegance! No, you will find nothing like it among us.' And he was ready to blush for his America. We glanced inside an immense drawing-room. The portraits of former owners, the pictures, the faded walls, the old furniture, the old heraldic crests, the stagnant atmosphere, the emptiness, and the old custodian in a black knitted cap and a threadbare black coat carrying a bunch of keys . . . all said as plainly as words that this was not a house but a curiosity, a sarcophagus, a sumptuous relic of past life.

'Yes,' I said to the Americans as we went out, 'you are perfectly right, these people *did* live well.'

March 1867.

LA BELLE FRANCE

*'Ah! que j'ai douce souvenance
De ce beau pays de France!'*

1

Ante Portas

FRANCE was closed to me. A year after my arrival in Nice, in the summer of 1851, I wrote a letter to Léon Faucher, then Minister of the Interior, and asked his permission to visit Paris for a few days. 'I have a house in Paris and I must look after it,' I said. A genuine economist could not but yield to this argument, and I received permission to stay in Paris 'for a very brief time.'

In 1852 I asked for the privilege of travelling through France to England: it was refused. In 1856 I wanted to return from England to Switzerland, and again asked for a *visa*: it was refused. I wrote to the Freiburg *Conseil d 'État* that I was cut off from Switzerland, and should have to travel by stealth, or come through the Straits of Gibraltar, or across Germany, which would most likely land me in the Peter-Paul Fortress and not in Freiburg. On which grounds I begged the *Conseil d'État* to apply to the French Minister of Foreign Affairs and ask for leave for me to pass through France. The Consul answered me on the 19th of October 1856 with the following letter:—

'Dear Sir,—In accordance with your desire, we charged the Swiss Minister in Paris to take the necessary steps to obtain for you an authorisation to pass through France on your way back to Switzerland. We forward you a copy of the answer received by the Swiss Minister: "M. Walewski has been obliged upon this subject to consult his colleague, the Minister of the Interior;

considerations of *special importance*, so the Minister of the Interior has informed him, compelled the latter to refuse M. Herzen the right of passing through France last August, and he cannot revise his decision, etc., etc"'

I had nothing in common with the French exiles except simple acquaintanceship; I had not taken part in any conspiracy or any society, and was at the time exclusively engaged in Russian propaganda. All this the French police—the one omniscient, the one national, and therefore the one infinitely powerful police—knew perfectly. They were angry with me for my articles and my connections.

Of this anger it cannot but be said that it went beyond all bounds. In 1859 I went for a few days to Brussels with my son. Neither at Ostend nor at Brussels was my passport asked for on arrival. Six days later, when I came back in the evening to the hotel, the waiter as he handed me a candle said to me that they had sent from the police for my passport. 'They have thought of it in time,' I observed. The man went with me to my room and took the passport. I had no sooner got into bed, between twelve and one, when there was a knock at the door; the same waiter appeared again with a big envelope. 'The Minister of Justice begs that M. Herzen will present himself at eleven o'clock to-morrow morning at the *Département de la Sûreté Publique.*'

'And you come and wake people up at night for that?'

'They are waiting for an answer.'

'Who?'

'Some one from the police.'

'Well, say that I will come, but say, too, that it is stupid to bring invitations after midnight.'

Then like Nulin[1] I put out my candle.

At eight o'clock next morning a knock at the door

[1] Nulin is the hero of a poem by Pushkin.—(*Translator's Note.*)

again. It was not difficult to guess that this was all the foolery of Belgian justice. '*Entrez.!*'

In walked a gentleman, excessively spick and span, in a very new hat and a fresh-looking black coat, with a long watch-chain, thick and apparently gold, and so on.

Not fully dressed—indeed, only partially clad—I presented the strangest contrast to a man who was obliged to be dressed so scrupulously from seven o'clock in the morning that he might be mistaken for an honest man. The advantage was certainly on his side.

'I have the honour to be speaking *avec M. Herzen père*?'

'*C'est selon*; as you look at it. On the one hand l am a father, on the other I am a son.'

That greatly diverted the spy.

'I have come to you . . .'

'Excuse me—to tell me that the Minister of Justice summons me at eleven o'clock to his department?'

'Just so.'

'Why does the Minister trouble you, and so early in the morning too? Is not it enough for him to disturb me so late at night, sending that envelope?'

'So you will be there?'

'Without fail.'

'You know the way?'

'Why? Have you been told to accompany me?'

'Upon my word, *quelle idèe!*'

'And so. . .'

'I wish you good day.'

'Good morning.'

At eleven o'clock I was sitting with the head of the Belgian Public Security Department.

He was holding some sort of a manuscript book and my passport.

'You must excuse me for our having troubled you, but you see there are two little circumstances here: in the first place, your passport is Swiss, while. . .' with police penetration, to test me, he fixed his eyes upon me.

'While I am a Russian,' I added.

'Yes. I must confess that has struck us as strange.'

'Why? Have you no law of naturalisation in Belgium?'

'And you . . .?'

'I was naturalised ten years ago at Morat of the Canton of Freiburg in the village of Châtel.'

'Of course, *if that is so*, in that case I do not venture to doubt . . . we will pass to the second difficulty. Three years ago you asked for permission to visit Brussels and received a refusal. . . .'

'*Mille pardons*, that did not happen and could not have happened. What should I have thought of *free* Belgium, if, though never banished from her, I could doubt my right to visit Brussels?'

The head of the Department of Public Security was a little embarrassed.

'However, here it is. . .' and he opened the manuscript book.

'It seems that not everything in it is correct. Here you did not know, for instance, that I was naturalised in Switzerland.'

'To be sure. The Consul, M. Delpierre. . .'

Don't disturb yourself, I will tell you the rest. I asked your Consul in London whether I could move the Russian printing-press to Brussels—that is, whether the press would be left alone if I did not interfere in Belgian affairs, which I had no inclination whatever to do, *as you will readily believe*. M. Delpierre asked the Minister. The Minister asked him to dissuade me from my plan of moving the printing-press. Your Consul was ashamed to communicate the Minister's answer by letter, and he asked Louis Blanc, as an acquaintance of both of us, to give me this message. Thanking Louis

Blanc, I asked him to reassure M. Delpierre and to tell him that I had with great fortitude received the news that my printing-press would not be allowed to enter Brussels, but "if," I added, "the Consul had had to inform me of the opposite—that is, that my printing-press and I would never to all eternity be allowed to leave Brussels—I might not have had the courage to bear it." You see, I remember all the circumstances very well.'

The guardian of public security cleared his throat a little, and reading the manuscript book observed: 'It really is so; I had not noticed the mention of the printing-press. However, I imagine that you must in any case obtain permission from the Minister; otherwise, much as we shall regret it, we shall be forced to ask you . . .'

'I am going to-morrow.'

'Oh dear no, no one insists on such haste; you may remain a week, a fortnight. We are speaking of permanent residence. . . . I am almost certain that the Minister will sanction it.'

'I may ask his sanction for some future occasion, but now I have not the slightest desire to remain longer in Brussels.'

There the afiair ended. 'I forgot one thing in the confusion of our explanation,' the apprehensive guardian of public security said to me, 'we are a small people, we are a small people, that's our trouble, *il y a des égards*. . .' He was ashamed.

Two years later my younger daughter, who was living in Paris, was taken ill. Again I asked for a *visa*, and again Persigny refused it. Just at that time Count Branicki was in London. Dining with him, I told him of the refusal. 'Write a letter to Prince Napoleon,' said Branicki, 'I'll see that he gets it.'

'I have no grounds for writing to the Prince.'

'That is true. Write to the Emperor. To-morrow

I am going, and the day after to-morrow your letter shall be in his hands.'

'That is very soon, let me consider it.'

On reaching home I wrote the following letter:—

'SIRE,—More than ten years ago I was compelled to leave France by ministerial order. Since then I have twice received permission to visit Paris.[1]

'Of late I have been steadily refused the privilege of visiting France, though one of my daughters is being educated in Paris and I own a house there. I venture to apply directly to your Imperial Majesty with a request for permission to visit France and to remain in Paris for the time necessary for my business, and I shall await your decision with confidence and respect.

'In any case, Sire, I give you my word that my desire to visit France has no political motive.—I remain, with profound respect, Your Majesty's obedient servant,

'ALEXANDER HERZEN.

'ORSETT HOUSE,
'WESTBOURNE TERRACE, LONDON.'

Branicki thought the letter was curt and would therefore probably not attain its object. I told him that I should not write another letter, and that if he cared to do me a service he might deliver it, but that if on reflection he had changed his mind he could throw it in the fire. This conversation took place at the railway station; he went off.

Four days later I received the following letter from the French Embassy:—

'PARIS, *June* 3, 1861,
'OFFICE OF PREFECT OF POLICE,
'BUREAU ONE,

DEAR SIR,—By command of the Emperor I have the honour to inform you that His Imperial Majesty

[1] The second time was in 1853 on the occasion of the illness of Mary a Kasparovna Reihel, I received this permit at the request of

sanctions your visit to France and your sojourn in Paris on every occasion when your business requires it, as you have requested in your letter of May 31st.

'You can consequently travel freely throughout the Empire, observing the accepted formalities.—Receive sir, etc., Prefect of Police.'

Then a signature written eccentrically slanting, impossible to decipher, and like anything rather than the name Boitelle.

The same day came a letter from Branicki. Prince Napoleon sent him the following letter from the Emperor:—

'DEAR NAPOLEON,—This is to inform you that I have just sanctioned the entrance of Monsieur[1] Herzen into France and have ordered him to be given a passport.'

After this 'Lift up!' the *Schlagbaum*, which had been down for eleven years, was raised, and a month later I set off for Paris.

2

INTRA MUROS

'Ma-ame Erstin!' a gloomy gendarme with enormous moustaches shouted at Calais at the barrier through which travellers who have only just landed from tie Dover steamer and been driven by the Customs House and other overseers into the stone-built barn have to pass one by one into France. The travellers went up, the gendarme served out the passports, the police com-

Rothschild. Mary a Kasparovna recovered, and I did not make use of it Two years later I was informed at the French Consulate that since I had not made use of it at the time, the permit was no longer valid.

[1] I have noted the word *Monsieur* because when I was banished the Prefecture invariably wrote *Sieur*, while Napoleon wrote *Monsieur* with his own hand in full,—(*Author's Notes*.)

missioner questioned with his eyes and, where necessary, with his tongue, and the traveller, approved and found innocuous to the Empire, vanished behind the barrier.

This time no traveller moved forward at the gendarme's shout.

'Ma-ame Ogly Erstin!' the gendarme shouted, raising his voice and waving a passport.

No one answered.

'Why, is there no one of the name?' shouted the gendarme, and looking at the passport, added: 'Mam'-zelle Ogly Erstin.'

Only then a little girl of ten, namely my daughter Olga, conjectured that the guardian of order was calling her with this ferocity. '*Avancez, donc, prenez vos papers!*' the gendarme commanded savagely. Olga took her passport, and huddling up to Malwide von Meysenbug, asked her in a whisper: '*Est-ce que c'est l'Empereur?*'

That happened to her in 1860, but something worse happened to me a year later, and not at the barrier at Calais, which no longer exists, but everywhere: in a railway carriage, in the street, in Paris, in the provinces, in my home, in my dreams, in waking life, everywhere I saw before me the Emperor, with long moustaches waxed to a thread, with eyes that did not see and a mouth that did not speak. Not only the gendarmes, who are to a certain extent emperors from their position, but the soldiers, the shop-boys, the waiters, and especially the conductors on trains and omnibuses, looked to me like Napoleons. It was only here in Paris in 1861, before the Hôtel de Ville, before which I had stood in respect in 1847, before Notre Dame, the Champs-Élysées and the Boulevards, that I grasped the meaning of the psalm in which King David with flattering despair complains to Jehovah that he cannot get away from Him, cannot escape Him: 'I go into the water,' he says, 'thou art there; into the earth, thou art there; into the sky, and of course thou art there also.' If I went to dine at the Maison d'Or, Napoleon in one of his incarnations was dining the other side of the table and asking for truffles *à la serviette*; if I went to the theatre, one would be sitting in the same row and one would walk on to the stage. If I ran away from him out of town, he followed on my heels beyond the Bois de Boulogne in a closely buttoned coat and moustaches with stiffly waxed points. Where was he not? At the ball in Mabille? At mass in the Madeleine? He was sure to be at both.

La révolution s'est faite homme. 'The revolution is embodied in a man,' was one of the favourite phrases of the doctrinaire jargon of the days of Thiers and the liberal historians of the Louis-Philippe period; but this is rather more cunning: the revolution and the reaction, order and disorder, the van and the rear, are incarnate in one man, and that man in his turn is reincarnated in the whole administration, from the ministers to the rural constables, from the senators to the village mayors, is scattered in the infantry and afloat in the navy.

This man is not a prophet, not a poet, not a conqueror, not an eccentricity, not a genius, not a man of talent; but a cold, silent, surly, plain, prudent, persistent, prosaic 'middle-aged gentleman, neither fat nor thin'[1]—*le bourgeois* of bourgeois France, *l'homme du destin, le neveu du grand homme*, the plebeian. He obliterates, he concentrates in himself, all the prominent aspects of the national character. all the tendencies of the people, as the topmost peak of a mountain or a pyramid ends in nothing.

In 1849 and in 1850 I had not grasped the significance of Napoleon 111. Carried away by democratic rhetoric,

[1] A phrase used by Gogol to describe the hero of *Dead Souls* —(*Translator's Note.*)

LIFE UNDER THE NEW RÉGIME

I did not appreciate him. The year 1861 was one of the very best for the Empire, everything was going well. Everything had reached equilibrium, was reconciled with and submissive to the new *régime*. There was precisely enough opposition and daring thought to give shadow and some spiciness to the mixture. Laboulaye[1] very cleverly praised New York to the disadvantage of Paris, Prévost-Paradol[2] Austria to the disadvantage of France. Anonymous hints were made with regard to the Mirés case.[3] People were quietly allowed to abuse the Pope and show some slight sympathy for the Polish movement. There were circles who met together to display their *frondeur* spirit, as we used to meet in the'forties in Moscow at the house of some old friend. They even had their dissatisfied celebrities, rather after the fashion of our Yermolov, but turned civilian, such as Guizot. All the rest had been beaten flat by the storm. And no one complained, they even liked the repose of it, as people like the first week of Lent with its horse-radish and cabbage after the seven days of feasting and drinking in Carnival. Those who did not like lenten fare were hard to find; they had vanished for shorter or longer periods, and would come back with taste corrected from Lambessa or from the Mazas prison. The police, *la grande police* which had replaced *la grande armée*, was everywhere at all times. Literary style was all at a dead level—wretched boatmen floating calmly in wretched boats over the once stormy sea. The inanity of the plays produced on every stage induced heavy sleep at night, which was maintained in the morning by the futility of the newspapers.

[1] Laboulaye, E. R. de (1811-1883), was a French lawyer and journalist.

[2] Prévost-Paradol, L. A. (1829-1870), was a French critic and journalist, author of *Études sur Us Moralities Français*.

[3] Mirés was a leading figure in the financial world, whose ruin through speculation led to a famous trial.—(*Translator's Notes*.)

Journalism in the former sense of the word did not exist. The leading papers stood not for views but for commercial firms. After the leading articles of London papers, written in condensed, sensible language, with 'nerve,' as the French say, and 'muscles,' one simply cannot read the Paris *premiers*. Rhetorical flourishes, faded and frayed, and the same old, high-flown phrases, made more than absurd, disgusting, through their obvious contrast with facts, took the place of subject-matter. Oppressed nationalities were continually being invited as before to rely upon France; she still remained 'at the head of the great movement,' and was still bringing the world-revolution freedom and the great principles of 1789. Opposition took its stand under the banner of Buonapartism. These are nuances of precisely the same colour, and they might all be indicated as sailors indicate the intermediate winds, N.N.W., N.W.N., N.W.W., W.N.W. . . . Buonapartism desperate, furious, moderate; Buonapartism monarchical; Buonapartism republican, democratic, socialistic; Buonapartism peaceful, military, revolutionary, conservative; and finally, Buonapartism of the Palais Royal and the Tuileries. . . . Late in the evening certain gentlemen run to the newspaper offices to set the weather-cock of the paper straight, if it should have turned a little too far to the east or west of the north. They check the time by the chronometer of the Prefecture, erase and add, and hasten to bring out the next edition.

Reading in a café an evening paper which stated that Mirés 'lawyer had refused to disclose how certain sums had been employed, saying that' very highly placed persons' were involved, I said to a man I knew: 'But how is it the prosecutor does not compel him to tell, and how is it the newspapers do not insist upon it?' My acquaintance gave a tug to my coat, cast a glance round, and signalled with his eyes, his hands and his cane. I had not lived in Petersburg for nothing. I understood him, and began discussing absinthe and seltzer-water.

As I came out of the café, I saw a minute man running towards me with minute arms outspread to embrace me. As he approached I recognised Darimon. 'How happy you must be,' said the deputy of the Left, 'to be back in Paris! *Ah, je m'imagine.*'

'Not particularly so!'

Darimon was petrified.

'Well, how are Madame Darimon and your little son, who must be by now your big son, especially if he does not take after his father?'

'*Touiours le même, ha-ha-ha, très bien*'—and we parted.

I felt oppressed in Paris, and I only breathed freely when a month later, through the rain and fog, I saw again the dirty white chalky cliffs of England. Everything that pinched like narrow shoes under Louis-Philippe pinched now like fetters on the legs. I had not seen the intermediate processes by which the new *régime* had been built up and made secure, but found it after ten years absolutely complete and established. . . . Moreover, I did not recognise Paris; its rebuilt streets, unfinished palaces, and, worst of all, the people I met were strange to me. This was not the Paris I had loved and hated, not the city I had longed to reach from childhood, not the city I had left with a curse on my lips. This was a Paris that had lost its individuality, had grown indifferent, and was no longer boiling. A strong hand oppressed it everywhere and was at every minute ready to tug at the reins—but that was not necessary; Paris had accepted the Second Empire *tout de bon*, it barely retained the external habits of older days. The 'discontented' had nothing serious and strong to set up against the Empire. The memories of the republicans of Tacitus and the vague ideas of the Socialists could not shake the throne of the Caesars. The *police de surveillance* did not combat these 'fantasies' seriously, they resented them not as a danger, but as disorderly and improper. They were more annoyed at the 'memories' than at the 'hopes,' they kept a stricter hand over the Orleanists. From time to time the autocratic police unexpectedly dealt some unjust and brutal blow as a menacing reminder of its power; it purposely aroused terror over two quarters of the city for two months, and then retreated again into the crevices of the Prefecture and the corridors of the Government Offices.

In reality, all was still. The two most violent protests were not French. The attempts of Pianori and Orsini were the revenge of Italy, the revenge of Rome. The Orsini affair, which terrified Napoleon, was taken as a sufficient excuse for dealing the last blow, the *coup de grâce*. It succeeded. A country which puts up with Espinasse's[1] laws concerning suspected persons has given its pledge. It was necessary to frighten people, to show that the police would not stick at anything; it was necessary to destroy all conceptions of human rights and dignity, to crush men's minds by injustice, to accustom them to it, and to prove the power of the authorities by it. When he cleared Paris of suspected persons, Espinasse ordered the prefects to discover a conspiracy in *each* department, to involve in it not less than ten persons known to be hostile to the Empire, to arrest them and to put them at the disposition of the Minister. The Minister had the right to send

[1] Espinasse, Charles, a French general, supported Louis Napoleon at the Coup d'État of the 2nd of December, was Minister of the Interior in 1858, and killed at Magenta in 1859.—(*Translator's Note.*)

them to Cayenne or Lambessa without legal proceedings, without rendering account or being held responsible. The man so exiled was lost, there could be no defence, no protest; he was not tried, and his only hope lay in the special mercy of the Emperor. 'I received these orders,' the prefect N. said to our poet Fyodor Tyutchev[1]—'what was I to do? I racked my brains. . . . The position was difficult and unpleasant. At last a happy thought struck me how to get out of it. I sent for the commissaire of police and said to him: "Can you at very short notice find me a dozen desperate rascals, unconvicted thieves and so on?" The commissaire said that nothing would be easier. "Well then, make up a list; we will arrest them to-night and send them to the Minister as revolutionaries."'

'Well, what then?' asked Tyutchev.

'We collected them, and the Minister sent them off to Cayenne, and the whole department was delighted and thanked me for getting rid of the rascals so easily,' added the worthy prefect, laughing.

The Government tired of the methods of terrorism and violence before the people and public opinion did. Times of peace, of tranquillity, *de la sécurité*, followed very shortly. Little by little the lines of care were smoothed out of the faces of the police; the insolent, provocative glance of the spy, the ferocious air of the *sergeant de ville* softened; the Emperor dreamed of various mild and clever forms of freedom and decentralisation. Ministers of incorruptible zeal restrained his liberal ardour.

From 1861 onwards the doors were open, and I passed several times through Paris. At first I was in

[1] Tyutchev, Fyodor (1803-1873), a minor poet, described as belonging to the 'Art for Art's sake' school, though of somewhat patriotic and Slavophil tendency, wrote lyrics marked by a deep feeling for nature and fine taste.—(*Translator's Note*.)

haste to leave it; afterwards that feeling too died away, and I grew accustomed to a new Paris. I was less angry with it. It was a different town, huge, unfamiliar. Learning and the intellectual movement, thrust back beyond the Seine, were not to be seen, political life was not to be heard. Napoleon had granted his 'broadened liberties'; the toothless opposition lifted its bald head and intoned the old phraseology of the 'forties; the working classes put no faith in them, kept silent and feebly tried co-operation and association. Paris was becoming more and more the general European market, in which everything in the world was crowding and jostling: merchants, singers, bankers, diplomats, aristocrats, artists of all countries, and masses of Germans unseen in old days. Taste, tone, expressions—all were changed. A glittering, oppressive luxury, metallic, golden, costly, succeeded the aesthetic feeling of old days: in dress and in trifles it was not choice nor taste that was the boast, but costliness, the power to waste, and people talked incessantly of profit, of gambling, of posts, of the funds. The *lorettes* set the tone for the ladies. The education of women sank to the level of Italy in the past.

L'Empire, I 'Empire . . . that is the evil, that is the trouble. . . . No, the cause lies deeper. *'Sire, vous avez un cancer rentré,'* said the physician. '*Un Waterloo rentré,*' answered Napoleon. And here we have two or three revolutions *rentrées, avortées*, stillborn.

Did France not bring them to the birth because she had too hurriedly, too prematurely conceived them, and wanted to be rid of her interesting position by a Caesarean operation? Was it because she had spirit enough for cutting off heads, but not enough for stamping out ideas? Was it because the Revolution was turned into an army and the rights of man were sprinkled with holy water? Was it because the masses were plunged in darkness, and the Revolution was made not for the peasants?

3

Alpendrücken

*'Hail to Light!
Hail to Reason!'*[1]

Russians who have no mountains near simply say that the *domovoy* choked them. It is perhaps a truer description. It certainly seems as though some one were choking you; your dream is not clear, but is very terrible; it is hard to breathe, yet one wants to draw deep breaths, the pulse is quicker, the heart throbs fast and painfully. . . . You are being hunted; creatures, not men, not visions, are just on your heels, you have glimpses of forgotten images that recall other years and an earlier age. . . . There are precipices, abysses, your foot slips, there is no escape, you fly into the void of darkness, a scream breaks unconsciously from your breast and you wake up. You wake up in a fever, drops of sweat on your brow; choking for breath, you hasten to the window. . . . Outside there is a fresh bright dawn, the breeze is carrying away the mist, there is the scent of grass and the forest, there are sounds and calls . . . everything that is ours and earthly. . . . And, comforted, you drink in deep draughts of the morning air.

The other day I had such a nightmare, and not in my sleep, but awake, not in bed but in a book, and when I tore myself from it to the light, I almost cried aloud: 'Hail to Reason! our simple earthly Reason!'

Old Pierre Leroux, whom I have been used to loving and respecting for thirty years, brought me his last work and begged me to be sure to read it, 'the text at least; the commentary will do afterwards, any time.'

---

[1] Quoted from a poem of Pushkin's.—(*Translator's Note.*)

'The Book of Job, a Tragedy in Five Acts, composed by Isaiah and translated by Pierre Leroux.' And not merely translated but applied to contemporary questions.

I read the whole text, and, overwhelmed with sadness and horror, made for the window.

What was the meaning of it?

What antecedents could have produced such a brain and such a book? What land gave birth to such a man, and what is its destiny? Such madness can only be that of a great mind; it is the last stage of a long and frustrated development.

The book is the delirium of a poet-lunatic, whose memory still retains facts and order, hopes and images, though no meaning is left; who has kept memories, feelings, forms, but not kept reason; or, if reason has survived, it is only to regress, to dissolve into its elements, to pass from thoughts into fancy, from truths into mysteries, from deductions into myths, from knowledge into revelation.

There is no going beyond it; the next stage is catalepsy, the stupor of the Pythian prophetess, of a Shaman, the frenzy of a dancing-dervish, the frenzy of twirling tables. . . .

Revolution and miracle-working, socialism and the Talmud, Job and George Sand, Isaiah and Saint-Simon, 1789 B.C. and A.D. 1789, all flung pell-mell into a cabalistic furnace—what could come out of these strained antagonistic combinations? The man has fallen ill with this undigested food, he has lost the healthy feeling for truth, the love and respect for reason. What is it that has driven him so far from his true course in his old age—a man who once stood among the leaders of the social movement, full of love and energy, whose words of indignation and sympathy for his poorer brethren moved our hearts? I remember those days. 'Peter the Red' (so we used to call him in the 'forties) 'is becoming my Christ,' Byelinsky, always carried to extremes, wrote to me. And here this teacher, this living, rousing voice, after fifteen years of seclusion in Jersey, appears with the Grève de Samarez and with the Book of Job, preaches some sort of transmigration of souls, seeks the solution in the other world, has no more faith in this one. France and the Revolution have deceived him; he pitches his tabernacle in the other world, in which there is no deception, and, indeed, nothing else, so that there is the more room for fantasy.

Perhaps it is an individual illness, an idiosyncrasy? Newton had his Book of Job, Auguste Comte his special madness.

Perhaps. . . but what is one to say when one picks up a second, a third French book, and always it is a book of Job, clouding the mind and weighing upon the heart? All set one seeking light and air, all bear the traces of spiritual turmoil and sickness, of something lost and gone astray; we can hardly put much of it down to individual insanity. On the contrary, we have to look for the explanation of the individual case in the general aberration; it is just in those who most fully represent the French genius that I see these traces of sickness.

These giants are lost, plunged in a heavy sleep, in long, feverish suspense, worn out with the woes of the day and burning impatience; they rave, as it were, half-asleep, and try to persuade us and themselves that their visions are reality and that real life is a bad dream, which will soon pass, particularly for France.

The inexhaustible wealth of their long years of civilisation, the vast stores of words and images, glimmer in their brains like the phosphorescence of the sea that lights up nothing. The whirlwind that comes before an approaching cataclysm has swept up and floated into these gigantic memories the fragments of two or three worlds, without cement, without connection, without science. The process by which their thought is developed is unintelligible to us; they pass from word to word, from antinomy to antinomy, from antithesis to synthesis, without solving them; the symbol is taken for the reality, the desire for the fact. There are vast yearnings with no practical means, no clear aims, unfinished outlines, thoughts half worked out, hints, approximations, prophecies, ornaments, frescoes, arabesques. . . . They have none of the clear coherence of which France boasted of old, they are not seeking the truth, it is so terrible in real life that they turn aside from it. False and strained romanticism, swollen and over-exuberant rhetoric have spoilt their taste for everything simple and sane. Proportion is lost, the perspective is false.

And it is not so bad as long as it is a matter of souls journeying about the planets, of the angelic settlements of Jean Reynaud,[1] of Job talking to Proudhon, and Proudhon to a dead woman; it) is not so bad as long as a fairy-tale is made out of the Thousand and One Nights of humanity, and Shakespeare from love and respect is buried under pyramids and obelisks, Olympus and the Bible, Assyria and Nineveh. But what are we to say to it when, on the very brink of shame and ruin, this rigmarole breaks into real life, throwing dust in the eyes and shuffling the cards in order to prophesy with them 'the nearness of happiness and the fulfilment of desire'? What is to be said when putrefying wounds are plastered over with the glittering rags of past glory, and syphilitic spots on the flabby cheeks are passed off for the flush of youth?

The old poet humbles himself in the dust before fallen Paris at the least pitiful moment of her degradation, when, pleased at the wealthy livery and lavishness of

[1] Reynaud, Jean (1806-1863), was a Utopian writer and follower of Saint-Simon.—(*Translator's Note*.)

PIERRE LEROUX AND VICTOR HUGO 259

her alien masters, she carouses in the market of the world. He greets Paris as the guiding-star of humanity, the heart of the world, the brain of history; he assures her that the bazaar on the Champs-de-Mars is the beginning of the brotherhood of nations and universal peace.

To intoxicate with praise a generation that has grown shallow, insignificant, complacent and conceited, pleased with flattery and self-indulgent, to maintain the pride of futile and degenerate sons and grandsons, veiling their paltry, senseless existence with the approval of genius, is a great sin.

To make of contemporary Paris the saviour and deliverer of the world, to assure her that she is great in her downfall, that she is not really fallen, is like the apotheosis of the divine Nero or the divine Caligula or Caracalla.

The difference is that the Senecas and the Ulpians were strong and powerful, while Victor Hugo is an exile.

Together with the flattery, one is struck by the vagueness of the conception, the confusion of the tendencies and the immaturity of the ideals. Men who walked in the van leading others are left behind in the twilight with no poignant yearning for the dawn. Talk of the transformation of humanity, the transmutation of all that exists . . . but of what and into what?

That is equally obscure in the other world of Pierre Leroux and in this world of Victor Hugo:—

'In the twentieth century she will be a marvellous land, she will be great, and that will not hinder her from being free. She will be famous, rich, profound in thought, peaceable, friendly to all the rest of mankind. She will possess the mild ascendancy of an elder sister.

'This central land which gives light to all, this model farm of humanity, on the pattern of which all the rest is moulded, has its heart, its brain, whose name is Paris.

'This city has one disadvantage: the world belongs

to him who rules her. Humanity follows her lead. Paris toils for the commonwealth of the earth. Whoever thou mayest be, Paris is thy master. . . she sometimes goes astray, she has her optical illusions, her errors of taste. . . and it is the worse for the sense of all the world: the compass is lost, and progress gropes its way.

'But the true Paris, I think, is different. I do not believe in that Paris—it is a phantom, and, moreover, a passing shadow is as nought in face of the vast radiance of the dawn.

'None but savages fear for the sun in an eclipse. Paris is a lighted torch; the lighted torch has will. . . . Paris will purge herself of all impurity; she has abolished the death penalty, so far as that lay in her power, and has transferred the guillotine to La Roquette. Men are hanged in London, in Paris they can no more be guillotined; if the guillotine were set up again before the Hotel de Ville, the very stones would rise up. To kill in these surroundings is impossible. It remains but to cast out of the law what has already been cast out of the city!

'1866 has been the year of the clash of nations, 1867 will be the year of their concord. The Exhibition in Paris is the great peace congress; all obstacles, all drags, all brakes on the wheels of progress will be shattered and fly into atoms. . . . War is impossible. . . . Why are dreadful cannons and other weapons of war exhibited?. . . Do we not know that war is dead? It died on the day on which Jesus said: "Love one another!" and has only lingered on like a ghost; Voltaire and the revolutionists slew it once more. We do not believe in war. All the nations have fraternised at the Exhibition, all the nations, flocking to Paris, have been France (*ils viennent être France*); they have learned that there is a city that is the sun of the world . . . and are bound to love her, to desire her, to submit to her rule!'

SCENES IN PARIS

And, moved to devotional tenderness before the nation which is evaporating in brotherhood, whose freedom is the testimony to the maturity of the human race, Hugo exclaims: 'Oh France! farewell! thou art too grand to be my fatherland! One must part from a mother who has become a goddess. Another step and thou wilt vanish transformed; thou art so great that soon thou wilt not be. Thou wilt not be France, thou wilt be humanity; thou wilt not be a land, thou wilt be universality. Thou art destined to pass out in light. . . . Boldly take up the burden of thy infinity, and, as Athens became Greece, Rome became Christianity, be thou, oh France, the World!'

As I was reading these lines there was a newspaper lying before me, and in it a simple-hearted correspondent had written as follows:—

'What is taking place now in Paris is extraordinarily interesting, not only for contemporaries, but for succeeding generations. The crowds that have gathered for the Exhibition are carousing. . . . All bounds are overstepped: there are orgies going on everywhere, in restaurants and private houses, most of all at the Exhibition itself. The arrival of the monarchs has finally intoxicated every one. Paris presents the spectacle of a colossal *Descente de la Courtille*. Yesterday (June 10) this intoxication reached its climax. When the crowned heads were feasting in the palace, which has seen so much in its day, the crowds thronged the surrounding streets and squares. Along the embankment in the rue Rivoli, rue Castiglione and rue St.-Honoré, as many as three hundred thousand people were feasting after their own fashion. From the Madeleine to the Théâtre des Variétés a most disorderly and unceremonious orgy was going on; big, open waggonettes, improvised omnibuses and chars-à-bancs, drawn by exhausted broken-down nags, moved at a snail's pace along the boulevards through the dense masses of heads. These vehicles were packed to overflowing: in them men and women with bottles in their hands were standing, sitting, and most often lying at full length in every conceivable attitude; laughing and singing, they talked with the crowds on foot; uproar and shouts met them from the crowds in cafés and restaurants, which were full to overflowing; sometimes the songs and bawling were interspersed with the savage oaths of a cabman or the friendly wrangle of drunkards. . . . Men were lying at the street-corners and in the back-alleys, dead drunk; the police themselves seemed to have retreated before the impossibility of doing anything. Never,' writes the correspondent, 'have I seen anything like it in Paris, and I have lived there for twenty years.'

This was in the street, 'in the gutter,' as the French express it, but what was being done within the palaces, illuminated by more than ten thousand lights . . . what was done at the banquets on which millions of francs were squandered?

'The sovereigns left the ball given by the city at the Hotel de Ville about two o'clock'—the official chronicler of the Emperor's festivities records. 'The carriages could not reach the building in time, nor drive home the eight thousand visitors. Hour after hour passed; the guests were weary, ladies sat down on the stairs, others simply lay down in the halls on the rugs, and fell asleep at the feet of the lackeys and *huissiers*, while gentlemen stepped over them, catching their spurs in their lace and flounces. When by degrees the rooms were cleared, the carpets could not be seen; they were all covered with faded flowers, broken beads, rags of blonde and lace, of tulle and muslin, torn from the ladies' dresses by the swords, hilts and stiff gold lace of the men.'

And behind the scenes the spies were catching men

who shouted: '*Vive la Pologne*,' beating them with their fists and passing them off for thieves, and in two instances the court condemned the latter to prison for *hindering* the spies from lawlessly, informally, arresting them with blows.

I purposely mention only trifles: microscopical dissection gives a better idea of the decay of the tissue than a big piece cut off a corpse.

4

The Daniels

In the days of July 1848, after the first terror and stupefaction of victors and vanquished, a thin, austere old man stepped forward as the embodiment of their stings of conscience. With gloomy words he cursed and branded the men of 'order' who had shot hundreds without even asking their names, had banished thousands untried, and had held Paris in a state of siege. When he had ended his anathema, he turned to the people and said: 'And you, be silent, you are too poor to have the right to speak.'

This was Lamennais. They were on the point of seizing him, but were awed by his grey hair, his wrinkles, his eyes, in which the tears of old age were quivering, and which would soon be closed for ever.

Lamennais' words passed, leaving no trace.

Twenty years later, other austere old men appeared with their stern words; and their voice too was lost in the wilderness.

They had no faith in the force of their words, but their hearts would not let them keep silent. Isolated in their banishment and their remoteness, these judges of the court of Vehm, these Daniels, pronounced their sentence, knowing that it would not be carried out.

They to their sorrow saw that this 'trifling cloud obscuring the grand dawn' was not so trifling; that this historical migraine, this drunkenness after revolution, would not pass off so quickly: and they said so.

'In the worst days of the ancient Caesarism,' said Edgar Quinet at the Congress in Geneva,' when every one was dumb except the sovereign, there were men who left their refuge in the wilderness to utter a few words of truth in the face of the fallen peoples. For sixteen years I have been living in the wilderness, and I in my turn should like to break the deathly silence to which our age has grown accustomed.'

What news did he bring from his mountains, and in the name of what did he lift up his voice? He lifted it up to tell his fellow-countrymen (whatever a Frenchman may be talking about, he always speaks of France): 'You have no conscience . . . it is dead, crushed under the heel of the mighty, it has disowned itself. For sixteen years I have been seeking traces of it and have not found it.

'It was the same under the Caesars in the ancient world. The soul of man had vanished. The peoples aided their own enslavement, applauded it, showing neither regret nor remorse. As the conscience of mankind vanished, it left an emptiness which was felt in everything as it is now, and to fill it a new god was needed.

'Who will in our day fill the abyss opened by modern Caesarism?

'In place of the worn-out, abolished conscience has come night; we wander in the darkness not knowing whence to seek aid, to whom to turn. All have helped to bring about our fall: church and law-court, the nations and society. . . . Deaf is the earth, deaf conscience, deaf the peoples; right has perished with conscience; only might rules. . . .

'What have you come for, what are you seeking in these ruins of ruins? You answer that you are seeking peace. Whence do you seek it? You are lost among the broken ruins of the fallen edifice of justice. You seek peace, you are mistaken, it is not here. Here is war. In this night without a dawn, nations and races are doomed to combat and destroy each other at hazard in obedience to the will of the rulers who have fettered their hands and their minds in bondage.

'The nations will rise again only when they are conscious of the depth of their fall!'

To diminish the horror of the picture the old man flung a few flowers for the children. His listeners applauded him. Even then they did not know what they had done. A few days later they went back on their applause.

Two months before these gloomy words rang out at the Geneva Congress, in another Swiss town another exile of old days wrote the following words:—

'I have no more faith in France. If ever she rises again to a new life and recovers from her terror of herself, it will be a miracle; no sick nation has risen up again from so deep a fall. I do not expect miracles. Forgotten institutions may be born again—but the spirit of the people, once quenched, will not revive. An *unjust* providence has not given me even that consolation which it so liberally deals out to make up for poverty to all exiles: perpetual hope and faith in their dreams. Nothing is left me from all I have passed through but the lessons of experience, bitter disillusionment, and an incurable weariness (*énervement*). There is ice in my heart, I have no more faith in right or human justice or common sense. I have turned away from it into indifference as into the tomb.'

The Girondist Mercier, with one foot in the grave, said at the time of the fall of the First Empire: 'I live only to see how it will end!' 'I cannot say even that,' added Marc Dufraisse. 'I have no special curiosity to know how the epic of the emperors will end.'

And the old man turned to the past, and with profound melancholy held it up to its degenerate successors. The present was strange, alien, revolting to him. From his cell rises the breath of the tomb, his words send a shiver through the listener.

Sayings of one, writings of another—all slid off, leaving no trace. Hearing them, reading them, the French had no 'ice in their heart.' Many were openly indignant: 'These men rob us of our strength and drive us to despair. . . . What salvation, what comfort is there in their words?'

It is not a judge's duty to comfort; he must unmask, must convict of sin, where there is no consciousness and no penitence. It is his work to stir the conscience. He is a judge and not a prophet, he has no Messiah in reserve for comfort in the future. He, like those he judges, belongs to the old religion. The judge stands for the pure and ideal side of it, while the masses represent its practical, evasive, attenuated application. While he condemns, the judge is practically forced to attack the ideal; while defending it, he proves its one-sidedness.

Neither Edgar Quinet nor Marc Dufraisse really knows of a solution, and they call us back to the past. It is no wonder that they do not see it; they stand with their back to it. They belong to the past. Revolted by the dishonourable end of their world, they seize their crutch, appear, uninvited guests, at the orgy of the haughty, complacent people, and tell them: 'You have lost all, you have sold all, nothing insults you but the truth. You have neither your old sense nor your old dignity, you have no conscience, you have fallen to the lowest depth, and, far from feeling your slavery, you insolently claim to be the deliverer of nations and nationalities. Decked with the laurels of war, you want to wear the olive-branches of peace. Take thought and repent, if you can. We, the dying, have come to call you to repentance, and if you do not, to break our rod upon you.'

They see their army retreating, deserting its flag, and with the scourge of their words try to drive it back to its old position, and cannot. A new banner is needed to rally them, and they have it not. Like heathen high priests they tear their garments, defending their fallen shrine. Not they, but the persecuted Nazarenes, bring tidings of a new birth and the life of the world to come.

Quinet and Marc Dufraisse sorrow over the defilement of their temple, the temple of representative government. They sorrow not only for the loss in France of freedom and human dignity, they grieve at the loss of the foremost place, they cannot resign themselves to the fact that the Empire did not prevent the unity of Germany, they are horrified that France has sunk into the background.

The question why France, in whom they do not themselves believe, should have the first place never once presents itself to their minds.

Marc Dufraisse with exasperated humility says that he does not understand the *new problems*, namely, the economic ones; while Quinet seeks a god to come and fill the emptiness left by the loss of conscience. . . . He has passed by them, they did not know him and let him be crucified.

Postscript.—As a commentary on our sketch there comes Renan's strange book on 'Contemporary Questions.' He too is frightened by the present. He sees that things are going badly. But what pitiful remedies! He sees a sick man, rotting with syphilis, and advises him to study well, especially the classics. He sees the inner indifference to everything except material profit, and weaves out of his rationalism some sort of religion—Catholicism without a real Christ and without a pope, but with mortification of the flesh. He sets up disciplinary, or rather hygienic, fences for the mind.

Perhaps the most important and boldest thing in his book is his saying about the Revolution: 'The French Revolution was a grand experiment, but it was an experiment that has failed.'

And then he presents the picture of the destruction of all the old institutions, which, though oppressive on the one side, did serve as a means of resistance against an all-devouring centralisation, and in their place man left weak and defenceless before an oppressive, all-powerful State and a Church that survived intact.

One cannot help thinking with horror of the union of this State and Church which is being accomplished before our eyes, and which goes so far that the Church is restricting medicine, taking doctors 'diplomas from materialists, and trying to decide questions of reason and revelation by decision of the Senate, to decree *libre arbitre*, as Robespierre decreed *l'Éire Suprême*.

To-morrow, if not to-day, the Church will capture education—and what then?

The French who have survived the reaction see that, and their position in regard to foreigners becomes more and more disadvantageous. They have never put up with so much as now, and from whom? From the Germans in particular. Not long ago an argument between a German *ex-refugié* and a distinguished French *littérateur* took place before me. The German was ruthless. In old days the Germans had a sort of tacit agreement of tolerance for English people, who were always allowed to say absurd things, out of respect and the conviction that they were a little crazy, and for Frenchmen, from affection for them and gratitude for the Revolution. These amenities have only survived for the English; Frenchmen find themselves in the position of elderly beauties who have lost their looks and have for years failed to observe that their charms have diminished, and that they have nothing more to expect from the fascinations of their beauty.

In old days their ignorance of everything that lay outside the frontiers of France, their use of hackneyed phrases, their tawdry tinsel, their tearful sentimentality, their aggressive domineering tone and *les grands mots*, were all allowed to pass—but now all this indulgence is over.

The German, setting his spectacles straight, slapped the Frenchman on the shoulder, saying: '*Mais, mon cher et très cher ami*, these are stock phrases that take the place of criticism, of attention, of understanding; we know them by heart; you have been repeating them for thirty years; they prevent you from seeing clearly the real position of affairs.'

'But anyway,' said the literary gentleman, obviously desirous of finishing the conversation, 'you, my dear philosopher, have all bowed your heads under the yoke of Prussian despotism. I quite understand that you look upon it as a means, that the Prussian domination is a step...'

'That is just where we differ from you,' the German interrupted him, 'that we take that bitter path, hating it and submitting to necessity, with an object before our eyes, while you have reached that position as though it were a haven of refuge; for you it is not a step towards the goal, but the goal itself—and besides, the majority likes it.'

'*C'est une impasse, une impasse*,' observed the Frenchman gloomily, and changed the conversation.

Unluckily he began speaking of Jules Favre's speech in the Academy; then another German turned grumpy and said: 'Upon my soul, can that empty rhetoric, that verbosity, hypocrisy, please you? It is hypocritical, and false to everything; how can a man deliver a panegyric for two hours on that pale Cousin? And what business had he to defend orthodox spiritualism? And do you suppose that such opposition will save you? They are rhetoricians and sophists. And how absurd is the whole procedure of speech and answer, of having to praise one's predecessor, all this mediaeval battle of words!'

'*Ah bah! Vous oubliez les traditions, les coutumes.*'
I felt sorry for the Frenchman. . . .

5

SPOTS OF LIGHT

But beyond the Daniels there are spots of light to be seen—faint, far away, and in Paris, too. I am speaking of the Quartier Latin, of that Aventine Hill to which the students and their teachers retreated, that is, those of them who remained faithful to the great tradition of 1789, to the encyclopaedists, to the Montagne, to the Socialist movement. There the gospel of the first revolution is preserved; there the acts of its apostles and the epistles of the holy fathers of the eighteenth century are read; there the great problems of which Marc Dufraisse knows nothing are familiar subjects; there men dream of the future Kingdom of Man just as the monks of the first centuries dreamed of the Kingdom of God.

From the side-streets of this Latium, from the fourth storey of its sombre houses, champions and missionaries continually go forth to combat and preach and perish—for the most part morally, but sometimes physically—*in partibus infidelium*, that is, on the other side of the Seine.

Objective truth is on their side, every sort of justice and real understanding is on their side, but that is all. 'Sooner or later truth is always triumphant.' But we imagine that it is very much later, and very rarely even then. From time immemorial reason has been unattainable or detestable to the majority. That reason might be attractive, Anacharsis Cloots had to dress it up as a pretty actress and to strip her naked. One can only work upon men by seeing their dreams more clearly than they see them themselves, and not by proving one's thoughts to them as geometrical theorems are proved.

The Quartier Latin recalls the mediaeval Carthusians or Camaldoli,[1] who turned aside from the noise of the crowd with their faith in brotherhood, mercy, and, above all, the speedy coming of the Kingdom of God. And this at tie very time when outside their walls knights and *ritters* were burning and slaying, shedding blood, plundering the villeins and outraging their daughters. . . . Then followed other times, also without brotherhood and the Second Coming—but the Camaldoli and the Carthusians still clung to their faith. Manners have grown softer still, the fashion of plundering has changed, women are outraged now for pay, men are robbed in accordance with accepted rules. The Kingdom of God has not come, but was inevitably coming (so it seemed to the Carthusians), the tokens were growing clearer, more direct than ever; faith saved the recluses from despair.

At every blow which sends the last fragments of freedom flying into dust, at every downward step of society, at every insolent step backwards, the Quartier Latin lifts up its head, *mezza voce* at home sings the Marseillaise, and, setting its cap straight, says: 'That is as it should be. They will reach the limit; the sooner

[1] A Benedictine order founded by St. Romuald at Camaldoli in Italy in 1009.—(*Translator's Note*.)

the better. 'The Quartier Latin believes in its course and boldly draws the plan of its' kingdom of truth,' running directly counter to the 'kingdom of reality.'

And Pierre Leroux believes in Job!

And Victor Hugo in the Exhibition of universal brotherhood!

6

After the Invasion

'Holy Father, it is your task now !'
       'Don Carlos'
    (Philip 11. to the Grand Inquisitor).

I keep wanting to repeat these words to Bismarck. The pear is ripe and the thing cannot be done without His Excellency. Do not stand on ceremony, Count!

I do not marvel at what is being done, and I have no right to marvel—I have long been crying out, Beware, beware! . . . l simply say farewell, and that is hard. There is neither contradiction nor weakness in it. A man may know very well that if his gout gets worse it will hurt him very much; what is more, he may have a presentiment that it will get worse, and that there is no way of stopping it: nevertheless, it will hurt him just as much when it does come on.

I am sorry for individual persons whom I love.

I am sorry for the country, whose first awakening I saw with my own eyes and which now I see outraged and dishonoured. I am sorry for the Mazeppa, who was untied from the tail of one empire to be tied to the tail of another.

I am sorry that I am right. I am, as it were, connected with the fact from having in outline foreseen it. I am angry with myself as a child is angry with the barometer that predicts a storm and spoils his picnic.

Italy is like a family in which some black crime has

AFTER THE INVASION

lately been committed, some horrible calamity that has betrayed ugly secrets has come to pass; a family which has been touched by the hangman's hand, or from which some one has been carried off to the galleys. . . . All are exasperated, the innocent are ashamed and ready for insolent defiance. All are tortured by an impotent desire of revenge, poisoned, weakened by a passive hatred.

Perhaps there are means of escape close at hand, but they cannot be found by reason; they lie in chance happenings, in external circumstances, they lie outside the frontiers. Italy's fate is not in her own hands, that is in itself one of the most insufferable humiliations; it so rudely recalls her recent captivity and the feeling of her own weakness and instability which had begun to be effaced.

And only twenty years!

Twenty years ago at the end of December I finished in Rome the first article of my *From the Other Side* and was faithless to it, carried away by the year'forty-eight. I was then in the heyday of my powers, and I watched with eagerness the unfolding of events. In my life there had not yet been one misfortune which had left one deep, aching scar, not one reproach of conscience inwardly, not one insulting word outwardly. With unreasoning light-heartedness, with boundless self-confidence, I floated lightly dancing on the waves with all sails set, and I have had to take them in one after another!

* * * * *

I was in Paris at the time of Garibaldi's first arrest. The French did not believe in the invasion by their troops.[1] I happened to meet with people of very

---

[1] Napoleon sent troops to Italy in 1861 to support the Pope, whose temporal power was maintained by a French garrison in Rome from that date to 1870.—(*Translator's Note*.)

different classes in society. The inveterate reactionaries and clericals desired intervention, clamoured for it, but yet doubted. At the railway station a distinguished French savant as he took leave of me said: 'Your imagination, my dear northern Hamlet, is so constructed that you see nothing but what is black; that's why the impossibility of war with Italy is not obvious to you. The Government knows too well that war for the Pope would set all thinking people against it; after all, you know, we are the France of 1789.'

The first news, not that I read but that I saw, was the fleet setting off from Toulon to Cività. 'It is only a military manœuvre,' another Frenchman said to me. '*On ne viendra jamais aux mains*, and besides there is no need for us to soil our hands in Italian blood.'

It turned out that there *was need*. A few lads from 'Latium' protested; they were clapped in the lock-up, and with that everything ended as far as France was concerned. Italy, blood-stained and taken unawares, thanks to the irresolution of the King and the trickery of the Ministers, made every concession. But the French, rendered savage, intoxicated by every victory, could not be stopped: to blood, to action, they had to add words of abuse.

And on these words of abuse being uttered and greeted with the applause of the Empire, its fiercest foes—the Legitimists in the form of the old attorney of the Bourbons, Berryer and the Orleanists in the form of the old Figaro of the days of Louis-Philippe, Thiers—shook hands with it.

I look upon Rouher's words as an historical revelation. Any one who did not understand France after that must have been born blind·

Count Bismarck, it is your task now!

And you, Mazzini, Garibaldi, last of the saints, last of the Mohicans, fold your hands and take your rest.

A PROPHECY

You are not needed now. You have done your part. Make room now for madness, for the frenzy of blood in which either Europe will slay herself or the Reaction will. What will you do with your hundred republicans and your volunteers with two or three cases of contraband guns? Now there are a million from here and a million from there with needle-guns and other artifices. Now there will be lakes of blood, seas of blood, mountains of corpses. . . . And then plague, famine, fire and devastation. *Ah, messieurs les conservateurs*, you would not have even so pale a republic as that of February, you would not have the mawkish democracy laid at your feet by the confectioner Lamartine, you would not have Mazzini the Stoic or Garibaldi the hero. You wanted order.

For that you will have a Seven Years 'war, a Thirty Years' war. . . .

You were afraid of social reforms, so now you have the Fenians with their barrel of gunpowder and their lighted match.

Who is the fool?

GENOA, *December* 31, 1867.

THE EMPEROR ALEXANDER I. AND V. N. KARAZIN[1]

To you, N. A., our latest Marquis von Posa, with all my heart I dedicate this sketch,

1

DON CARLOS

DURING the first years of the reign of Alexander 1., that is, when the lessons of Laharpe[2] were still fresh in his memory and the lesson given to all the monarchs in Paris and to the Russian autocrats in particular in the Mihailoysky Palace[3] had not been forgotten, the Emperor Alexander 1. used to have literary soirées, and some of the persons of the Tsar's circle, well known as capable of reading and writing, used to be invited to them.

---

[1] In my early youth I saw Vassily Nazarovitch Karazin two or three times. I remember that my father used to talk of his letter to Alexander 1., of his close association with the Tsar, and of bis rapid fall. In 1860 I read a remarkable life of the man in the *Northern Bee*. In the impetuous, enterprising career of Karazin everything arrests attention, most of all what was not in the *Northern Bee*, that is, what was left on the other side of the censor's shears. I happened to get hold of a letter of Karazin's to the Emperor (it was published in the *Russian Messenger* in 1810) and some other documents. At first I only thought of publishing the letter to complete the above-mentioned article. Then I felt inclined to make a few general observations regarding Alexander 1.'s attitude to Karazin, and this I have done. The biography of V. N. Karazin is far from being covered by the article in the *Northern Bee* and these notes; they are only materials for it. I have hardly touched upon Karazin's life, I have only tried to sketch the surroundings and block in the background against which his figure stands out. This article was published in The Polar Star, vol. vii. page 7.—(*Author's Note.*)

[2] Laharpe, F. C. de (1754-1838), a Swiss politician, was the tutor of Alexander 1.

[3] Where Paul 1. was murdered.—(*Translator's Notes.*)

A LITERARY SOIRÉE

At one of these evenings there was a reading which lasted a long time; they read aloud a new tragedy of Schiller's.

The reader finished and stopped.

The Tsar sat silent with downcast eyes. Perhaps he was thinking of his own fate, which had so closely resembled the fate of Don Carlos, perhaps the fate of his Philip. A complete silence lasted for some minutes. The first to break it was Prince Alexandr Nikolayevitch Golitsyn; bending down to the ear of Count Victor Pavlovitch Kotchubey, he said to him in an undertone, but so that every one could hear it: 'We have our Marquis Posa!' Kotchubey smiled and nodded. The eyes of all the company turned to a man of thirty who was sitting a little way off.

The Tsar started, looked at the circle about him, cast a distrustful, searching glance upon the man who had become the object of general attention, frowned, stood up, gloomy and displeased, took leave of his guests and went out.

Prince Alexandr Nikolayevitch, the future Minister of Education and Religion, the inquisitor and the freemason, the protector of Magnitsky and Runitch, the President of the Bible Society and the Post Office Department, the friend of the Emperor Alexander, who mercilessly sacrificed him to Araktcheyev, the friend of the Emperor Nicholas, who never gave him any commission of importance, smiled; he was satisfied. Knowing Alexander's suspicious character, he was certain that his words had gone home—and he was not mistaken. Why he had injured the man he could not have said: that lay hidden in his courtier's nature; it is never amiss to thrust aside a superfluous person.

There is no doubt that, at that moment, of all the company present only two had a sincere and ardent desire for the good of Russia—the Tsar and V. N. Karazin, who had been called the Marquis Posa.

These two personages—one 'crowned and exalted' in the Uspensky Cathedral by the Metropolitan Platon, the man who had crushed Napoleon and was himself crushed under the burden of glory and of helpless, hopeless autocracy; and the other, the inexhaustible worker for the common weal who undertook everything with extraordinary energy, pushing at every door and meeting everywhere opposition, hindrances, and the impossibility of doing anything real in those surroundings—these two personages cast two melancholy gleams of light on the frozen wastes of Russia, in which energy and character, talents and powers, were sunk, and are still sunk, lost, unrecorded, in the swampy bogs, like the piles on which Petersburg is built.

The character of the Emperor Alexander1. has never been fully explained. Our historians could not write of him, foreigners neither could nor can understand his tragic significance. This is not due either to his rank as Tsar or to his personal misfortunes; on the contrary, he was exceptionally fortunate as a Tsar, fortunate even after his death. No ruler could stand out in greater relief than he does. To succeed Paul was enough, apart from being succeeded by Nicholas. Between the tiger of Gatchina butchered like a wild beast and the boa-constrictor buttoned up to the chin who stifled Russia for thirty years, the stooping figure of the Emperor Alexander is strikingly humane and mild, now lighted up by the fire of Moscow, now by the illumination of Paris, now restraining the princely German thieves, now checking the wild vengeance of the conquerors when they had burst into their enemies' capital.

And this figure of an Agamemnon, reconciling Europe, at the height of its grandeur grows dimmer, visibly fades, and is obliterated behind the awful shadow of Araktcheyev. It is lost in solitude on the shores of the Black

A HEART-RENDING TRAGEDY

Sea, giving the hand of belated reconciliation to the woman whose whole life, veiled in the Imperial purple, had been one humiliation, and who, kneeling a lonely figure before the dying man, closed his eyes.[1]

Every inch[2] a heart-rending tragedy.

No need to seek the solution in the death of Paul; that may have added another thread of gloom to his life, but the background is broader, wider, deeper. Some implacable fatal element hovers over it and enfolds it far and wide. In the surroundings there is a feeling of an ominous breath, the presence of crime—not crime committed, not past, but crime persisting and inevitable; it is in the blood, the walls are saturated with it. Before birth, the blood has been poisoned in the veins. The air which people breathe here is full of corruption; every one who steps into it, whether he will or no, is sucked into a gulf of ineptitude, ruin, sin. The path to every evil is wide open. Good is impossible. Woe to the man who stops and thinks, who asks himself what he is doing, what people are doing about him! he will go mad; woe to the man who within these walls suffers a human feeling to enter his heart: he will be broken in the struggle.

Well, the Emperor Alexander 1. was among the Russian crowned heads the first after Peter who did so stop and think. That is why he is the only one of all the Romanovs who has been punished, punished humanly, by inner struggle, punished before he was guilty, though he reached that guilt in the end.

Compare his fate with the fate of Peter 111., of Paul, of Nicholas, if you like, and you will understand why that man, called the blessed, who died in his bed and was never conquered, was a far more tragic figure than all his predecessors. What is there tragic in the drunken

[1] The Empress Elizabeth is meant.
[2] English in the original.—(*Translator's Notes*.)

idiot[1] being killed and robbed by a dissolute woman? That is happening all the time in the grimy houses of the dark London by-streets. Or what is there tragic in the fact that a man defending himself from a madman[2] brought a snuff-box down on the latter's head and others finished him off? Those were not tragic catastrophes, but acts of the criminal court and houses of correction.

The tragic element is not given by pain nor bruises nor blows, but by those spiritual conflicts that are independent of the will and run counter to the reason, with which a man struggles but which he can never overcome; on the contrary, he almost always yields to them, crushed against the granite rocks of apparently insoluble contradictions. To be shattered in that way needs a certain degree of humane culture, needs a special grace of a sort. There are natures so commonplace, so conventional, so narrow and mediocre, that their happiness and unhappiness is trivial, or at any rate not interesting. The cold eyes, the deadly prose, of the drill and discipline of Nicholas' despotism, his limited outlook continually fixed upon trifles and details, his subaltern's precision and partiality for straight lines, for geometrical figures, exclude everything poetical. It is vain to try to make something majestically gloomy out of his latter days. The man never stopped at anything, never doubted of anything; he might hesitate, but he could not repent; he had no ideals, he knew that he reigned by the will of God, that the post of Emperor was a military officer's, and he was completely satisfied with himself. He did not suspect that the moral life of the State was being degraded by him, that, shut in and robbed right and left, he was leaving Russia on the edge of the abyss. When he did discover this last fact, he

---

[1] Peter 111., who was murdered, possibly with the connivance of Catherine 11., is meant.

[2] Paul 1. and his assassination is meant.—(*Translator's Notes.*)

ALEXANDER I. A DREAMER

saw with vexation that he was not equal to coping with his first failure, and at once died of impotent fury. That was a lesson, an example, a warning, but not a tragedy. If that is not so, one may make a tragic type not only of every robber who is punished, but even of the splenetic coward, Araktcheyev,[1] dying at Gruzino, hated and abandoned by all, beside the foul grave soaked with the blood of a whole household of servants.

The Emperor Alexander was very different. The Empress Catherine, who concentrated upon him all the dynastic interest and the motherly feeling she had never had for her own son, gave him a very humane education and, as is common with old sinners, brought him up in ignorance of what was going on around him. Alexander was a dreamer, a youth of romantic ideas, with the vague philanthropy which was then in fashion, and which was a sort of Aurora Borealis or cold glimmering reflection of that other, warmer philanthropy preached in those days in Paris. But for all that, his education ended early, and with Laharpe's teaching in his head he appears on the royal stage, surrounded by the grey-headed, putrefying corruption of the last years of the reign of Catherine.

'I am greatly dissatisfied with my position,' he writes as Grand Duke to Kotchubey on May 18, 1796, that is, when he was eighteen. 'I am extremely glad that the subject has come up of itself, or I should have found it very hard to begin upon it. Yes, dear friend, I repeat: my position does not satisfy me at all. It is too conspicuous for my character, which finds pleasure exclusively in quietness and tranquillity. Court life is not made for me. I suffer every time I have to appear on the stage of the Court, and I am out of humour at the sight of the mean things done by others at every step for the sake of gaining external distinctions, in my eyes

[1] See Vol. II. page 202.—(*Translator's Note.*)

not worth a farthing. I feel unhappy in the company of such people, whom I should not care to have as lackeys; and yet here they fill the highest posts, as for instance, Z., P., B., both the S. M., and numbers of others not worth mentioning, who are haughty with their inferiors but cringe before those they are afraid of. In short, my dear friend, I am conscious that I was not born for the high position which I endure now, and still less for that destined for me in the future, which I have inwardly vowed to renounce in one way or another.

'This, dear friend, is a grave secret which I have long meant to tell you. I think it unnecessary to beg you not to speak of it to any one, for you will understand of yourself how dearly I might have to pay for it. I have asked G. Garrick to burn this letter if he should not succeed in handing it to you in person, and not to give it to any one else to pass on to you.

'I have considered the subject from every point of view. I must tell you that the first idea of it had arisen in my mind even before I came to know you, and that I was not long in reaching my present decision.

'The disorder prevailing in our affairs is incredible; there is robbery on every side, all departments are badly governed; order seems to have been banished from everywhere—and in spite of that, all the energies of the Empire are devoted to nothing but widening its frontiers. When that is the position of things, it is scarcely possible for one man to govern the State, even less so to reform the deeply rooted abuses existing in it. . . . The task is beyond the powers not only of a man endowed like me with ordinary abilities, but even of a genius, and I have always clung to the principle that it is better not to undertake a task at all than to perform it badly. It is in accordance with that principle that I have taken the resolution I have mentioned to you above. My plan is, after renouncing this difficult career (I cannot yet with certainty fix the date of this renunciation), to settle with my wife on the banks of the Rhine, where I shall live quietly as a private man, finding my happiness in the society of my friends and in the study of nature.

'You are at liberty to laugh at me and say that this design is impracticable; but wait till it has been carried out and then pronounce judgment. I know that you will blame me, but I can do nothing else, for I make the peace of my conscience my first rule, and it can not be at rest if I undertake a task beyond my strength. This, my dear friend, is what I have long wished to tell you. Now when it has all been uttered, there is nothing left for me, but to assure you that wherever I may be, whether happy or unhappy, rich or poor, your affection for me will always be one of my greatest comforts; mine for you, believe me, will end only with my life.'

Catherine died. Paul dragged the body of Peter III. into the Peter-Paul Fortress in a hard frost to bury it beside his dead mother, and made Count A. Orlov[1] and Baryatinsky carry the former Tsar's crown. Alexander was moved one step nearer to that pinnacle surrounded by the clouds of corruption of which he wrote. Everything was already transformed by one death, everything grew even viler, though in a different way. It was his lot to regret the courtiers 'whom he would not have cared to have for his lackeys.' The spoilt and sated household of the old mistress was filled with the army captains and *kammerdieners* of her successor, who brought the atmosphere of the barracks and servants' hall into the palace. In place of the haughty palace robbers there were thieves who were police spies; in place of the lackeys there were hangmen. The palace was transformed from a brothel into a torture-chamber.

[1] Count Alexey Orlov was the murderer of Peter III.—(*Translator's Note.*)

The orgy of sensuality was followed by an orgy of ferocity and cruelty.

Overwhelmed with horror, the Tsarevitch stood in alarm and distress at the foot of the savage throne; powerless to help and unable to get away, Alexander wandered like Hamlet through the palace-halls, unable to decide on anything; others decided for him.

With the same alarm and distress, and with a black stain, moreover, on his conscience, he mounted to the dreadful pinnacle from which the mutilated corpse of his slain father had just been thrown down. He wanted the good of Russia and he was trusted. Men gazed on his mild and youthful features with ardent hope; he too hoped that he would make a paradise of Russia; he would give her his best years, his utmost strength, the people should bless him; he would expiate the sin of his share in the bloody deed, and then, like Trajan and Marcus Aurelius, he would do what he had written to Kotchubey and retire to his vineyards on the banks of the Rhine.[1]

Alexander was sincere in these dreams; he believed in them, and not he alone, all Russia believed in them, that is, the Russia of decent people, the Russia recognised as human. The *dark* masses of Russia, the Russia of the poor, had nothing to do with it. As at all celebrations and holidays, they were excluded from the general rejoicing, and, indeed, made no effort to take part in it, remembering their Little Mother, the Empress, and seeming instinctively to divine that the new reign would only pay for the blood of every twelfth man among them with the gift of Araktcheyev's military settlements.

It was easy to begin a new epoch supported by such love, such faith, such joy at the death of the miscreant. . . .

[1] He dreamecd of abdication up to the time of his death.—(*Author's Note*.)

> 'Now give me a man, O Creator....
> Thou hast given me much: a true man
> Is all that I ask Thee for now ...
> I pray for a friend; I am not such
> As Thou the All-Knowing. The servants
> Thou hast sent me, Thou knowest
> Their hearts what they are,
> For money alone do they serve me
> Truth and faith is all that I ask.'[1]

Ten days had passed after the death of Paul. There was a great reception in the palace; people with joyous faces, clothed in deep mourning, came and went, bowing low, repeating slavish phrases. Alexander, shy, unaccustomed to this job and to playing the part of a god, before whom every one falls down, upon whom every one rests his hopes, went after the reception exhausted to his study, and sank into an easy-chair before his writing-table. On his table in his study, which no one dared to enter, there lay a thick letter, sealed and addressed to him.

He broke the seal and opened the letter; as he read it, his eyes filled with tears, his cheeks burned. He put down the letter, and big tears still rolled down his cheeks. They were seen by Count Pahlen and Troshtchinsky. 'Gentlemen,' the Tsar said to them, 'some one unknown has put this letter on my table; there is no signature; you must find out for me who wrote it.'

2

The Letter

Here is what the Emperor read:—

'With what a lovely day has Thy reign begun! It seemed as though Nature herself were greeting Thee

[1] Quotation from Schiller's tragedy, *Don Carlos.*—(*Translator's Note.*)

with rapture![1] Alexander, beloved of our hearts! For ten days now the spring sun has been shining on Thy subjects, who are full of hopes, and day by day, hour by hour, Thou hast done more to justify those hopes. What a joyful future awaits us!

'At this time of universal rejoicing, who would spare his life for Thy defence? But Thou hast no need of it. . . . Forgive me, then, if I, remote from Thy Court and all dreams of reward, an obscure Russian, seeking to bring Thee an offering, trace certain truths with audacious hand. Forgive, forgive me for this unworthy offering, an offering from the heart; accept it as a testimony of trust in Thy virtues, as a sign of the true love of Thy subjects. Doubtless all that I could say to Thee is more or less clearly printed already on Thy noble heart, or is well known in the counsels of the wise men with whom Thou surroundest Thyself. But this thought could not keep me from offering my widow's mite to the treasury, even as the most dazzling conception of Thy glory will never keep me from zealously proclaiming it wherever I may go.

'My Sovereign! Thou reignest over forty million men, from of old accustomed to pay boundless homage to authority, apart from which they cannot picture their weal. A mere glance from their Tsar is often enough to diffuse universal joy, and of course, a mere command is enough to give the greatest happiness man can enjoy on earth. . . .

'The Empire which will call Thee its own is not an ordinary State. There is no other like it either in the Europe of to-day or in the other parts of the earth, nor perhaps in the chronicles of past ages. It includes ten

[1] It happened that the 11th of March 1801 was a most unpleasant wintry day in Petersburg; on the 12th the weather turned mild, warm and bright, as though the spring had suddenly come.—(*Author's Note.*)

climates, and is inhabited by a people for the most part
of one language and of one religion. From north to
south and from west to east it abounds in innumerable
riches of all kinds supplementing each other; and this
gives it the possibility of complete independence in its
relations with foreign countries. It has spacious lands
for producing the materials peculiar to it, and the trusty
hands of its sons for working upon them. Hence its
wealth, resting on no chance foundations but on Nature
herself, is bound to increase with time. It may be compared to a mine that has only been opened on the surface,
the wealth of which is gradually revealed as it is sunk
deeper. It abounds in rivers which, flowing from its
centre into five seas,· await only the protecting hand of
government to unite them in order to carry the products
of Europe to Asia and the products of Asia to Europe
by the shortest ways. It is bounded for the most part
by the Arctic Ocean or by lands as unapproachable;
on its other frontiers it has neighbours accustomed to
respect the might of Russia. What new thing can I
say to Thee, Sire, of the civic virtues of Thy people,
which even in the period of coarsest ignorance had
already given evidence of its power; of the people, which
in the present state of the moral world is perhaps less
corrupted than any other nation?. . . I will only
recall one of these virtues, which secures the stability
of the Fatherland. The sacrifice of life for one's
country has at all times and in all places been deemed
worthy of everlasting praise; but this sacrifice with no
prospect of the glory which comforts dying heroes, this
great devotion, is characteristic only of rare souls, and the
Russian soldier is more capable of it than any warrior
of ancient or modern times. The heroic leader goes
to his death: I respect him; but I see that the glory
which beyond the grave will strew its laurels on him
fills his mind with the admiration of his fellow-country-

men and of posterity, and that glory softens the horrors of death. He is intoxicated by ambition, the desire of winning the highest distinction. The very necessity of acting in accordance with the traditions of the class to which he belongs leads him on. But the humble soldier who does not dream of laurels, who has none of the conventional ideas of noble birth that compel a man to distinguish himself, expects no reward; the soldier, whose lot is unchanged after twenty battles won, and who, with no thought of eye-witnesses, of posterity, of history, dies *altogether*, for whom his sacred duty is the one impelling force, is to my mind a great hero indeed! Such is the Russian soldier; and of such Thou hast hundreds of thousands. Time has developed the wisdom of man; time, which perfects all things, is making it possible for the lawgiver to be the benefactor of all mankind. If Catherine, if Marcus Aurelius himself had lived in the Iron Age of the reign of Ivan Vassilyevitch when all Europe was still shrouded in the darkness of superstition and oppressed by the tyranny of feudalism, could they have done much for the benefit of their subjects? Even assuming that they had evolved laws from their own benevolent hearts, from their own all-embracing wisdom, assuming that they could have found the possibility of vigorous action and of deep reflection, could, without any preliminary study, have fully understood the organisation of society and the hearts of the people, where could they have found men worthy to carry out their plans? Neither the men nor the means for public education had yet been evolved. In our day, Sire, legislation, together with other branches of learning and the progress of reason which has inevitably advanced in the course of ages, offers Thee in the works of the greatest minds a thousand new ideas. These ideas, embraced by Thy beneficent spirit, and tested by Thy religious ardour as gold by fire, may be the foundation of the happiness of the Russians. Great is the service of the sage who laboriously discovers the truth; but he who uses the power given him by Heaven to apply that truth to real life is deserving of an altar! He is like God Who gathers the mists that float profitless in the air into the fructifying rain that brings fertility to the plains and water to the rivers irrigating them. If earthly rulers may be likened to the Great Inconceivable Being Who has created millions of worlds, it can only be when they imitate Him in their beneficence. . . .

'Look at the present state of Europe; can there ever have been a time fitter for the raising of Thy "Russia to the pinnacle of glory and happiness" in accordance with Thy promise? The pretensions and aims of all the Powers are so different, so opposed to one another, that Thou canst never be forced to take up arms if Thou hast Thyself peaceful intentions, if the vain praises of idle minds (the so-called glory of conquerors) are never by Thee held worthy to be weighed beside the blessings of thousands and thousands of men whose fate depends on Thee. The French Revolution, so fatal in itself, so menacing to the stability of many Governments, far from doing harm to Russia, into which its principles could never penetrate, has brought it palpable advantage: in the first place, by turning away the envious attention of the Powers at the moment most critical for Russia, and then, by the new grouping of their alliances, freeing our Court from the necessity of adhering to one or the other party, both of whom now, regarding our alliance as the determining factor, are bound to compete for our goodwill. Through this unexpected concatenation of circumstances Russia has emerged from the state of concealed warfare with all the European Powers which has always existed since the days of Peter the Great. The very youth of Russia, which would hardly have been forgotten for another whole century, has been for ever effaced from the memory of man by the Revolution.

'In this position of affairs, the internal and external debts of Thy Empire are not so great in comparison with the still unexhausted sources of Thy revenues that the Treasury could not be extricated from every difficulty in a few months by simply cancelling some proposed expenses.

'Such are the means, Sire, which Thou hast at Thy disposal for becoming a great and happy monarch in the midst of the happiest people on earth. . . .

'At night as I passed by Thy palace I drew this picture of Thy blessed political position and pondered on what would be Thy ways.

'Can it be, I said to myself, can it be that He will wantonly destroy the rare harmony of heaven and earth in His favour, and will leave uncompleted the blessed work that has been prepared by the last half-century? Can it be that for the pleasure—created for common souls—of despotic power He will coldly sacrifice the people's hopes, the immortal glory and the reward which in the Land of Bliss awaits virtuous monarchs after a long untroubled life filled with domestic joys?

'*No! He will open the great book of our destiny and the destiny of our descendants to which Catherine only pointed with her finger. He will give us inviolable laws. He will confirm these laws for generations on generations with the oath of allegiance of his numerous subjects. He will say to Russia: "This is the limit of my autocratic power and that of my descendants, and is immutable for ever. . . ." And Russia will at last become one of the monarchical powers,· and the iron sceptre of arbitrary tyranny shall not be able to break the Tables of her Covenant.*

'Towards this goal He will move slowly, as Nature moves in the mysterious ways I made ready for her by the Creator, He will call to His aid the Eternal Reason that can shed light on His soul; guided by that, He will examine the whole code of laws hitherto existing, that He may not without need or through mere love of novelty destroy what has been confirmed and justified by time. In the name of the Fatherland He will require advice from the wise men happily placed by destiny at His side, and from others whose voice from the remotest borders of His Empire may make the truth known to Him. *Under vow of strictest discretion* He will question them; with the light of His own pure conscience He will go through the works of the lawgivers of the world, ancient and modern, and will compare them with the circumstances of His people, with their manners, customs and religion, with their local conditions, with the true enlightenment promised us by the coming age after the cruel trials of the past. . . . He will compile in secret, but publish in the face of an attentive world, an Imperial Code, the basis of laws which may of themselves imperceptibly pave the way for the diffusion of its underlying principles. He will command throughout the expanse of Russia the election of elders, worthy of the unlimited confidence of their fellow-citizens; and, putting them beyond the sphere of ambition and fear, bestow upon them the excess of His authority—that they may preserve the Holy of Holies of the Fatherland. . . . He will take other measures too, drawn from the experience of ages, to confirm the rights of his subjects. He will be the first to use autocracy for the bridling of despotic power; He will be the first who from the purest impulse of the heart will sacrifice His own interests for humanity! And humanity, sobbing with joy, will raise His image higher than the images of other rulers, and multitudes of foreign people will flock to kiss its pedestal and to enjoy happiness in our midst!

'Doubtless, our Alexander, the Friend of Humanity, knows that nothing but confidence in the Government, resting on the certainty of its immutable principles, begets mutual confidence among the citizens, that it alone is the life of commerce, the mother of public virtue and the source of social prosperity. . . .

'Beside confidence in the Government, and on a level with it, He will set faith in the justice of law. Without these two principles, the honoured words "Citizen" and "Fatherland" are empty sounds in our language!. . .

'He will despise these new false politicians who maintain that private wrongs do no harm to society, that it makes no difference to the State "how property passes from hand to hand." Leaving all the administration of justice to the elected of the people, He will remove the judges from temptation, not by laws, inevitably ineffectual, but by providing them with an abundant maintenance, commensurate with their disinterestedness and their zeal for the public service. To the same end He will subject the judges to the influence of public opinion. It has always been more impartial, more implacable than the higher authorities, which were not rarely moved by the same motives as their subordinates, to the still greater discredit of the laws! A court with open doors, the right for the litigants to publish the decisions, will be one of the most reliable guarantees of justice.

'He will lay the State property on a firm basis once for all: He will reckon out the wealth of His spacious dominions; He will determine the powers and liabilities of His subjects upon an immovable scale, unaffected by the rise and fall of the currency, and will say: "Such are the dues of one class to another; such are the dues to the public Treasury; such are the means at the personal disposal of the Tsar." Then only extraordinary needs of State that cannot be foreseen by any human wisdom will remain undetermined: but to

LETTER TO ALEXANDER

meet these there will be the national—so to speak—natural riches of the country, which in a state of peace increase indefinitely.

'He will not command steps to be taken for laying on new taxes in order to increase the nominal revenue indefinitely, but with goodwill will take steps tending to diminish expenditure. And by this surest of means He will, accompanied by the blessings of the citizens who toil in the sweat of their brow, secure a continual surplus in the Treasury of which no single Power can yet boast.

'He will restrict particularly the expenditure which does not serve the welfare of His Empire, nor really exalt the glory of His crown. He will diminish His Court; He will dismiss from it the crowds of servitors and flatterers who shamelessly imagine that the property of the Empire belongs to them, and that they have a pre-eminent right to the Tsar's favour, simply because chance has placed them in proximity to His person.

'He will restrict vain display—the desire to adorn the streets and squares of the capitals while all the rest of the Empire presents the spectacle of roofless huts. He will not call art to His aid to provide monuments for Himself, but will find them in the wisdom of His institutions and the love of His people. These memorials will not perish with time, and will awaken not the wonder of idle curiosity but the reverence of all ages and all peoples!

'He will not merely protect the arts capriciously and only in His own palace, on condition that they pay Him homage, but will truly encourage them, increasing the general welfare and setting free intellects and talents. In general, He will prize the toil, the bloody sweat of His subjects, that is devoted to the public benefit; and moral beauty will be His first care. He will not deign to occupy Himself with details, and waste on trifles the precious time which will barely, very barely, suffice for the all-embracing cares of the Ruler of the greatest Empire in the world. His glance will embrace whole masses. He will give the right direction to the chief wheels of the political machine, and all the rest will run their course rightly! As even the most perfect laws will remain useless to a corrupt people and will lack meaning for an ignorant people, He will doubtless turn all His attention to the education of His subjects in accordance with the local and personal needs of each. He will entrust the higher supervision of this to the class of the guardians of the law, and they will act through the men who have the most moral influence over the people. The clergy will be employed for the enlightenment of the people, and will first themselves be enlightened to that end; schools will be founded for the latter, free from the tedious principles of scholasticism; and distinctions will be given not to those preachers of the Word of God who with poetic enthusiasm glorify the Tsar in town churches, but to those who show in practice the good influence they have had on the morals of their flocks; to those who, founding schools, will faithfully preach in them the pure teaching of Christ and by their example will exhort the man and the citizen to his duties. In this way not the sword, wielded, day and night, by power, will compel the fulfilment of the law, but far more effectively the personal conviction of each man of his usefulness. In this way law will be preserved by morals and morals by law.

'On the other hand, He will do something, too, for the moral improvement of those who are called the lowest. He will secure to the landowners' serfs the rights of man; He will give them the rights of property; He will set limits to their dependence. And this not by a law which might dangerously shake the stability of the present bonds of society, but by the gradual influence of custom, which would strengthen them the more. To the simple peasants He will give the means of tasting at times the sweetness of life in reward for their toil, without resorting to wantonness, to beverages that deaden the sense, to other temptations of depravity, sometimes of despair, and of hopeless slavery. . . .

'Agriculture will flourish under His gentle rule. Little by little He will cover the wide steppes of Russia with settlements, not moving whole families by force over thousands of versts to lands terrible from being unknown and deadly from extreme contrast of climate, but by attracting them from adjacent over-populated parts and encouraging them with rewards and privileges.

'The waterless but fertile mountain-ranges of favourable climates He will make habitable and will turn to blossoming gardens, cutting canals from neighbouring rivers, turning spacious lakes to advantage, or gradually clothing the slopes of mountains with forest. Is it only enlightened capital cities that have claims on government expenditure? Is it not bound to prepare dwellings for future generations and . . . a refuge for those who will probably come one day from the West to seek a home among us?

'He will not set crowds of greedy officials to take charge of the forests, those ornaments of the land and treasure-stores of water, but by judiciously distributing them as private property will preserve them for the country. Only the wild steppes and impassable forests should be the estate of the Government; they must become the property of private persons as soon as they are made fit for husbandry. Woe to the Governments whose institutions serve only as a source of temptation without eradicating the evil in its very foundation!

'He will assign solemn rewards for peasants distinguished either by rare virtues or by industry or by the invention or introduction of anything new in agriculture or manufactures. He will not leave the decision of this and the like in the hands of local authorities swayed by partiality or narrow political considerations, but will organise occasional expeditions about the Empire of persons qualified by special knowledge in the department investigated and worthy to represent His Imperial Eye. He will Himself not infrequently abandon the monotony of Court life in order to see and hear in person; He will not confine the rule of the lovely and spacious realm entrusted Him by God within the narrow limits of work at the papers laid before Him. He will encourage handicrafts, not by sudden and arbitrary prohibition of the importation of foreign produce (it is possible to combine the welfare of the Fatherland with peace and goodwill towards foreign countries), but by privileges given to manufacturers and factories, and especially by the removal of oppressive taxes which discourage new enterprise. Russia can, however, without the slightest disadvantage to herself, generously yield many branches of industry and manufacture to nations more scantily provided with land. Is it for her, so lavishly endowed with essential riches, greedily to appropriate all the sources of existence? Is it for her to desire to make everything for herself, when she can incomparably more cheaply employ *hired* labour outside her frontiers? How long are we going to measure ourselves by foreign standards and to imitate like children?

'Internal trade, strengthened by the progress of agriculture and handicrafts, will of itself in the course of a few years, with no artificial encouragement, increase our foreign trade to our advantage. Morality and love for everything belonging to one's own country, encouraged by examples in high places, will also tend to diminish the demand for foreign produce. The price of essential Russian goods, and at the same time also the rate of exchange, will rise inevitably.

LETTER TO ALEXANDER

'For the sake of internal and external trade, for the sake of completing the great work of legislative reform, He will, of course, strive to keep the peace with the Powers. To this end, He will employ the happy means furnished Him now by Providence, which is unmistakably extending to Russia a blessing hand. It will doubtless be His task to outline a bold plan of permanent policy appropriate to the Russian Government and peculiar to it. Has He not the most hopeful resources for keeping all the Courts respectful to Him, without swerving from one side or the other? Will He, in the present position of His Empire, with its unbroken frontiers and its strength, find the slightest reason for entering into their disputes? Is the population of Russia, still in its flower, such as to justify the sacrifice of men without the utmost necessity? . . . Oh, what a destiny, to draw upon oneself the grateful love and respect of all peoples! To have unlimited power and to do good. . . . If the Almighty loathes murder and the other abominable results of war, if it is pleasing to Him that there should ever be a truly Christian Power, it is most of all likely in Russia and in the reign of Alexander.

'In that happy time the armed forces will not remain useless. On the contrary, then they will fulfil their true purpose, the preservation of public tranquillity. While waiting till some frantic foe really attacks, means will be found, without forcing them to shed blood in foreign lands and affairs that do not concern them, to occupy the millions of strong, healthy hands which cost annually more than a third of the Imperial revenues. . . . First of all, He will fence the western frontier of His Empire with a double shield of fortresses: and they will seem to neighbouring peoples like the terrible rows of teeth of a lion in repose. Then, after the example of the Romans, who, though they esteemed the trade of arms above all others, did not hesitate to employ soldiers on public works, building their splendid aqueducts and roads; after the example of some European sovereigns who in more modern times have undertaken similar experiments, and among them of the founder of this capital, who secured its welfare by the Ladoga Canal, He will employ part of our sturdy soldiers, accustomed from their youth to obedience and labour, on the tasks of the State. Some addition to their ordinary pay will stimulate their energy; and how many really profitable works there will be to show for it in the course of a few years! On all sides means of communication by water and by land will be opened. Rivers will be made navigable, marshes will be turned to fertile valleys. . . . Meanwhile the frontiers of the Empire will not remain undefended, and the force of Russia will be seen and understood by enemies.

'He will unite the warrior with the peasant, and the peasant with other classes, by bonds of mutual profit, the feeling of which, together with brotherly love and allegiance to the Sovereign, will be the same feeling under three different aspects.

'He . . . but can I fathom the designs of God? Can I picture, can I enumerate, all the activities of which the seed lies in the humane heart of Alexander?. . .

'Nations will always be what it pleases the Government they should be: the Tsar, Ivan Vassilyevitch, wanted to have submissive slaves—abject with him, brutal among themselves; he had them. Peter wanted to see us imitating foreigners; unhappily we have done so to excess. The wise Catherine began to educate the Russian. Alexander will complete that great work. Rejoicing in the fruits of His youth, He will be the most blessed of mortals. His glory, resting securely on the love of His subjects, passing down from generation to generation, based on the universal esteem of all races of the earth, will be the envy of the greatest monarchs!

'I have heard that our young Ruler receives with indifference the hackneyed phrases of poets who shamelessly apply them to all monarchs, assuring each one that he is better than his predecessor: I have made bold to outline these thoughts. . . .

'O Thou whom my heart adores, do not reject this gift of it, offered Thee in simplicity and with disinterested feelings. . . .

'Sire! In my soul I throw myself at Thy feet, I water them with tears of the purest everlasting devotion. . . . Beneficent Genius of my beloved Fatherland!'

3

MARQUIS VON POSA

Next day Troshtchinsky announced to the Tsar that he had brought the author of the letter, that he was a clerk in one of the offices of his department, called Vassily Nazarovitch Karazin. The Tsar, dismissing Troshtchinsky, invited Karazin into his study, and as soon as he was alone with him asked:—

'You wrote that letter to me?'

'Pardon, my Sovereign,' answered Karazin.

'Let me embrace you for it, I thank you; I should be glad if I had more subjects like you. Continue always to speak as frankly to me, continue always to tell me the truth!'

The Tsar pressed him to his heart, and Karazin, sobbing like a child, flung himself at his feet with the words: 'I swear that I will always tell you the truth.'

Alexander made him sit down, had a long conversation with him, bade him write directly to him, the doors of his study were to be open to him. . . .

'Als der Marquis weggegangen, empfing ich den Befehl ihn künftighin unangemeldet vorzulassen.'

Our Marquis von Posa had begun his political career two years before. At five-and-twenty he had left the army. Well educated, of an unusually many-sided culture, he said good-bye to the Semyonovsky Regiment in order to study Russia and devote himself to the exact sciences. This was at the time when the frenzy of Paul's reign was at its height. When the young man had looked into the position of luckless Russia, scourged at random by her torturer, he was overcome by such horror, such loathing, such despair, that he made up his mind at all costs to go away to another country. Foreign passports were forbidden. Karazin could not obtain permission to go. He determined to get over the frontier without a passport. As he was crossing the Niemen, he was caught by the dragoons and brought to Kovno. Karazin's fate seemed inevitable. He clutched at the most risky and incredible means of saving himself, and it saved him. Before the official report had been despatched, he sent on the 14th of August 1798, by express messenger, the following letter to Paul:—

'Sire,—A luckless criminal makes bold to write to Thee, a criminal against Thy commands, O Sovereign Ruler of Russia, not against honour, conscience, religion, or the laws of his country. Deign to listen before condemning. And may one ray of Thy clear vision be shed upon me before the lightnings of Thy wrath consume me!

'I have tried to leave my country, the great land of Thy sovereign rule; I have transgressed Thy Will, doubly expressed, that is, for the whole people and for me personally. On the night of the third of this month, while crossing the Niemen to Kovno, I was seized by a patrol of the Ekaterininsky Grenadier Regiment; the official report will reach Thee shortly.

'No doubt information will be collected about me

in St. Petersburg, where I have spent a short time, and in the province of Ukraine, where I was born and have my estates. I make bold to assure Thee beforehand that they will in no wise prove me guilty. I had no need to take refuge in flight. It will be the only weapon for my prosecutors.

'Receive my confession: I wanted to escape from Thy rule, dreading its cruelty. Many examples, carried by rumour over the expanse of Thy Empire, in all likelihood exaggerated tenfold by rumour, terrified my thoughts and my imagination day and night. I knew of no guilt in myself. In the solitude of my country life I could have neither opportunity nor occasion to offend Thee. But even the free turn of my thoughts might be a crime. . . .

'Now it is in Thy power to punish me—and justify my fears—or to forgive and make me shed tears of repentance that I have cherished thoughts so false of a great and merciful Sovereign.'

It was not often Paul's lot to read such letters. The horror of his despotism, which had compelled the young man to flee, and the simple-hearted confession of it, took Paul by surprise. Standing in the third position of dancing, and leaning with intentional awkwardness on his cane, Paul said in his husky voice to the *criminal* who was brought before him: 'I will show you, young man, that you are mistaken, that service in Russia under my rule may not be so bad; in whose department would you like to serve?' 'Though Karazin's design to escape over the frontier was no proof of a very strong desire to test the charms of service under Paul, there was no discussing the question. Karazin mentioned Troshtchinsky. Paul commanded that he should be given a post and left in peace.

For Alexander such a man was a treasure, and it

seemed as though he understood that. Karazin's inexhaustible energy and his broad scientific education were striking. He was an astronomer and a chemist, a statistician, a scientific agriculturalist, not a rhetorician like Karamzin, nor a pedant like Speransky, but a living man, who brought into every question a quite new point of view and advised exactly what was needed.

At first the Emperor was continually sending for him and writing notes to him with his own hand.[1] The intoxication of success increased Karazin's energy tenfold; he drew up programmes of reform, among others the plan of a Ministry of Education, sent in a note concerning the *eradication of slavery* (that is, of serfdom), in which he says plainly that after the nobles had been set free by special decree[2] it was the peasants 'turn; at the same time, he wrote about elementary schools, himself composed two catechisms, one secular, one religious, and all at once, in the very heyday of his favour, asked for leave and was lost in his native district in Little Russia. It must not be imagined that he went for a rest to gather fresh energy; such men are never tired. No, he returned to Petersburg a few weeks later with six hundred and eighteen thousand roubles which he had wrung by tears and entreaties from the nobles and merchants of Harkov and Poltava for founding a university in Harkov. The Tsar wanted to reward him for it, but Karazin refused.' I have been on my knees, Sire, before the nobles and the merchants, I entreated the money from them with tears, and I will not have it said that I did all that hoping to gain a reward.' Alexander was pleased with him and everything went

---

[1] How glad we should be to see these notes. Such historical materials should not be kept under lock and key.—(*Author's Note.*)

[2] A decree of Peter 111. relieved the nobles from the obligations to serve the State introduced by Peter the Great.—(*Translator's Note.*)

well, but already a hostile force could be discerned which at times rolled a log under the wheel, at times put on the brake....

The plan for a Ministry of Education was ratified, but by now it was not the same; the scheme of the Harkov university was ratified too, but Karazin's colossal plans were narrowed down to the commonplace proportions of a German provincial *Hochschule*. Karazin was dreaming of a great educational centre, not only for all Little Russia, but also for the south-eastern Slavs and even the Greeks. He wanted to attract to it the greatest celebrities of the world of learning. Laplace and Fichte agreed to go at his invitation, but the Government found them too expensive.

Scarcely noticing the failure of his success, Karazin summoned from foreign lands to Harkov at his own expense thirty-two families of printers, bookbinders and other workmen, visited the palace of the widowed Empress, wrote for her treatises concerning female education, articles on pedagogy, and so on. This did not in the least distract him from carrying out other commissions of Alexander's and persisting with other labours he had undertaken. In a little more than two years he had, in addition to all we have mentioned, already succeeded in writing constitutions for an academy, for universities and for various educational institutions, collecting materials for the history of finance and for the history of medicine in Russia, superintending the collecting of the first statistical information, and bringing the State archives into order.

In 1804 Karazin returned from an inquiry which he had been conducting, in combination with Derzhavin, into the doings of the Governor Lopuhin. The misdeeds of this man, who was under powerful protection, were laid bare. Lopuhin was put on his trial. All that remained to do was to reward the investigators;

but by now the rope that had been allowed Marquis von Posa was almost at its end.

Unaware of anything, he presented himself before the Tsar. The Tsar received him with knitted brows. Karazin stood as though struck by a thunderbolt.

'You brag of my letters?'

'Sire . . .' But the Tsar would not let him answer.

'Other people know what I have written to you alone and have shown to no one. You can go.'

Karazin withdrew, and all was over between them. Karazin asked to be relieved of his duties; the Tsar accepted his request.

And so in 1804 the Emperor did not know that the contents of letters become known through the Post Office.

One cannot help recalling the melancholy anecdote that used to be told by N. I. Turgenev, that at some congress Alexander, receiving the petition of a peasant who had been sold by his owner, asked Turgenev: 'Surely the law does not permit the sale of men apart from land, and the sale of serfs individually?' Turgenev, who knew the chaotic state of the law on that subject, tried to take advantage of the question to abolish such sale of serfs, and of course did not succeed. After the sitting of the Council at which Turgenev spoke heatedly on the subject, V. P. Kotchubey went up to him, and, smiling bitterly, said: 'And do you imagine that anything will come of this?. . . What you should rather be surprised at is that after reigning twenty years the Tsar does not even know that serfs are sold individually in Russia!'

4

THE SINS OF THE FATHERS

The Russian Government since the days of Peter the Great has been exceptionally free. It has views, interests, relations, but no sort of *moral obligations*.

When it freed itself from the stagnant traditions of the parental home, it simultaneously severed all ties of blood, without assuming any others; it handed over its own mother into bondage to a stranger, but did not submit to him either.

The complex elements of Western life, derived from various different sources, were selected to suit its purposes. Of a whole phrase in which the very discords softened its one-sidedness, took the edge off its extremes and made a harmony of a sort, a few notes were retained, destroying the concord and the significance. All that exaggerated authority and all that oppressed the individual was adopted; every defence of personal liberty was laid aside; the casuistry of the inquisition was enriched by Tatar torture, German discipline, Byzantine servility.

Even speech, absolutely oppressed and despised, gained the power of fatal menace, of inflicting boundless misfortune, the power of action, only when 'word and deed'[1] meant denunciation!

There has never in history been such a Government, relieved from all moral principles, from every duty undertaken by authority except that of self-preservation and maintaining the frontiers. The Russian Government of this period is the most monstrous abstraction to which the German metaphysics *eines Polixeistaates* could rise. The Government exists for the sake of the Government, the people for the sake of the State: a complete disregard for history, for religion, for tradition, for the heart of man; material force in place of an ideal, material power in place of authority.

Had Russia been conquered by Poland, let us suppose, there would have been a struggle. The Polish nobility would have brought in their tradition of aristocratic

---

[1] The reference is to the phrase 'word and deed,' which was the accepted form of denunciation to the police, introduced by Peter the Great.—(*Translator's Note*.)

freedom; it would, as in Little Russia, as in the time of the Pretenders, have called forth from outraged national feeling Lyapunovs,[1] Minins,[2] Pozharskys and Hmyelnitskys.[3] The two elements would have measured their strength. The conqueror would have seen what the conquered was, what were his peculiarities, where his national characteristics lay. But the conquest of Russia by the Government of Petersburg, without an enemy of a different race, without a hostile flag, without an open battle, took the whole country unawares. The people only grasped that it was conquered by the time that all the strong places were in the hands of the enemy; for the conquerors the vanquished people had not even the interest of novelty, of the unknown; on the contrary, the estranged oppressor despised the ignorant Russian people, was convinced that it knew them and felt that it was the same flesh and blood, but purified by civilisation and called to rule the ignorant masses.

About Peter the Great there gathered a crowd of destitute nobles who forgot their birth, of foreigners who

[1] Lyapunov was one of the national heroes who fought against the Poles in 1610. The Rurik dynasty became extinct on the death of Fyodor, son of Ivan the Terrible, and Boris Godunov was elected Tsar by the people of Moscow. At his death, after a reign of eight years, a time of anarchy followed, when many pretenders claimed the throne. The Poles took advantage of this 'Time of Trouble,' as it is called by Russian historians, to attempt to annex Russia.

[2] Minin was a meat-merchant of Nizhni-Novgorod who roused the people to form a national army, deliver Russia from the Poles and elect a Tsar. At his suggestion the command of the army, to which men flocked from all parts of Russia, was entrusted to Pozharsky, a nobleman of good reputation and great military ability. Under his command the Russians succeeded in driving the Poles out of Moscow, and eventually out of Russia. A *zemsky sobor* was summoned which elected Michael Romanov as Tsar.

[3] Hmyelnitsky was a Hetman of Little Russia who, seeing the only chance of peace and safety lay in union with Russia, secured the allegiance of the Little Russians to the Tsar Alexey (father of Peter the Great) in 1654.—(*Translator's Notes.*)

forgot their native land, of orderlies and sergeants, interspersed with the old Boyar aristocrats and the everlasting intriguers who crawl at the feet of any one in power and take advantage of any one's favour. This circle grew and multiplied rapidly, sending out its parasitic branches in all directions. Little by little this blight spread all over Russia, it trailed through the mud and the snow carrying an officer's commission, an appointment from the senate, or a deed of sale, hungry and greedy, ferocious with the common people and abject with the higher officials.

It formed a sort of net, maintained by soldiers, joined together at the top in the knot of the Winter Palace, and holding tight peasants and townsmen in every mesh below. This was a sort of fortuitous state made up of nobles and government functionaries, with a flavour of army discipline and serfdom. In it everything was shaved off: beard, regional independence, individuality. It wore German dress and tried to speak French. The people looked with horror and repulsion on the traitors, but power was on the side of the latter, and however the people moaned, and however they revolted, the census and the recruiting, the forced labour and pay in lieu of labour, knout and rods went on unchecked. The people murmured, made frequent efforts to revolt; joining with the Cossacks and the Tatars, a whole countryside rose in insurrection—but there were troops and troops of soldiers. . . and order was restored by the knout. Stunned with pain, crushed by despair, the people were felled to the earth and lay stupefied for nearly a hundred years. It is only from that time that Russiahasbecome that dead, dumb sea which no hurricane will stir.

Up to the'seventies of last century the Petersburg orderlies and sergeants had not fallen into step. These people of haughty insolence and no feeling of honour, drunk with wine and blood, accustomed to the executioner's axe and the moan of the tortured, after tasting the sweets of power and being beaten with the stick, remembered well how easy it is in a state without a people to put any worthless creature on the throne or turn it off again.

They knew that they too had their share in the Imperial 'We.' . . . The far-sighted among them wanted to limit the power of the autocracy for their own benefit, but the true sergeants preferred simply to strangle Tsars and put their mistresses in their place. The insolent courtiers were dangerous, exacting. It was not enough for Prince Grigory Grigoryevitch Orlov to have Catherine, he wanted the title of her husband. Knowing how light are the chains of matrimony, Catherine consented, but the other orderlies and sergeants would not dream of allowing it. The name of Ivan Antonovitch[1] was pronounced: she bade them kill him like a cat; the name of Princess Tarakanov[2] was recalled: she bade them steal her as puppies are stolen.

All this was done from terror. Feverish, irresistible terror took possession of every one who sat on Peter's blood-stained throne. It was hard to rely on such faithful subjects as the orderlies and sergeants, as the German adventurers; still more so to rely on the people, on the voiceless people, trampled in the mud, handed over as a gift to the nobility: they did not exist. Those who wore the crown kept up appearances, tried to forget themselves, but panic got the upper hand, and suddenly

[1] Ivan the Sixth was in 1740 proclaimed Tsar as a baby, and after a reign of six months was incarcerated in the Schlüsselburg till, in 1764, Mirovitch attempted to release him and he was shot by his guards.

[2] Princess Tarakanov, the morganatic daughter of the Empress Elizabeth, was living abroad when Count Orlov, at Catherine's instigation, succeeded in decoying her to Russia, where she was put in prison and there died.—(*Translator's Notes*.)

they would be overcome by the terror of the rope-walker: below, a black mass of downcast heads that never look up, no voice can reach it; near at hand . . . it would be better if there were no one. . . near at hand, sergeants, orderlies, and no one akin. . . . They were terrified by their own infertility, and sent seeking everywhere among German *landgrafs* and archbishops a drop of Peter's blood in the fourth or fifth generation, or hurriedly ordered children, as Elizabeth did from Catherine, and kept looking about them, afraid that a drunken orderly would come . . . with the ribbon of Saint Andrew on his breast and a rope in his hand.

Another figure appeared on the scene, and everything was changed. The storm-clouds had parted, men could see clear again. A picture of the greatest family happiness was displayed to the world: the godlike Felitsa,[1] 'the mother of her country,' stood serenely at the pinnacle of power and authority, graciously smiling on her kneeling orderlies and sergeants, senators and cavaliers; every one worshipped her, every one did homage to her. Radiant with paste gems, after the manner of the *encyclopaedic* diamonds, she sparkled with the wisdom of Beccaria[2] and the profound thought of Montesquieu, delivered classical speeches to the landowners of the steppes, put Roman helmets on her *balafrés* . . . sent for legislators who took her will for law. . . . Her generals brought her victory on land and on sea, Derzhavin sang her praises in heavy verse, Voltaire exalted her in light prose, and she, drunken with power, weighed down with love, gave everything to *her own* people, everything: her body, the souls of the free Cossacks, the estates of the monasteries. 'Glory, glory to you, Catherine!'

[1] The name given to Catherine 11. by the court poet, Derzhavin.
[2] Beccaria, Cesare de (1738-1794), an Italian philosopher, was the author of a celebrated work on criminal law.—(*Translator's Notes*.)

Who had performed this miracle, who had roped in the Russia of the renegades and the Germans? Who wedded the mutinous orderlies and blood-stained sergeants to Felitsa?

An unknown old lady, a landowner of the steppes after the style of Korobotchka,[1] had bewitched them. What happened, it was said, was this.

Pugatchov came to her farm; the old woman was frightened and went out to offer His Majesty bread and salt.

'Well, what sort of a mistress has she been to you, good Christians?' the Tsar-Cossack asked the peasants.

'We will not take a sin on our souls, Your Majesty; we have always been satisfied with our mistress, she has been a mother to us.'

'Good! I will come to you, old lady, and drink your vodka, since the people praise you.'

The old lady regaled him as best she could. Pugatchov took leave of her and went to his sledge. The peasants stood waiting for him; their faces were dissatisfied.

'If you have some favour to ask, speak boldly.'

'Well, Your Royal Majesty, how is it left then for us?'

'What do you mean?'

'Why, here, you see, Sire, you were at such a place and there you hanged the master and his children too, and at the other village, too. . . and how about us?'

'Why, you say yourselves your old woman is a very good one.'

'That is so, Your Majesty, she is a good woman, but still, perhaps it would be better to do for her.'

'Well, brothers, if you want to—as you like, we can do for her.'

[1] A character in Gogol's *Dead Souls.—(Translator's Note.)*

'It is a pity, it is a pity, but there is no help for it,' said the peasants, going to fetch the old lady, who was calmly clearing away the plates and dishes, delighted at having been spared by the Tsar, and to her great surprise they hanged her from the crossbeam. It was she, they said, who cast a spell over the mutinous orderlies and sergeants of the Government.

They pondered, seeing such impartial justice. 'Is that how we did for them? I say, but you know, might not this happen to any one of us? No, enough of mutiny; what could we do without the help of the Tsar?'

And the family feud was ended.

From that time forward the Government dared not hold out a hand to the peasants in any way. The nobles lost all sense of civic courage in face of the Government, and all feeling of moral shame in regard to the peasants. The two Russias completely ceased to recognise each other as human beings. There was no human tie, neither compassion nor justice between them. Their morality was different, what they held sacred was different. The terrified peasant crouched in his village, afraid of the landowner, afraid of the police-captain, afraid of the town where every one could beat him, where his full coat and jerkin were looked on with contempt, where he saw a beard only on the images of Christ. The landowner, who shed genuine tears over the novels of Marmontel, flogged the peasant in his stable for arrears with perfect equanimity; the peasant with untroubled conscience deceived the landowner and the judge. 'Are you a gentleman?' an old woman would say in the coach-house to Mitka or Kuzka, 'that you eat meat in Lent? As for the master, it's not expected of him, but why don't you keep the law of God?' The division could be no wider.

The people were broken. Without murmur, without revolt, without hope, they passed with clenched teeth *through the next thousand blows*,[1] sank exhausted, died; their children were driven the same way, and so one generation followed another. Tranquillity prevailed, the masters 'tribute was paid, the forced labour was performed, the horn sounded for the hunt with hounds, the serfs' band played, the motherly heart of the Empress rejoiced.

The Petersburg throne was made secure. It was supported on the graduated table of ranks, made fast to the earth with bayonets and butt-ends of guns; it was supported by the provincial nobility, who battened upon the peasants. The light from the West shed its pale, cold beams on the top of the pyramid, lighting up one side of it only; on the other, behind its shadow, nothing could be discerned—and, indeed, there was no need to look: there lay a scourged body covered with sacking, waiting for *some one* to come and decide whether it was dead or not. It seemed as though the conquest was complete.

But the revolution made by Peter the Great introduced a double-edged element into the life of the Russian nobility. Peter liked the material side of civilisation, practical science. The rich resources it provided increased the power of government tenfold. But he did not know what thorns lie hid in these West European roses, and, maybe, had too much contempt for his own people to dream that they could assimilate something else as well as constructing fortifications, building ships and establishing official routine. Science is as bad as any wood-worm which gnaws day and night until somewhere it comes forth into the light, struggles into

[1] The reference is to the punishment known as the 'Green Street,' in which the condemned man walked between two rows of soldiers, each of whom dealt him a blow. It was the favourite form of torture of Nicholas 1. (hence nicknamed 'the Stick'), and numbers of men died under it in his reign.—(*Translator's Note*.)

consciousness. And some thought, like the gnawing of conscience, begins to ferment, until the whole dough rises.

In 1789 the following incident took place. A young man[1] of no importance, after supping with his friends in Petersburg, drove in a postchaise to Moscow. He slept through the first station. At the second, Sofya, he was detained a long time before he could get horses, and consequently, it may be supposed, was so thoroughly awakened that when the fresh team carried him off with the bells ringing, instead of sleeping he listened to the driver's song in the fresh morning air. Strange ideas came into the mind of the young man of no importance. Here are his words:—

'My driver sang a song, as usual a mournful one. Any one who knows the airs of the Russian peasants' songs will recognise that there is something suggestive of spiritual sadness. Almost every tune of these songs is in a minor key. The Government should be based on this peculiarity of the peasants' musical taste. In it you will find the character of our people's soul. *Look at the Russian and you will find him melancholy*. If he wants to shake off his dreariness, or, as he himself says, if he wants to enjoy himself, he goes to the pot-house. . . . The barge-hauler going with hanging head to the pot-house and coming back red with blood from blows in the face may provide the solution of much that has hitherto been enigmatic in the history of Russia.'

The driver went on wailing his song: the traveller went on thinking his thoughts, and before he had reached Tchudovo suddenly recalled how he had once in Petersburg struck his Petrushka for being drunk. And he burst out crying like a child, and, without blushing for his honour as a nobleman, had the shamelessness to

[1] Radishtchev, author of the famous *Journey from Petersburg to Moscow*, is meant,—(*Translator's Note.*)

write: 'Oh, if only, drunk as he was, he had plucked up spirit enough to answer me in the same way!'

This song, these tears, these words, cast at hazard on the posting-road between two stations, must be regarded as one of the first signs of the turning tide. The seed always germinates in silence, and at the beginning there is no trace of it.

The Empress Catherine saw the point of it, and was graciously pleased 'with warmth and feeling' to say to Hrapovitsky: 'Radishtchev is a rebel worse than Pugatchov!'

To wonder that she sent him in chains to Ilimsky Prison is absurd. It is much more wonderful that Paul brought him back, but he did that to spite his dead mother, he had no other object in it.

Thenceforward, from time to time, stray gleams of light flash on the horizon with no clap of thunder. Men appear on the stage who embody in themselves the historical gnawings of conscience, helpless and guiltless victims expiating the sins of their fathers. Many of them are ready to give up everything, sacrifice everything, but there is no altar, no one to accept their sacrifice. Some knocked at the palace doors, and on their knees besought their rulers to take heed to their ways; their words seemed to trouble the rulers, but nothing came of it. Others knocked at the hut but could say nothing to the peasant, since they spoke a different language. The peasant looked with sullen distrust at these 'Greeks bearing gifts,' and the conscience-stricken turned away bitterly, feeling that they had no fatherland.

Bereaved of all through thought, bereaved of all through love, foreigners at home, cut off from communication with each other, the five or six best men in Russia perished in idleness, surrounded by hatred, indifference, misunderstanding. Novikov[1] was in the

---

[1] Novikov, one of the most learned and cultured men of

fortress, Radishtchev in Ilimsk. A fine place Russia must have seemed to them when Paul released them!

There is no wonder that all men looked with ecstatic hope to Alexander.

Young, handsome, with a mild and pensive expression, shy and extremely gracious, he might well fascinate them. Was he not suffering for the ills of Russia as they were? Was he not trying to heal them as they were? And, moreover, he *could* do it—so at least they fancied.

And Radishtchev, who had paid so dearly for his pity of the dark masses of Russia, went with the same faith as Karazin to offer his services to the young Emperor, and he too was accepted. Zealously Radishtchev plunged into work and drew up a series of legislative projects for the abolition of serfdom and corporal punishment. But all at once, after a short discussion, not with the sledge-driver but with Count Zavadovsky, he stopped short, hesitated, was overcome by doubt and dread, pondered, poured himself out a glass of sulphuric acid and drank it. Alexander sent his own doctor, Villiers, but it was too late. Villiers only said, looking at his features as he lay in agony: 'This man must have been very unhappy!'

He must have been!

This was in the autumn of 1802. Karazin was then in power. He knew Radishtchev very well, and indeed on one occasion lost the manuscript of his proposed reforms—but his alarming example had no effect on him. Dismissed from the palace, Karazin came back five years later, ten years later, twenty years later, thirty

Catherine's reign, published satirical sketches and then historical researches, and did much for the promotion of education. He was a freemason and a mystic. Catherine, towards the end of her reign—frightened by the French Revolution—imprisoned him in the Schlüsselburg because he was opposed to serfdom, Paul released him.—(*Translator's Note.*)

years later, with his plan for the emancipation of the serfs and a representative assembly of the nobles, his programme for a revolution from above. Not even observing that Nicholas was reigning, he knocked at his door too, and urged upon that dull-witted martinet that 'storms were rising, there would be trouble; that to save the throne concessions must be made,' and could not imagine why, in 1820, Alexander had ordered him to be put in the fortress, and the head gendarme Benckendorf ordered the gendarmes to turn him out of Nicholas' anteroom. He should have asked Speransky how the 'steep hills break the spirited steed' even in flat Petersburg, and make of him a respectable harnessed nag, gravely jogging along in blinkers.

But how was it these people could be so deceived, or was it Alexander who deceived them? But that was not the case at all. We have not, at any rate before 1806 or 1807, the slightest right to doubt his genuine desire to alleviate the lot of his subjects: to protect his peasants from maltreatment by their owners, from maltreatment by officials, from the venality of the law-courts and the injustice of the mighty. Alexander did not set before himself as the exclusive aim of his reign the futile preservation and increase of his power, as Nicholas did. It was not his desire that his word should have the effect of strychnine; he strove not only to be feared but to be loved. In his most passionate moments he could not only listen to another man's opinion, but even accept it. When he had decided to shoot Speransky in 1812, he commuted the senseless sentence after talking to the academician, Parrot. All that is so, but he *could not* do anything real for the Russian people. That was just the tragedy of his position.

And who can tell whether he did not rush into foreign wars because he had begun to discern the magic circle which grew wider every time that he ordered a levy or increased the taxes on the peasants, and at once contracted when he undertook anything for the peasants? He became irresolute, he was oppressed by mistrust of others, lack of confidence in himself; his hesitation grew with defeat and grew with victory. From Paris he returned a gloomy mystic: he no longer wanted to transform or to improve; he brought back Speransky, but his projects of reform were pigeonholed in the archives. To Engelhart, who said something to him about bringing order into the civilian side of the Government, he answered gloomily: 'There is no one to undertake it!'

He was accustomed to power, he had glory enough, all he wanted now was peace, and among all his ministers and grandees, among the generals covered with glory and courtiers about his person, he chose the heartless torturer, Araktcheyev, and handed Russia over to him, and, what is more, arranged that even after his death it should pass into the hands of another Araktcheyev.

He did not trust the nobles, the peasants he did not know—and that is no matter for wonder, since about him stood men like Speransky and his rival Karamzin; like Shishkov, the forerunner of Slavophilism, who might have known the peasants but did not know them; since the most intelligent statesmen, like Mordvinov, talked of the nobility as the one prop of the throne; since honest senators, like Lopuhin, were indignant at the idea of the emancipation of the serfs.

It is a pity that Alexander was rather deaf and did not drive about in a chaise alone on the high-roads. He too might have been awakened at dawn by the song of the sledge-driver and might have sought the key to the mysteries of the people in that instead of in Eckhartshausen.

To understand the Russian people it was not enough for Alexander to kill his father. He would have had

318 *THE MEMOIRS OF HERZEN*

to renounce his wise grandmother, to renounce Peter the Great, to renounce his whole family and kindred. He would have had—horrible to say—to renounce even Laharpe, who had made a man of him, but who could never have grasped that one could learn more of Russian history from the barge-hauler who goes gloomily into the pot-house and comes out of it covered with blood than from the records of Governments.

5

FAREMO DA SE

When the doors of the Tsar's study had been shut upon Karazin he still made an effort to write to the Tsar, taking advantage of the privilege that had been accorded him. But the Marquis von Posa had no further interest for the crowned Don Carlos; moreover, Alexander was now engrossed and absorbed by questions of far different importance, European questions; he was measuring himself against Napoleon, and blundering into the war which was to end in our defeat at Austerlitz.

Karazin, too, began to be engrossed with other tasks; like a rejected lover, he flung himself *par dépit amoureux* into amazingly many-sided activities. His ardent, restless brain was filled with ideas floating by in rapid succession—political plans, agricultural projects, learned theories, machines, observation, apparatuses, new and improved methods of distillery and of leather tanning, horticultural experiments with foreign seeds, easy ways of drying and preserving fruit, and so on. War broke out: Karazin wrote on the methods of increasing the output of saltpetre, he preserved meat, and at the same time was engaged in founding stations for meteorological observations in Russia. He absolutely clearly formulated in 1808 the scientific needs of that department, which

GROWING DISSATISFACTION

have not been satisfied to this day, investigated the possibility of utilising the electricity in the atmosphere, founded a technological society in Ukraine, looked after his Harkov university, and so on.

But his chief thought, his chief anxiety, the leading note of his life, lay not in these things. While he was improving distilleries and trying to utilise the electricity of the atmosphere, Karazin was passionately watching other events and seeking other means of averting the storm. And meanwhile time was passing and passing.

Alexander had been reigning now for twenty years; all sorts of things had happened since, with tears in his eyes, he had read Karazin's letter . . . Tilsit and 1812. . . Moscow and Paris, the Congress of Vienna and St. Helena. Public opinion, stirred by so many shots and shocks, had moved forward while the Government had fallen back. Alexander had not carried out his promises. Dissatisfaction was growing. The people, who had given so much blood and received in return a manifesto written in Shishkov's prose, murmured against the new levy of recruits, the more as there was talk of a senseless war in support of the Austrian yoke in Italy, of a repetition of the futile campaign of Suvorov.

The younger men of energy and education looked on sullenly. Karazin saw it all, but still believed that Alexander could and would prevent the gathering storm.

At the beginning of 1820 the Tsar forgave Karazin's father-in-law some government debt. Karazin asked permission to offer his thanks in person, but was refused. He wrote a letter to the Tsar, in which among other things he said:—

'I am not going to write anything special, but I only beg you, gracious Sovereign, ask Count Viktor Pavlovitch[1] for the note of some pages I wrote for him on the 31st of March, apropos of a conversation with him,

[1] *I.e.* Kotchubey.—(*Translator's Note.*)

and also Prince Vyazemsky for the letter written to him from his Masalsky estate by the merchant Rogov on the 1st of April, which he read to me the other day. One cannot without horror see the striking similarity of the thoughts of a man (so far removed from me in every respect) with my thoughts and with all that has been filling my soul continually since the year 1817, when I had the audacity to reveal the same in my letter from Ukraine to Your Majesty. One cannot help remembering that just in the same way warnings from the well-disposed resounded from various parts of France before the coming of the fatal revolution, and that in just the same way they were neglected! *"Il est singulier que dans ce siècle de lumières, les souverains ne voient venir Forage que quand il éclate"* Napoleon said to Las Cases[1] on the Island of St. Helena. Such striking agreement in the views of different minds that have nothing in common between them deserves attention. There *must* be something true in them; and the more so as similar feelings have been for some time past apparent in private conversations in both Petersburg and Moscow! It is quite enough if there are grounds for one half, for a fraction of what is thought!'

'. . . Time,' he says in a note given at the Tsar's command to V. P. Kotchubey—' time will strengthen the weakened framework of our State; time will replace the *religious* reverence for the Throne by another founded on the laws. . . .

'Of course it may linger on a year or two, perhaps more, but it is just for that reason I am writing now, it is for that reason that I am disregarding myself entirely. My fate is bound to be either exile beyond Lake Baikal, while there is still power to exile, or death with a weapon

[1] Las Cases, Emmanuel, Comte de (1766-1842), a French historian who went with Napoleon to St. Helena and published the *Mémorial de Sainte-Hélène*.—(*Translator's Note*.)

in my hand defending to the last the entrance to the Tsar's apartments. Only then I shall write no more.'

Karazin beseeches the Tsar not to believe the sayings with which the governors meet him that 'All is well, all is as before. . . .'

'A great change,' he says, 'has taken place and is daily taking place in men's minds. . . .'

In the Semyonovsky mutiny, in which he justifies the soldiers and admires them, he sees distinctly 'the first step of the ladder which the spirit of the age is raising for us.'

But what were his means of averting the storm? Here they are:—

'The gradual emancipation of the peasants and the summoning of elected persons from the whole of the nobility as representatives of public opinion to the private councils of the Government.' By this Duma Karazin supposes 'all will be saved and without detriment to the power of the Monarch, if only the time has not passed. O my Country, unique in Thy character, Thou mayest even on the threshold of Thy greatest catastrophe be saved by a sincere, warm union of Thy Tsar with His nobility! But God's Will be done in this as in all!

'. . . And, indeed, what can the Autocracy lose from trusting the class whose fate is so closely bound up with it? . . . All the measures of the police and ecclesiastical censorship are insufficient to check the growth of opinion. Excessive seventy only revolts men's hearts. All at once the strained cord will snap. Among the many freed serfs and men of no definite class I foresee the miscreants who will surpass Robespierre. There are noblemen, too, who have squandered their estates and been reared in debauchery and evil principles, who are dissatisfied with their lot and are consequently ready to join the ignorant mob. The times of Pugatchov, of the Moscow mutiny in the time of Yeropkin,[1] and the outbreaks of lawlessness at the invasion in 1812 in various parts of the Moscow and Kaluga provinces have shown us already what our mob can be when it has had too much to drink! Alas for us! the Throne will drown in the blood of the nobility!'

In answer to this cry of horror and warning, the Emperor Alexander bade V. P. Kotchubey demand from Karazin 'details, proofs, names'—in other words a denunciation. The 'Trajan and Marcus Aurelius' had developed in the twenty years of his reign!

Karazin refused to give them. The Tsar ordered him to be thrown into the fortress and afterwards to be banished to his estate in Little Russia.

What for?

For having meddled in what was not his business, but that Karazin was quite unable to understand.

'How long has the welfare of the country in which I live,' he says, 'in which my children and grandchildren will live, ceased to be my own business?[2] From what Asiatic system is this idea borrowed? *Teaching* the *Government* is an expression purposely invented to mortify the vanity of the persons who make

---

[1] Yeropkin was a general who put down the mutiny in Moscow during the plague in 1776, when the people rose in revolt against the sanitary measures imposed by the Government. Catherine rewarded him with the ribbon of Saint Andrew and four thousand peasants. He accepted the ribbon but refused the peasants.—(*Translator's Note*.)

[2] Nicholas in his simplicity did not share Karazin's opinion. This is how the Governor of Harkov informed the latter on November 24, 1826, of the Most High's permission to leave his estate: 'His Excellency, the commanding officer of the Chief Staff, has informed me that His Majesty the Emperor graciously grants you full right to live where you choose, with sanction to stay even in Moscow, saving, however, Saint Petersburg, until further commands, and with the condition that you refrain from every sort of opinion not concerning you!'—What a jargon and what a brain!—(*Author's Note*.)

up the Government. But must not the authors of books on the best systems of legislation, of finance and so on, be called even more guilty? We all teach and are taught up to the day of our death. The Government is a centre, to which every thought concerning the commonweal must flow. Woe to us if we begin passing judgment in the market-place as other nations do! . . . And are there so many of us now in Russia desirous and capable of saying something to the Government and daring enough to do so? There is no need to be uneasy on that score: there will not be enough to become wearisome!'

However that may be, Karazin was in the fortress and was able at his leisure to ponder on the question whether there was more danger in saving the mighty of this world, or in thrusting them into the abyss.

While Karazin in those sleepless nights was writing his political rhapsodies to Kotchubey, there were other men, too, who could not sleep: in the barracks of the Guards, in the staff of the Second army, in old-fashioned signorial Moscow houses, there were men who did not sleep. They grasped the fact that Alexander would not go beyond two or three Liberal phrases, that there was no place in the Winter Palace for a Marquis von Posa nor Struensee[1]; they knew that no salvation for the people could come from the same source from which the military settlements had come. They expected nothing from the Government and tried to act independently of it; they brought all that was enlightened lower down in the social pyramid; its

[1] Struensee, Johann Friedrich, Count, was court physician to Christian VII. of Denmark and gained complete ascendancy over that monarch and his wife Caroline, sister of George III. of England. He used his power for the advancement of liberty and enlightenment and succeeded to some extent in abolishing serfdom (1771). Offending the nobility and clergy by his liberalism, he was accused of adultery with the Queen, and in 1772 he was beheaded.—(*Translator's Note*.)

324 *THE MEMOIRS OF HERZEN*

summit had grown dim in the mist. Culture, intelligence, the thirst for freedom, all now was to be found in a different region, in different surroundings, away from the Palace! In these were to be found youth, daring, breadth, poetry, Pushkin, the scars of 1812, fresh laurels, and white crosses. Between 1812 and 1825 there appeared a perfect galaxy of brilliant talent, independent character and chivalrous valour (a combination quite new in Russia). These men had absorbed everything of Western culture, the introduction of which had been forbidden. The period of Petersburg Government produced nothing better. They were its latest blossoms, and in spite of the fatal scythe that mowed them down at once, their influence can be traced flowing far into the gloomy Russia of Nicholas, like the Volga into the sea.

The story of the Decembrists becomes a more and more solemn prologue, from which we all date our lives, our heroic genealogy. What Titans, what giants, and what poetical, what sympathetic characters! Their glory nothing could diminish or distort, neither the gibbet nor the prison, nor the treachery of Bludov, nor the memorial words of Korf. . . .

'Yes, they were men!

When, thirty years afterwards, a few of the old ones who survived Nicholas came back, bent and leaning on crutches, from their long, weary exile—the generation of broken-spirited, splenetic, disillusioned men who had lived under Nicholas looked at these *youthful* figures, who, at the fortresses, at the mines, in Siberia, had kept the old warmth of heart, young enthusiasm, unconquerable will, unflinching convictions, at these young figures with their silver hair that still bore traces of the crown of thorns which had kin for more than a quarter of a century on their heads. It was not they who sought support and comfort at the hearth that had grown chill—

no—they consoled the weak, they gave a hand to the sick children, cheering them on, supporting their strength and their hopes!

As Faust, wearied, turned for peace and rest to the eternally beautiful types of motherhood, so our younger generation turn for new energy and strengthening example to these Fathers.

The Petersburg period was purified by the holy company of Decembrists; the nobles could go no further without going out to the people, without tearing up their patent of nobility.

It was their Isaac sacrificed for reconciliation with the people. The crowned Abraham did not hear the voice of God and drew the noose. . . .

The people did not weep for them.

The tragic element of the Petersburg period attained its furthest, most heart-rending expression—further it could not go.

The sacrifice was complete, and the last touch to its completeness was given by the indifference of the people.

Only now a way of escape and reconciliation became possible. The separation from the people was truly expiated by so much love and strength, purity and penitence, so much self-denial and devotion to others. The readiness of this group of aristocrats and noblemen not only to give up their unjust heritage, *se faire roturiers de gentilskommes*, as Count Rostoptchin expressed it, but to face death, to go to penal servitude, wipes out the sins of the fathers!

6

ON THE FURTHER SIDE

When in 1826 Yakubovitch saw Prince Obolensky with a beard and wearing the greatcoat of a soldier, he could not help exclaiming: 'Well, Obolensky, if I am like Stenka Razin, you certainly must be like Vanka Kain![1]. . .' Then the officer came up, the convicts were put in fetters and sent to Siberia to penal servitude.

The common people did not recognise the likeness, and dense crowds of them looked on indifferently in Nizhni-Novgorod as the fettered prisoners were driven by at the time of the fair. Perhaps they were thinking: 'Our poor dears go there *on foot*, but here the gentry are driven by the gendarmes!'

But on the other side of the Ural Mountains lies a mournful equality in face of penal servitude and in face of hopeless misery. Everything is changed. The petty official whom we knew here as a heartless, dirty bribe-taker, at Irkutsk, in a voice trembling with tears, begs the exiles to accept a gift of money from him; the rude Cossacks who escort them leave them in peace and freedom so far as they can; the merchants entertain them on their way. On the further side of Lake Baikal some of them stopped at the ford at Verhno-Udinsk; the inhabitants learnt who they were, and an old man at once sent them by his grandson a basket of white rolls, while he hobbled out himself to talk to them of the region beyond the Baikal and to question them about the wide world.

While Prince Obolensky was still at the Usolsky Works, he went out early in the morning to the place where he had been told to chop down trees. While he was at work, a man appeared out of the forest, looked at him intently with a friendly air, and then went on his way. In the evening, as he was going home, Obolensky met him again; he made signs to him and pointed to the forest. Next morning he came out from the bushes

---

[1] Vanka Kain (equivalent to Jack Cain—from Cain of the Bible) is a slang term of abuse for a desperate fellow, ready for anything.— (*Translator's Note*.)

again and signed to Obolensky to follow him. Obolensky went. Leading him away into the forest, he stopped and said to him solemnly: 'We have long known of your coming. We have been told of you in the prophecy of Ezekiel. We have been expecting you, there are many of us here, rely upon us, we will not betray you!' It was an exiled Duhobor.

Obolensky had for a long time been fretted by the desire for news of his own people through Princess Trubetskoy who had come to Irkutsk. He had no means of forwarding a letter to her. Obolensky asked the help of the Duhobor, The latter did not waste time in deliberation. 'At dusk to-morrow,' he said, 'I will be at a certain spot. Bring me the letter, it shall be taken. . . .' Obolensky gave him the letter, and the same night the man set off for Irkutsk; two days later the answer was in Obolensky's hands.

What would have happened if he had been caught?

Among comrades one does not count the risk.

The Duhobor paid the people's debt for Radishtchev.

And so in the forests and mines of Siberia the Russia of Petersburg, of the landowners, of the officials, of the officers, and the Russia of the ignorant peasants of the village, both exiled and fettered, both with an axe in the belt, both leaning on the spade, both wiping away the sweat, looked each other for the first time in the face, and recognised the long-forgotten traits of kinship.

It is time that this should take place in the light of day, aloud, openly, everywhere.

It is time that the nobility, artificially raised into a different channel by the German engineers, should mingle with the surrounding sea. Fountains are no marvel now, and Samson's spout of water from the lion's mouth is no wonder beside the infinity of the rippling sea.

The Peterhof fête is over, the court masque in fancy

dress is played out, the lamps are smoking and going out, the fountains have almost run dry—let us go home.

'All that is so, but . . . but. . . would it not be better to raise the people?' Perhaps; only it is as well to grasp that the one sure method of doing so is the method of torture, the method of Peter the Great, of Biron, of Araktcheyev. That is why the Emperor Alexander accomplished nothing with the Karazins and the Speranskys—but when he got to Araktcheyev, he did not give him up again.

There are too many of the common people for it to be really possible to raise them all to the fourteenth grade,[1] and indeed every people has a strongly defined

---

[1] The Old Believers of the English school, bound by their creed to preserve all the historical gains of the ages, even indeed when they are pernicious, do not agree with this. They think that every sort of right, however wrongly obtained, must be preserved and others grafted on to it. For instance, instead of depriving the nobles of the right of flogging and beating the peasants, the same right should be given to the peasants. In old days they used to say it would be a good thing to promote all the common people into the fourteenth * grade so that they should not be beaten; would it not be better to promote them straight away to being captains in the guards or hereditary noblemen, since heredity among us is reckoned in the opposite direction?† Yet the Ukrainians in the seventeenth century did not reason like that when there was a plan of ennobling them, and a plan not suggested by bookish scholars, but by the brilliant, gorgeous, exuberant nobility of Poland. They thought it better to remain Cossacks. There is something like that Cossack principle in organic development generally (which our doctrinaires are very fond of taking as an example). One side of the organism can under certain circumstances develop specially and get the upper hand, always to the detriment of all the rest. In itself the organ may be well developed, but it becomes a deformity which one cannot

---

* The fourteenth is the lowest grade in the government table of ranks.

† In Russia an 'hereditary nobleman' (so-called) is one who has not inherited his noble rank, but whose heirs will inherit it. (*Translator's Notes.*)

physiological character which even foreign conquest rarely changes. So long as we take the common people as clay and ourselves as sculptors, and from our sublime height mould it into a statue *à l'antique*, in the French style, in the English manner, or on the German model, we shall find nothing in the people except stubborn indifference or mortifyingly passive obedience.

The pedagogic method of our civilising reformers is a bad one. It starts from the fundamental principle that we know everything and the peasantry knows nothing: as though we had taught the peasant his right to the land, communal ownership, organisation, the artel and the mir.

It goes without saying that we can teach the peasantry a great deal, but there is a great deal that we have to learn from it and to study in it. We have theories, absorbed by us and representing the worked-out results of European culture. To determine which to apply, and how to fit them to our national existence, it is not enough to translate word for word; the lexicon is not enough. One must try in the first place to do with it what social thinkers are trying to do in Western Europe—to make their institutions comprehensible to them.

get rid of in the organism by artificially developing the remaining parts to the point of grotesqueness.

This reminds us of a remarkable instance from the religious-surgical practice of Prince Hohenlohe. Prince Hohenlohe was one of the last mortals endowed with miraculous powers. This was in those blessed days of our century when everything feudal and clerical was rising up again with powder and incense on the ruins of the French Revolution. The Prince was summoned to an invalid, one of whose legs was too short; his relations had failed to grasp that in fact the other leg was too long. The miracle-working Prince set to work praying. . . the leg grew, but the Prince did not know where to stop and prayed too excessively—the short leg overdid it —how annoying; he began praying for the other and then that outdid the other—he went back to the first . . . and it ended in the Prince leaving his patient still with legs of unequal length and both of them as long as living stilts.—(*Author's Note.*)

The common people cling obstinately to their habits—they believe in them; but we cling as obstinately to our theories and we believe in them, and, what is more, imagine that we know them to be true, that the reality is so. Passing on after a fashion what we have learnt out of books in conventional language, we see with despair that the common people do not understand us, and we bewail the stupidity of the people, just as the schoolboy will blush for poor relations, because they do not know when to put 'i' and when 'y,' but never troubles to wonder why two different letters should be used for the same sound.

Genuinely desirous of the good of the people, we look for remedies for their ailments in foreign pharmacopœias; there the herbs are foreign, but it is easier to find them in a book than in the fields. We easily and consistently become liberals, constitutionalists, democrats, Jacobins, but not Russians, believers in the common people. All these political shades one can acquire from books: all that is understood, explained and written, printed, bound. . . . But here one must go without a track. . . . The life of Russia is like the forest in which Dante lost his way, and the wild beasts that are in it are worse than the Florentine ones, but there is no Virgil to show the way; there were some Moscow Susanins,[1] but even those led one to the graveyard instead of to the peasants' cottage. . . .

Without knowing the people we may oppress the people, we may enslave them, we may conquer them, but we cannot set them free.

Without the help of the people they will be freed

---

[1] Susanin, a peasant, saved the elected Tsar Michael Romanov from the Poles who sought to assassinate him. Susanin undertook to lead them to the monastery in which the Tsar was concealed, but led them instead into the forest, where they killed him but were themselves frozen to death. It is the subject of Glinka's opera, 'Life for the Tsar.'—(*Translator's Note*.)

neither by the Tsar with his clerks, nor the nobility with the Tsar, nor the nobility without the Tsar.

What is happening now in Russia ought to open the eyes of the blind. The peasantry have borne the terrible burden of serfdom without ever acknowledging its lawfulness; seeing the force opposed to them they have remained dumb. But as soon as others attempted in their own way to set them free, they passed from murmuring, from passive resistance, almost to open mutiny, and yet they are obviously better off now. What new signs do the reformers wait for?

Only the man who when called to action understands the life of the people while keeping what science has given him; only one who voices its strivings and founds on the realisation of them his work for the common cause, will be the bridegroom that is to come.

This lesson is repeated to us alike by the mournful figure of Alexander with his crown; by Radishtchev with his glass of poison; by Karazin flying through the Winter Palace like a burning meteor; by Speransky who shone for years together with a glimmer like moonshine, with no warmth, no colour; and by our holy martyrs of the Fourteenth of December.

Who will be the predestined saviour?

Will it be an emperor who, renouncing all the traditions of the Petersburg Government, combines in himself Tsar and Stenka Razin? Will it be another Pestel? Or another Emelyan Pugatchov, Cossack, Tsar and heretic? Or will it be a prophet and a peasant, like Antony Bezdninsky?

It is hard to tell: these are details, *des détails* as the French say. Who ever it may be, it is our task to meet him with warm welcome!